IMAGES
of America

BARDSTOWN

I0806379

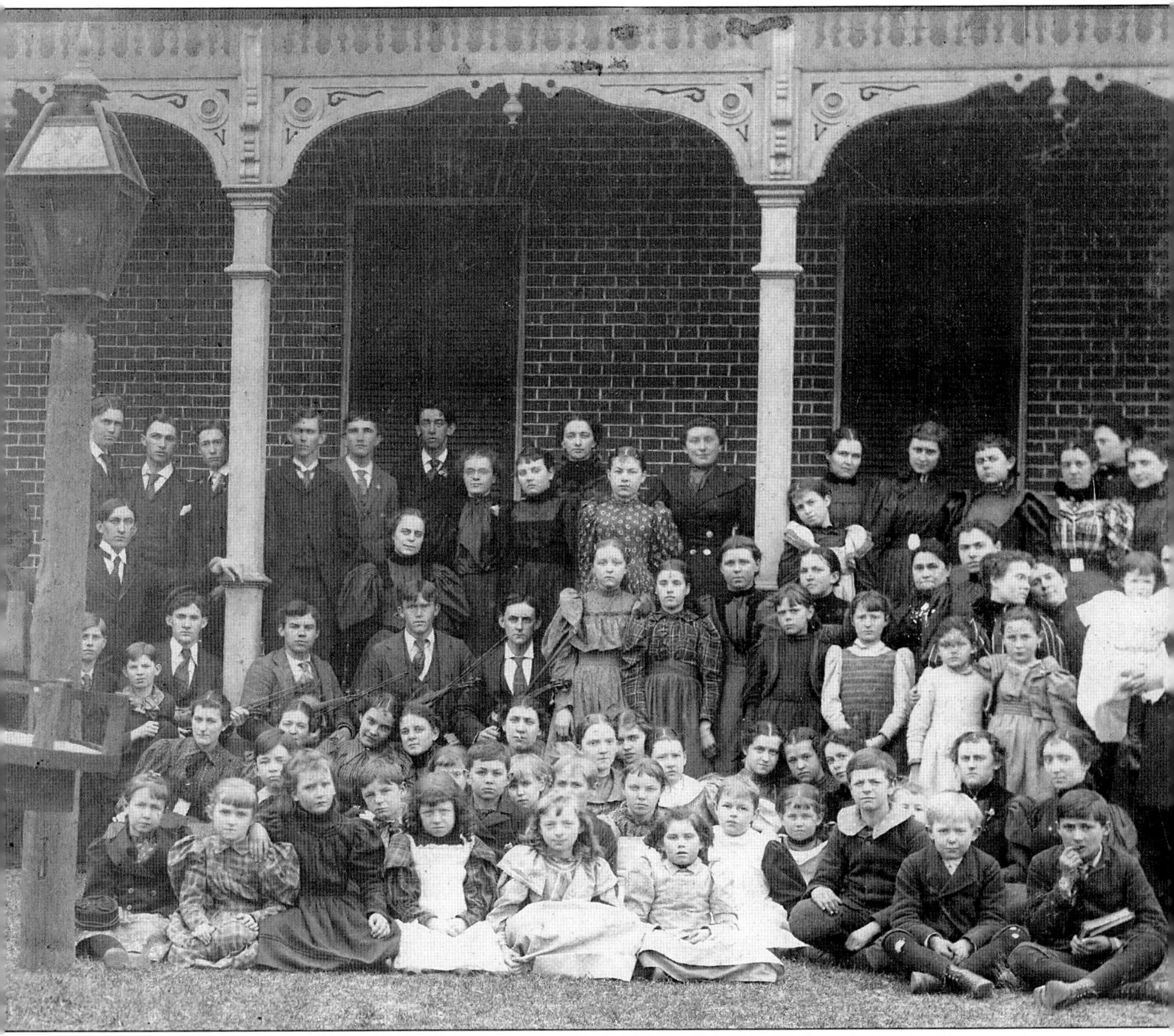

The Professor Cook School, c. 1897, was located on the east side of South Third Street on outlot 12. The school, a private Protestant institution, was earlier known as the Bardstown Female Institute and the Bardstown Male and Female Academy. It was managed by a Methodist Church Board of Trustees. It was taken over by the Baptists in 1865.

Professor Robert N. Cook ran the school from 1896 to 1898. This school later became known as the Bardstown Baptist Institute. It was torn down after the Bardstown Public School building was erected.

COVER IMAGE: Dan Talbott's Drugstore was located in the Johnson Building on the northwest corner of the public square. This 1922 interior view shows the marble-topped soda fountain, leaded-glass fixtures, and gum ball machine. Mr. Talbott, druggist, is seen in the center.

IMAGES
of America

BARDSTOWN

Dixie Hibbs

ARCADIA
PUBLISHING

ISBN 978-0-7385-8991-6

Published by Arcadia Publishing
Charleston, South Carolina

Printed in the United States of America

Library of Congress Catalog Card Number: 98-86670

For all general information contact Arcadia Publishing at:
Telephone 843-853-2070
Fax 843-853-0044
E-mail sales@arcadiapublishing.com
For customer service and orders:
Toll-Free 1-888-313-2665

Visit us on the Internet at www.arcadiapublishing.com

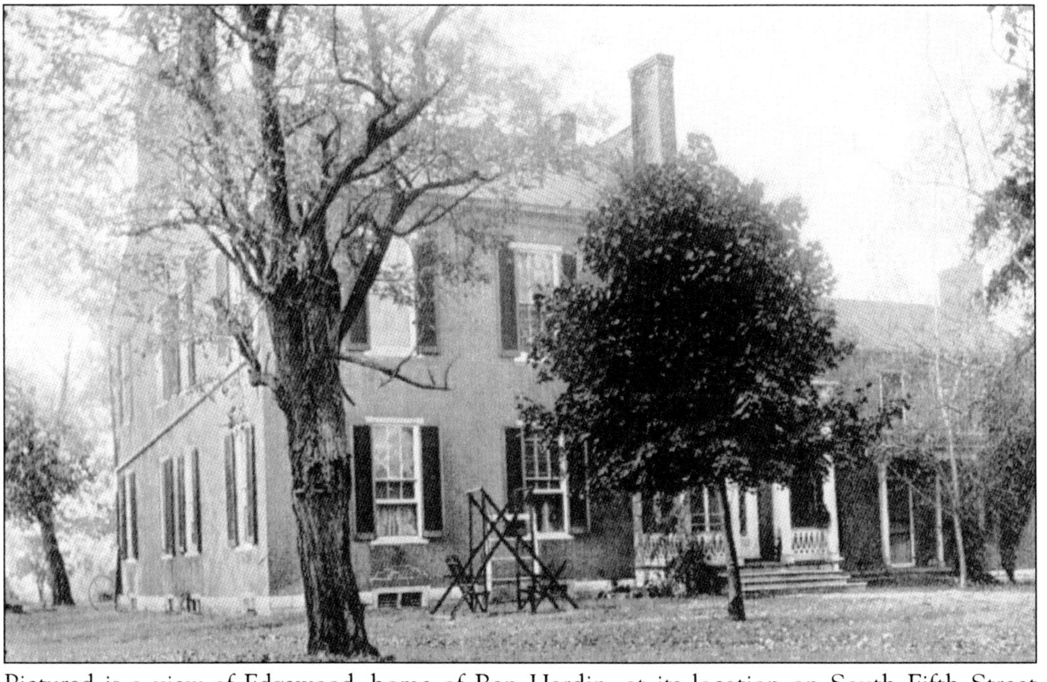

Pictured is a view of Edgewood, home of Ben Hardin, at its location on South Fifth Street in 1915, 100 years after its construction. The house was the headquarters of Gen. Braxton Bragg during the Confederate occupation of Bardstown in September 1862. The Victorian-style porches on the front were added by 1886. In the years after the Hardin family left the home, it served as the residence for the Linthicum, McKay, and Muir families. In the 1930s, Harry Tuer replaced this porch with a two-story, columned porch.

CONTENTS

ACKNOWLEDGMENTS

I follow in the footsteps of two noted Nelson County historians, Jack Muir and Sarah Smith, in preserving in print the images and stories of the past. Although both are deceased, their collections continue to contribute to our understanding of local history. Mr. Muir's interest in the history of the community and his lifetime habit of clipping news items allowed me to find the elusive details that straight-line research often fails to uncover. Many of the photos in this book came from his collection. I also wish to thank the following people for allowing me to copy their photographs: Arch Pendergrass, W.J. Case, Midge Barnes Ballard, Tom Isaac, Carol Shelburne, Ann Marks, Larry Cass (Heaven Hill Distillery), Frances C. Strange, Guffy Wilson, William Pike Conway, Haydon Spalding, the Bardstown Methodist Church, Alfred Mattingly, Don Parrish, Beth Johnson, Rebekkah Ray, Ron Greenwell, Neal Cornett, and Carl Howell of Hodgenville. I used photos from the public collections of the Kentucky Historical Society, the University of Louisville Photographic Archives, the Montfort Collection at Spalding Hall, Bardstown, the Sisters of Charity Nazareth Archives, Old Kentucky Home State Park, the Nelson County Circuit Court, and the Nelson County Historical Society.

I have an extensive collection of photographs and original papers of local historic interest. Over the years, many people have given me items that they wanted preserved and used. This generosity has allowed me to compile two books about Nelson County.

I must thank the Hibbs Engineering Office crew who put up with my talking to myself and their computer for two weeks. The conversation became very loud when two weeks of work went on an unauthorized coffee break! Three hours later, my computer expert friend, Janice Donan, rescued my manuscript and allowed me to meet my deadline. JoAnne Blincoe helped with copies, typing, and opinions. My mother, Christine Polley, and my sister, Marie Taylor, fed us periodically. My family is used to my erratic projects, but this one seemed to overflow in every direction.

My husband, Franklin, must also be thanked for his patience with the confusion and last-minute proofreading that was essential to my peace of mind. The facts are as accurate as I could find but, being human, I may have used the wrong references, so please read with charity. I didn't get every picture and every fact I wanted in, but I completed the project on time, and I have gathered the pieces into a whole.

Introduction

Bardstown, Kentucky, is a progressive but historic community dating back to 1780. Located about 45 miles southeast of Louisville and 60 miles west of Lexington, Bardstown is presently the home of approximately 8,000 residents. Settled by immigrants from Pennsylvania, Maryland, and Virginia, it would rise from the primitive wilds of western Virginia with the building of log, brick, or stone homes. In 1785, it became the county seat of Nelson County, Virginia. In 1792, Kentucky's statehood opened up more economic opportunities for the area. Although it was called Salem by the original owners, David Bard and John C. Owings, very soon it was known as Bard's Town.

By 1789, property owners had asked the city trustees for a map to define the boundaries of their lots. George Calhoun surveyed the young settlement and his map is still the reference today. Later maps reflect the area's growth and changes. Historically, agriculture has been the largest industry, with manufacturing second and tourism third. Bardstown has welcomed travelers since the 1780s. During the early part of this century, Southern hospitality became an industry.

The intent of this collection of pictures is to reflect the changes that have occurred in this community, particularly in the 20th century. The early economic success of Bardstown funded the construction of impressive examples of Federal, Greek Revival, and Georgian architecture. Commercial buildings in the business area, private residences, and educational buildings were designed and completed by skilled craftsmen. The quality of their work is reflected in the longevity of the buildings. Those buildings which did not survive have been removed by man through neglect or so-called progress. It is encouraging to see the adaptation and reuse of the older structures.

The theme "Gone, but not Forgotten," fueled my search for images to illustrate the changing streetscape. The search and review also revealed how it has been preserved. As you turn the pages of this book, look at the pictures and compare the different views. Place yourself in the scene. Local readers will remember and reminiscence while others will relate to personal experiences in their own communities.

In 1967, Bardstown passed a historic zoning ordinance to protect the physical heritage of the community. It came too late for most of the buildings noted as being gone, but it is protecting 300 buildings in our community that are listed in the National Register of Historic Places.

As this book evolved, it was evident that it needed to be expanded to cover more than lost buildings. Nelson County is the center of Bourbon Whiskey production in Kentucky. Whiskey-making history goes back to the Pennsylvanians of 1780. A review of the distilleries in 1896 reveals many familiar brands. Prohibition struck for 13 years. After repeal, not all of the distilleries were able to recover but many new ones began. The industry continues to produce the world-renowned Kentucky product.

Tragedies produce photographs. The use of newly found pictures of the famous 1917 train wreck, the 1996 distillery fire, and two 1998 fires at local landmarks visually records history for future generations. Compiling images of our community is a serious responsibility. Choosing which images to include was a difficult decision-making process. Many lost buildings may have been photographed, but the images lie undiscovered in trunks and drawers. Perhaps this book will encourage families to carefully investigate family photos and create their own accounts of "Gone, But Not Forgotten."

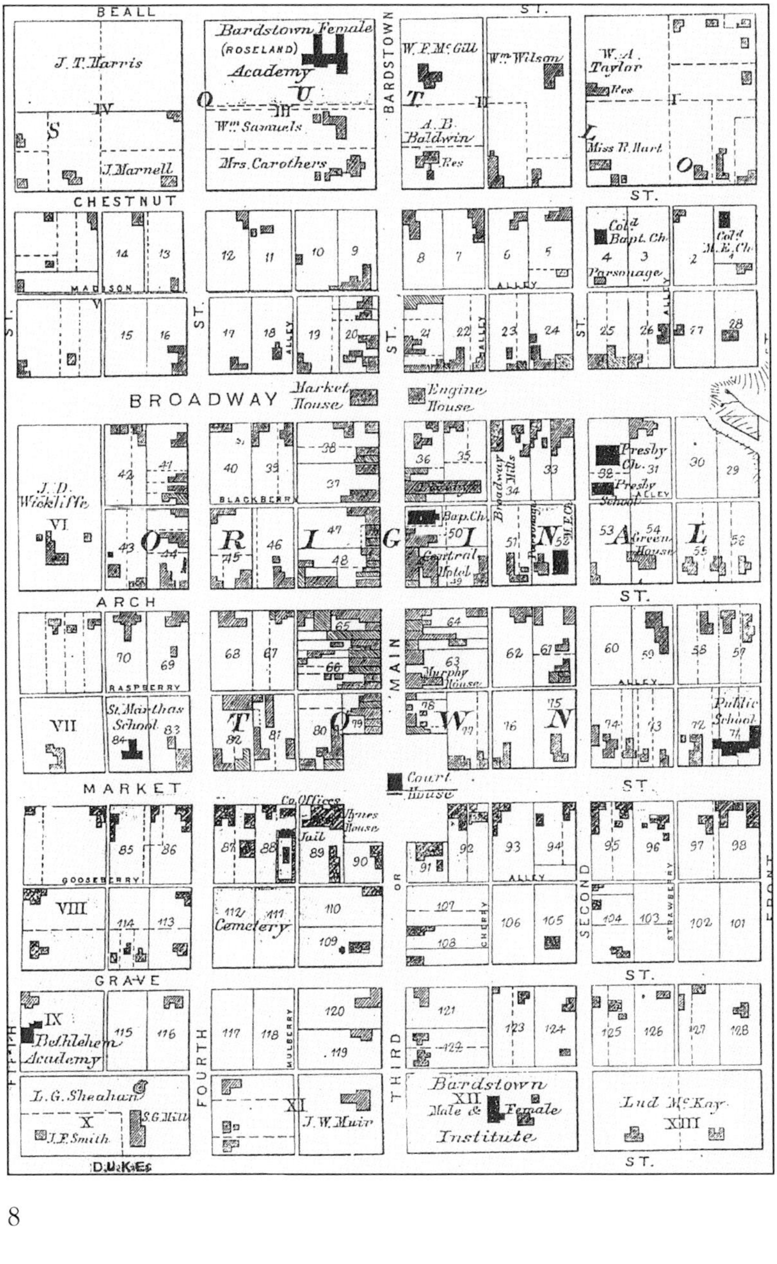

This 1882 map of Bardstown has been trimmed in order to fit on this page. The areas south of Duke and north of Beall have been omitted. These street names will be used to locate the pictures until the 1940 period. In the late 1930s, the east-west street names were changed. References to street names after 1940 use the new names. The following list will help you remember the names: Beall and Broadway remained the same; Chestnut Street became Brashear; Arch Street became Flaget; Market Street became Stephen Foster; Graves Street became John Fitch; and Duke Street became Muir.

One

Changes on Main Street

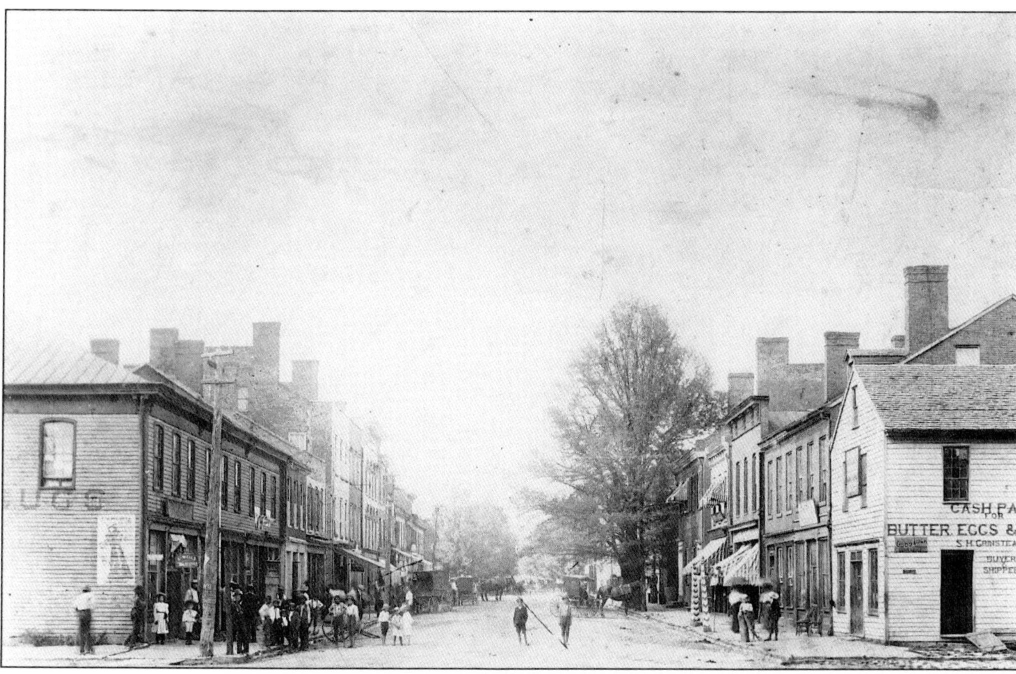

The blocks north of the Court Square are and have been the main business section of Bardstown. From the early frame buildings of 1800, such as the John Caldwell "Yellow House" (left) and the Grinstead store (right), to the 1820 Beall's Row commercial 2- and 3-story brick structures and early-1900 rebuilds, the downtown area preserves the past while serving today. New facades screen the age of many of the buildings. These 1890–1950 views show how many structures have survived by adapting to the demands of a changing commercial climate. They also show how the same businesses often continue at the same locations.

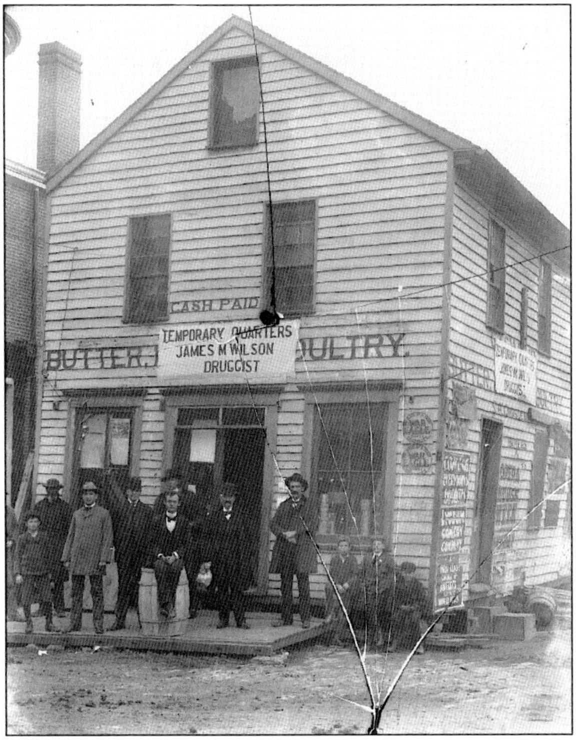

This cracked glass negative from the W.F. Monfort Collection shows druggist James M. Wilson using the Grinstead's store building as temporary quarters. The frame building has been jacked up from its foundation and moved so that a new building could be constructed. Note the brick wall of Wilson's new building on the left edge of the photograph.

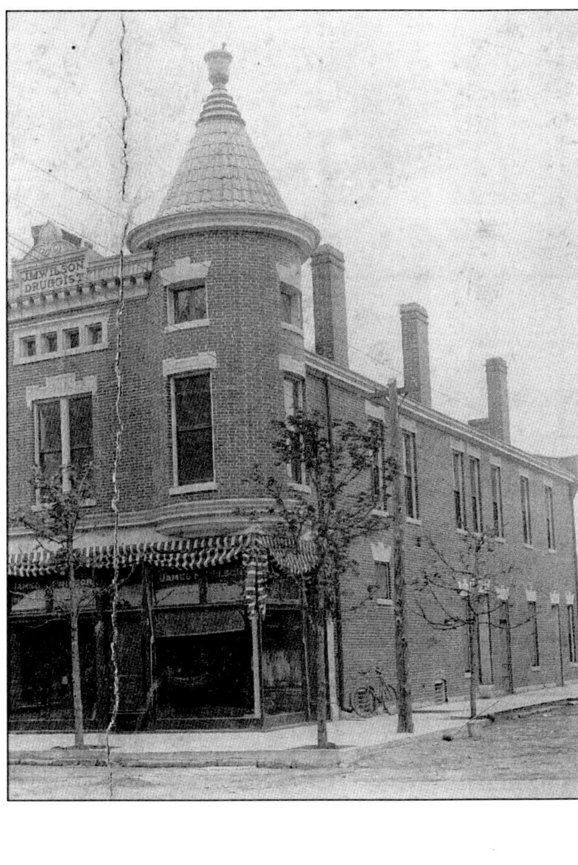

The cornice sign reads "J.M. Wilson, Druggist." Mr. Wilson has just completed his new brick building, poured new sidewalks, and planted trees. Notice the mortar and pestle on top of the tower. Crume Drugstore, located at the opposite end of the block, would also have had the mortar and pestle atop its roof. Mr. Wilson was also a photographer whose postcards are found throughout this book. All of the views were made before 1922.

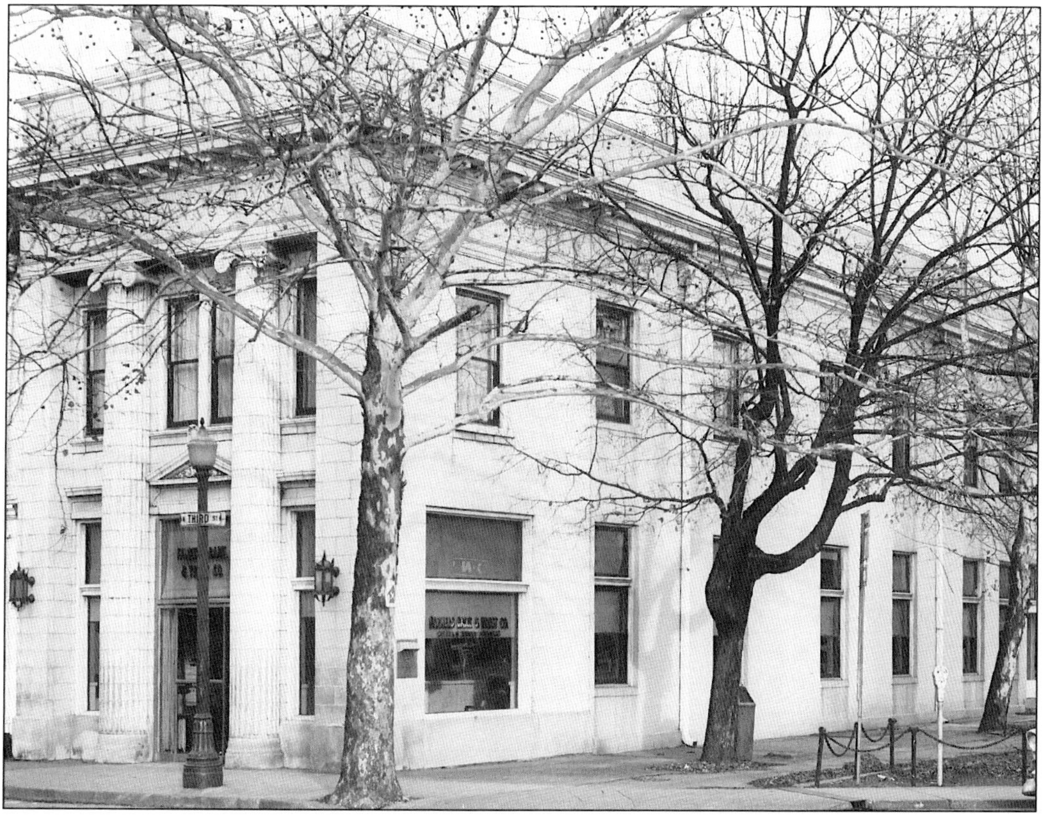

In 1924, Farmers Bank purchased the Wilson Drug Store and remodeled it. Stone columns and facings replaced the brick walls and tower of the earlier building. The bank operated at this location until 1970, when the business was moved to a new building on the corner of Third and Flaget Streets.

The Johnson Building (left) replaced Caldwell's building in 1900. The balustrade on the roof line no longer exists but the building remains in use. It was originally built by Ben Johnson for commercial use on the first floor. The upper floors were occupied by offices and apartments.

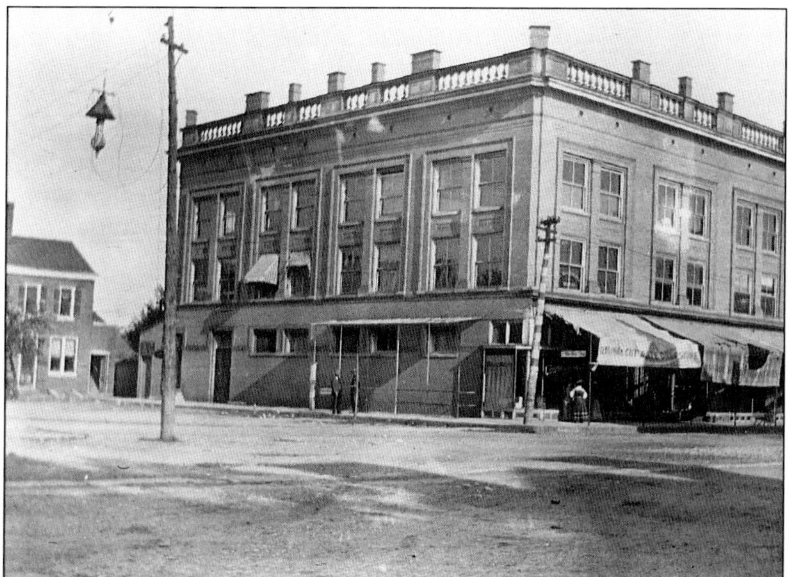

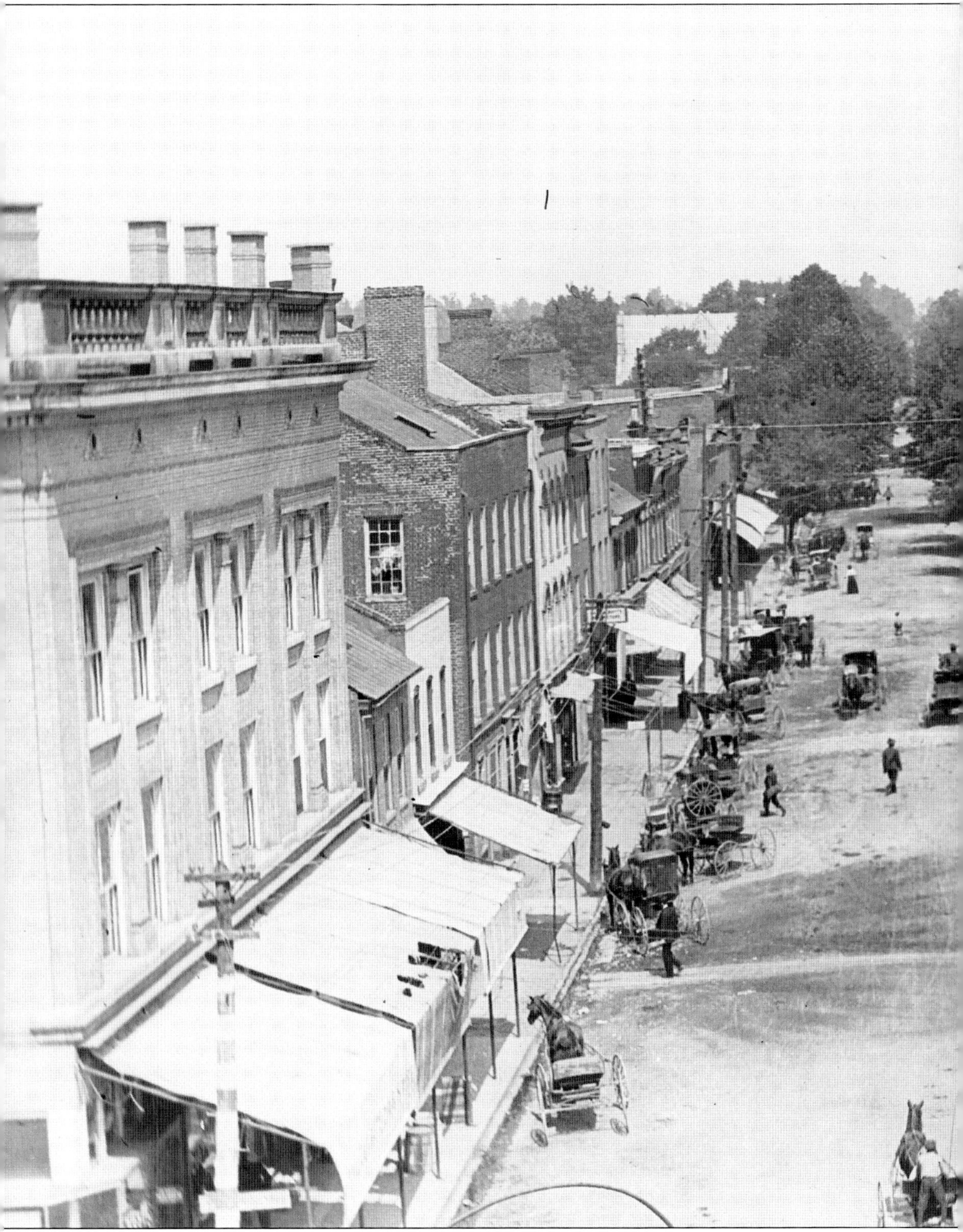

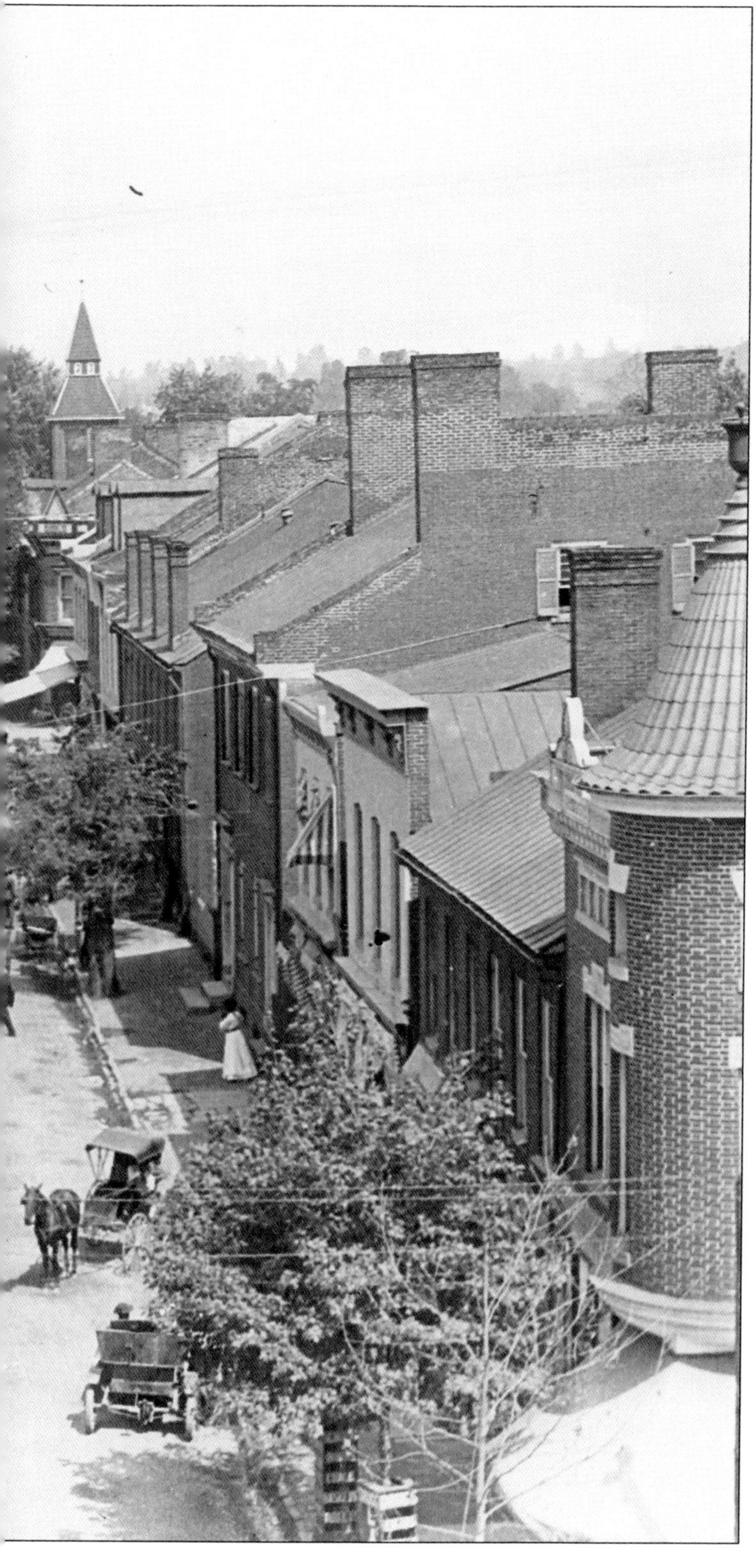

This bird's-eye view of the streetscape was photographed from the bell tower of the courthouse c. 1905. This view looking north spans one and one-half blocks. A 1910 map indicates the type of businesses in these buildings. The Johnson building (left) housed two grocery stores, a dry goods business, a jewelry store, and Mann's wallpaper and furniture store (beside the alley). The three-story brick building also had a grocery store and a pool hall in its two shops. Beside it is a dry goods shop, a drugstore, grocery store, and Spalding's dry goods. Heyman's dry goods, located beside the last building on the block, had a millinery shop and a drugstore.

On the right is Wilson's Drugs and a brick building with a confectionery and fruit shop and a barber shop. Farmer's Bank is in the next building with the flat cornice. Wilson and Muir is next door, along the alley. The Murphy Hotel with its large, brick chimney wall is directly behind the lady in white. The hotel was torn down in 1910. There is a small side yard, then a cobbler shop, meat shop, and four saloons. People's Bank is located on the corner. The spire seen here is part of the Christian Church.

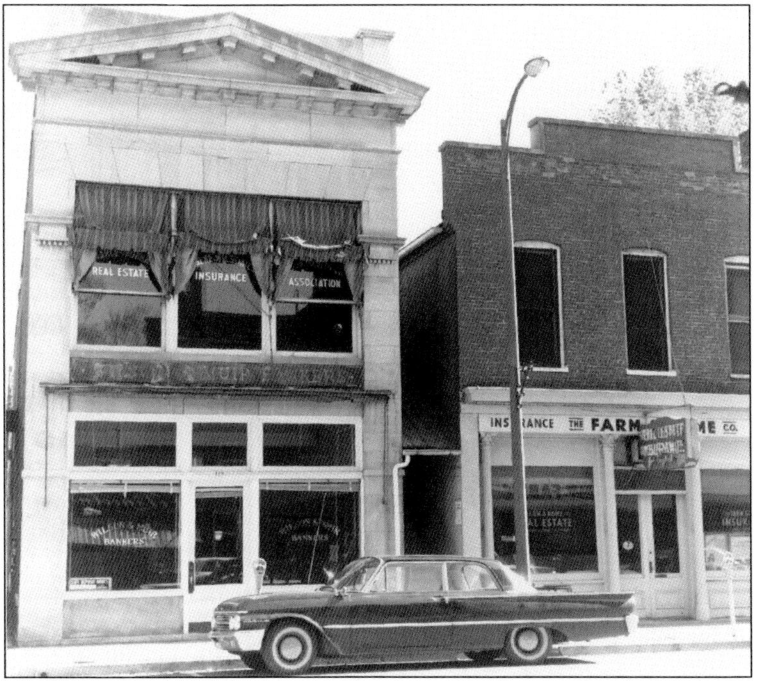

These two buildings, located on lot 78 (east side of Main Street), were torn down in 1962 to make room for the new Wilson and Muir Bank building. The building on the left was originally owned by William Russell as a watch repair shop. It was purchased in 1865 by Richard Shipp, who dealt in gold and silver and loaned money. The building was sold in 1867 as a "banking house" and in 1869, with the partnership of William Wilson and Jasper W. Muir, became the Wilson and Muir Bank. In 1900, the handsome stone face was put on the building. The interior was remodeled in 1926. During the 1962 reconstruction, the banking operations were moved to the old People's Bank building on the corner of Third Street and Flaget Avenue. The Farm and Home building was used by Farmer's Bank from 1907 to 1924, and the Wilson and Muir banking operation moved here in 1926.

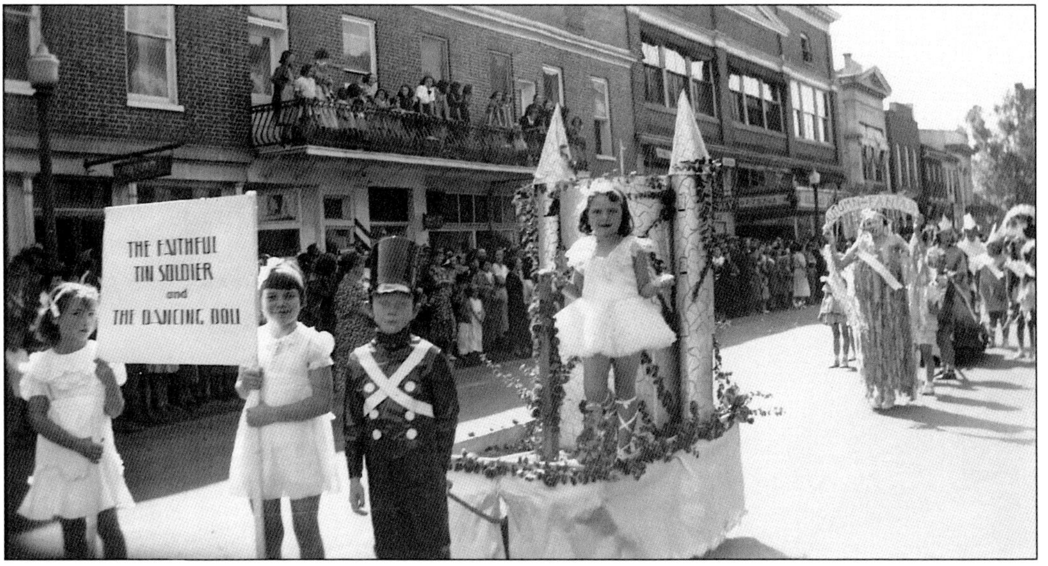

Storybook characters were the theme of this school parade in 1937. The balcony and sidewalks are filled with viewers. The balcony allowed the apartment dwellers of the building to have a porch as well as a hallway. This view is looking southeast to the first block north of the courthouse. The Crystal Theatre's marquee can be seen on the right. The acorn-shaped, globed street lights (installed in 1929) gave this business section the name "The Great White Way."

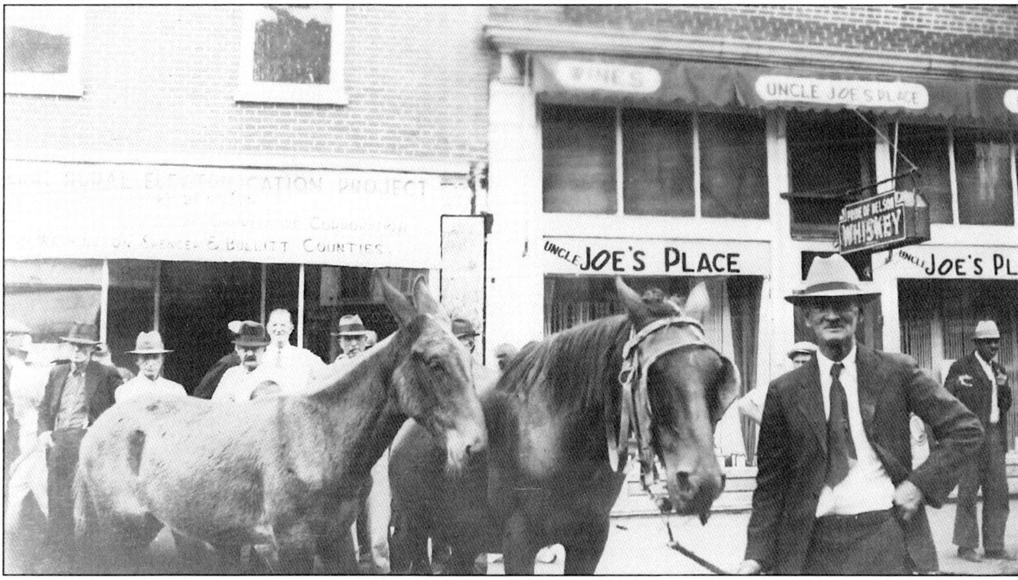

Looking for a buyer? An unidentified mule trader is standing in front of Uncle Joe Hurst's Liquor Store on the east side of North Third Street. His store was filled with interesting items, from marbles to arrowheads. It was located in the north third section of the Crystal Building. Next door is the first office of the Federal Rural Electrification Project, which became the Salt River RECC. Organized in 1937, the group moved to a brick building on West Stephen Foster Street after leaving this location.

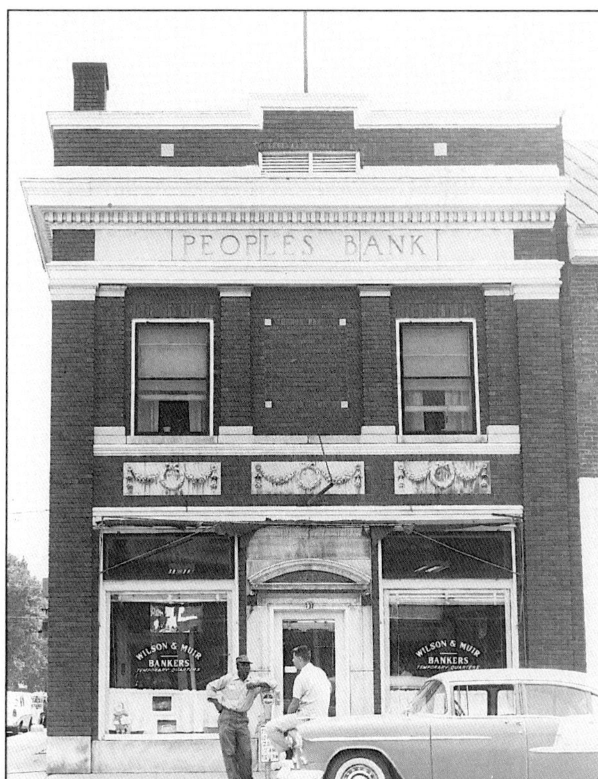

Pictured is the People's Bank building, located on the corner of Third and Flaget Streets, as it looked when used by Wilson and Muir Bank in 1963. People's Bank was organized in 1897 and sold to Farmer's Bank in 1933. In 1935, the Venture Inn restaurant was in this building, and later, the Wathen Bottom Jewelry Store and the Hilton and Keeling Barber Shop were located here. Benny and Crew's Barber Shop presently occupies the building.

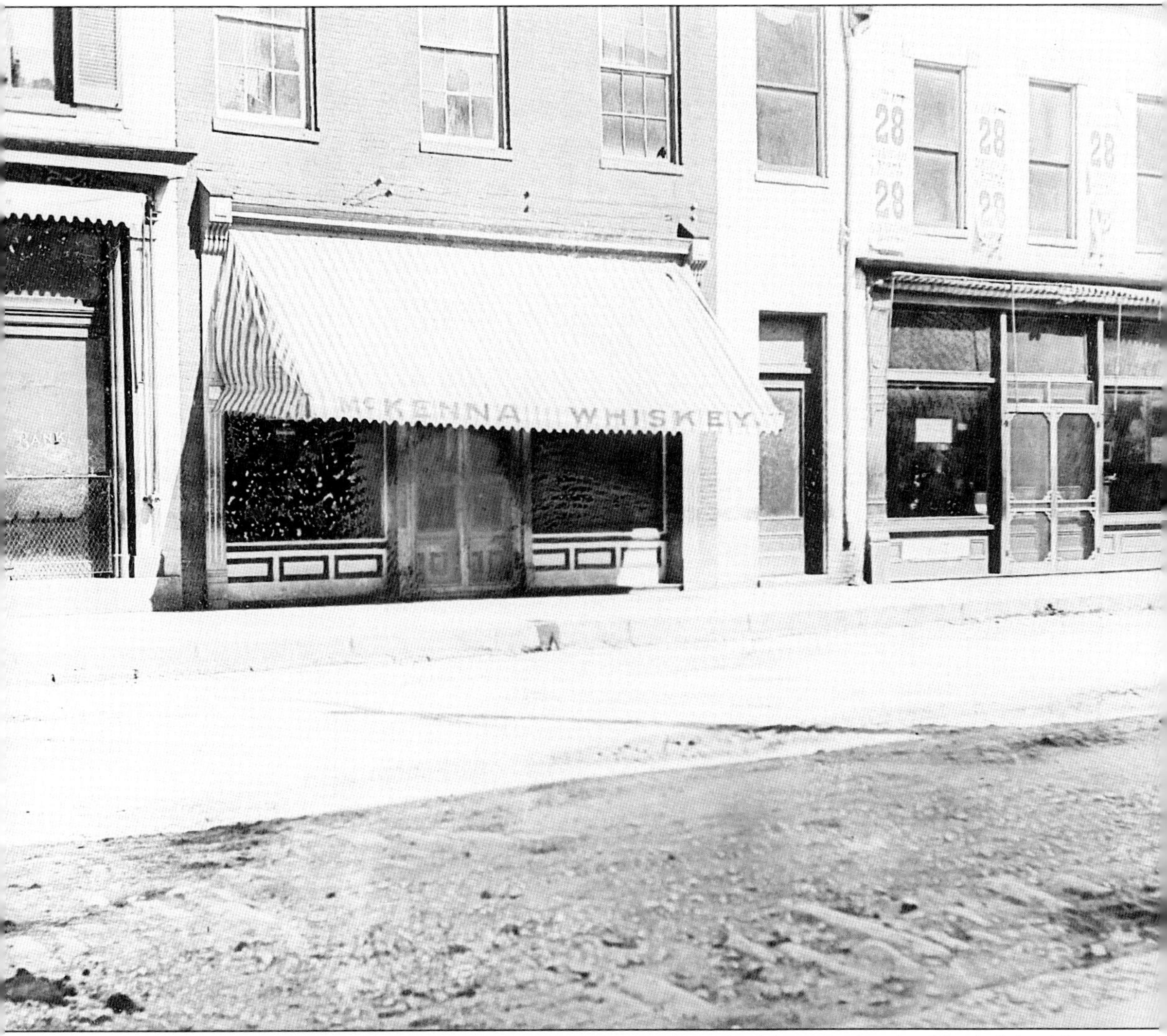

This 1900 photo of the east side of Main Street shows three buildings on lot 64. The left building is now occupied by the People's Bank. In the 1820s, it was occupied by the Bardstown Branch Bank of Kentucky. Moses Black purchased these three buildings and combined them as Black's Tavern. He ended up owning most of the buildings on this lot. In 1820, he managed a store at the location and later, the Tavern House. In the 1840s, Isaac Eastham leased the building from Black and called it the Lafayette Hotel. This side of the street had several coffeehouses and taverns and was not generally used by ladies in the late 1800s. The building on the right was destroyed by fire in January 1977. It had been occupied by the Louisville (dry goods) Store since the early 1900s. The name McKenna on the awning refers to the whiskey produced in Fairfield, Kentucky, by H. McKenna.

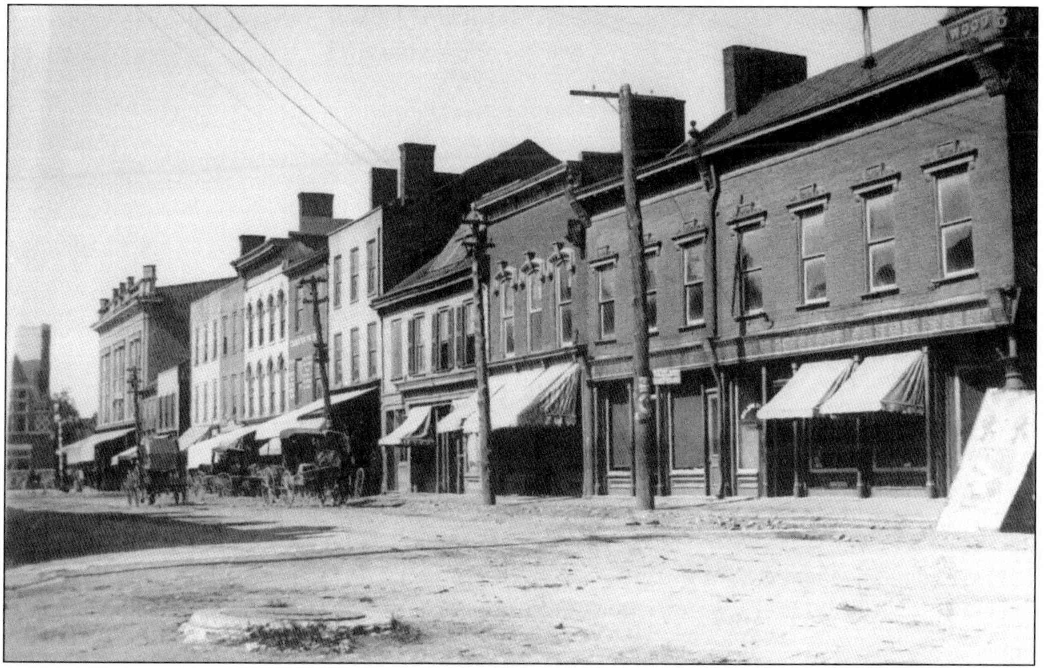

Looking south from the corner of Arch and Main Streets, there are 11 buildings housing 15 different businesses. The third building from the right is Spalding Dry Goods, which has a skylight in the roof. The street was not paved until 1918 but stone walkways were at each corner. The round object in the foreground is a well cover for one of the many reservoirs used for fighting fires.

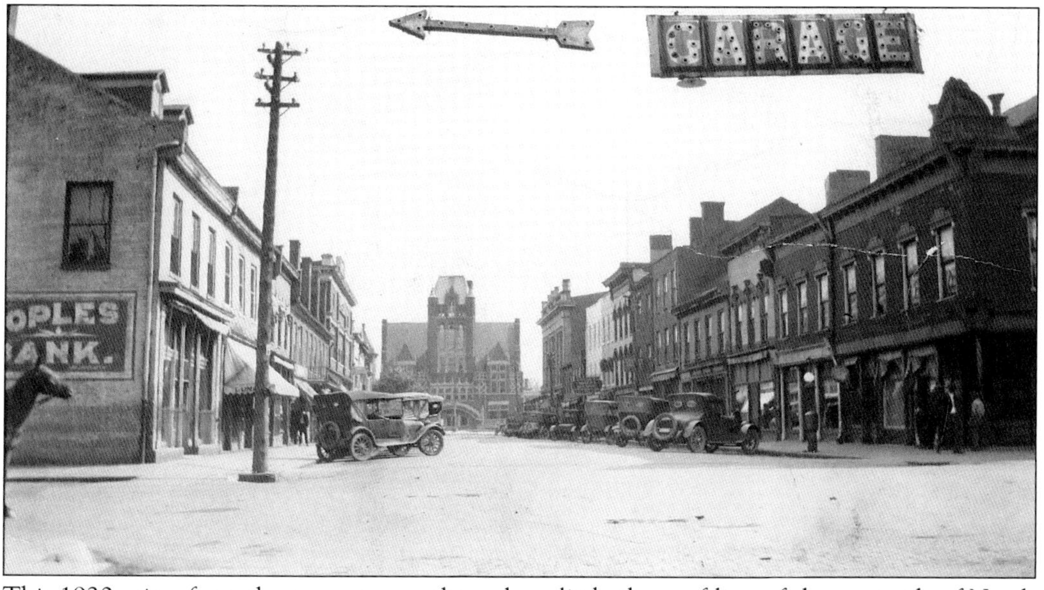

This 1920s view from the same corner shows how little the roof line of the west side of North Third Street (looking south from Flaget Street) has changed. Horse and buggy rides like the one seen here would only be for amusement today. The People's Bank (left) was sold in 1933 to the Farmer's Bank and Trust Company. The reflector sign is pointing to the Wilson Brothers' Garage on East Flaget Street.

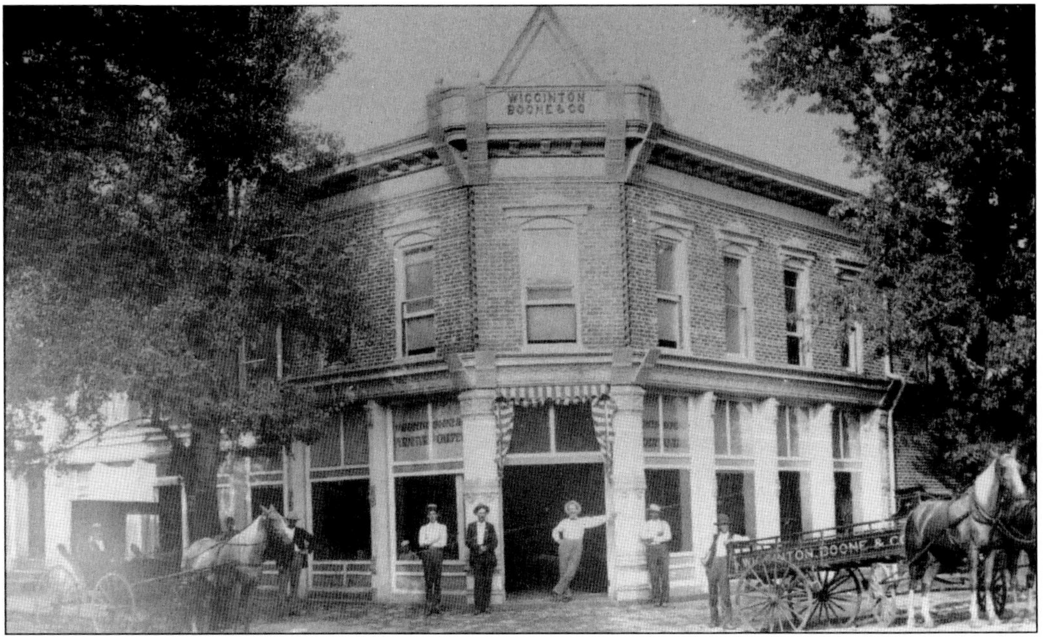

According to the Insurance Map of 1910, Wigginton, Boone, and Company sold furniture, carpets, and coffins. The combination of furniture sales and undertaking was common. William Hart manufactured saddles and harnesses here before this business began. The shop was located on the northeast corner of Arch and Main Streets. Next door, to the north, is the Central Hotel, which was torn down in 1914. At the lower right corner is a cistern or well used for fire protection.

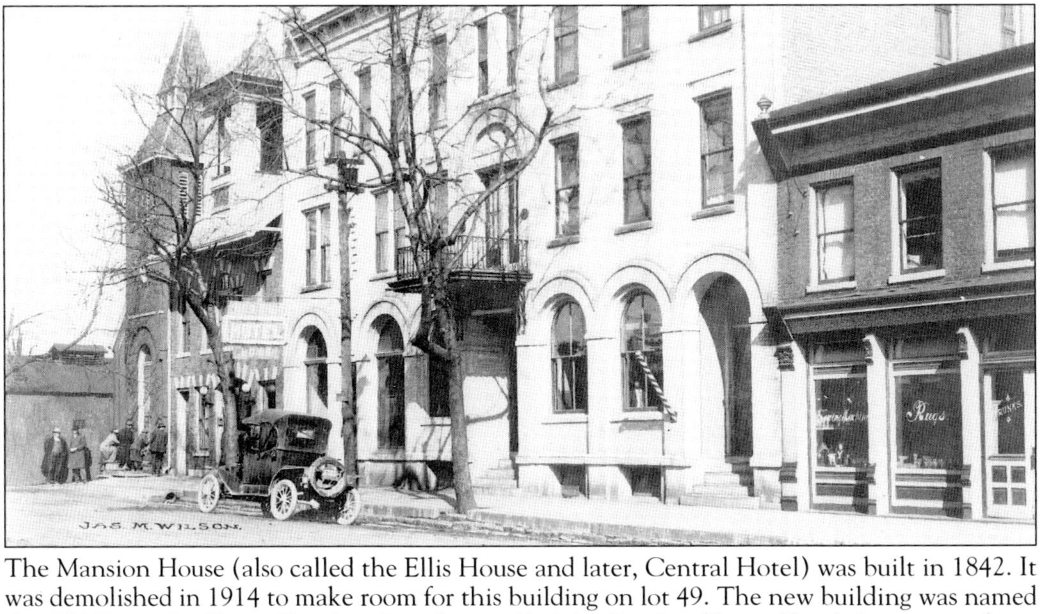

The Mansion House (also called the Ellis House and later, Central Hotel) was built in 1842. It was demolished in 1914 to make room for this building on lot 49. The new building was named the Old Kentucky Home Hotel and was later called the Stephen Foster Hotel. It was torn down in 1967 to build the new Farmer's Bank building. The long shed building past the Christian Church (left) is the livery stable where a Civil War skirmish took place in 1863 between John Hunt Morgan's men and Union soldiers.

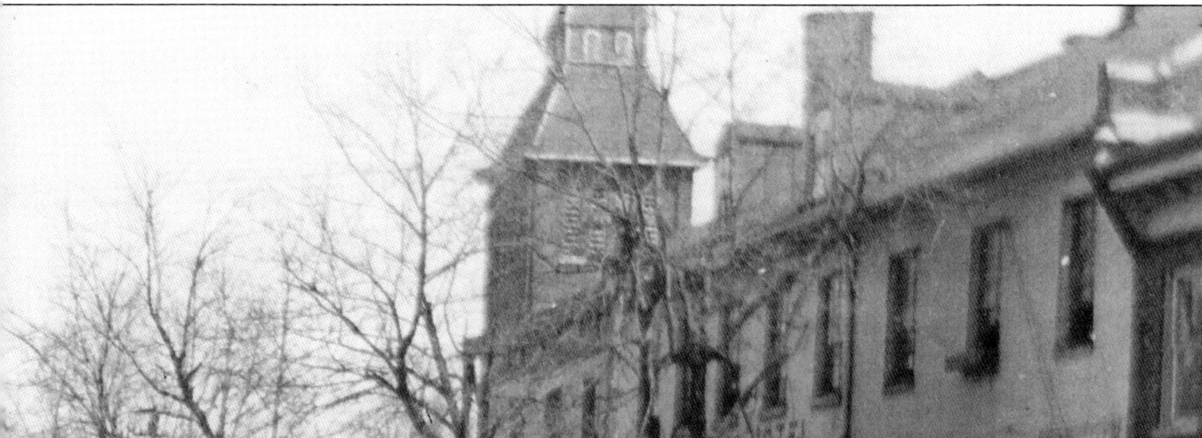

The two-story, light-colored building on the right is the Central Hotel. In this lobby, in 1881, Jesse and Frank James narrowly missed being arrested by detectives Yankee Bligh and George Hunter. The detectives brought two others for reinforcement as they went into the hotel but Donnie Pence and Ben Johnson joined the James brothers. Jesse walked through the lobby with his arms crossed over his chest and his hands under his coat. He turned and stood while the others walked out the door. After they brought the horses from the nearby livery stable, they quickly mounted and left. Knowing a gunfight would be deadly, the detectives backed off and the James boys rode away. T.D. Beam operated his "Old Tub" Saloon inside the same building in 1894.

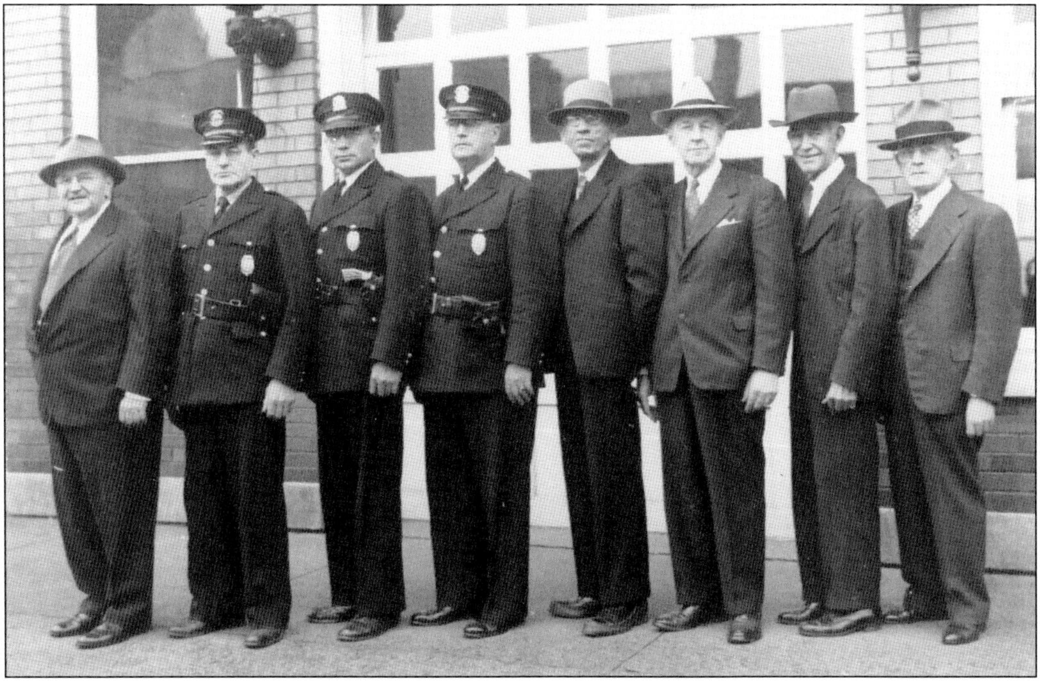

Photographed in 1945, these Bardstown city officials are posing in front of city hall on North Third Street. They are, from left to right, as follows: Judge James M. Carothers, Irvin Royalty, Clifton Gibson, Chief C.P. "Heavy" Tong, city engineer Charles Edelen, Mayor J.F. Conway, city treasurer George Barkhurst, and city clerk Bernard Hurst. The fire department's equipment was housed behind the door on the first floor of this building.

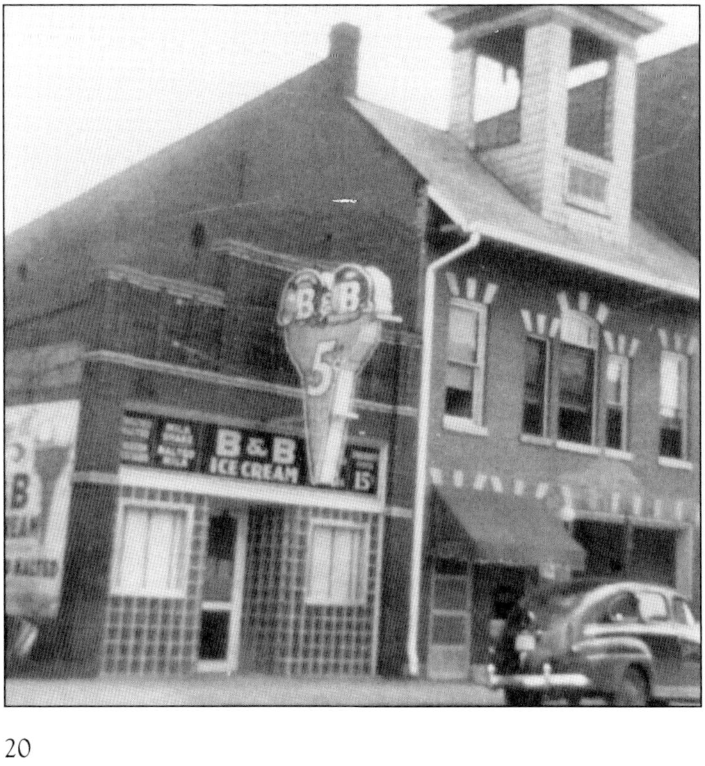

Brothers Marion and Frank Bohn opened this ice cream shop in 1939. It soon became a gathering spot for students. No visit downtown was complete without checking out the "B and B" to see who was there. In 1971, after 30 years and several million cones, the landmark business closed. It was located on North Third Street (lot 50) beside city hall.

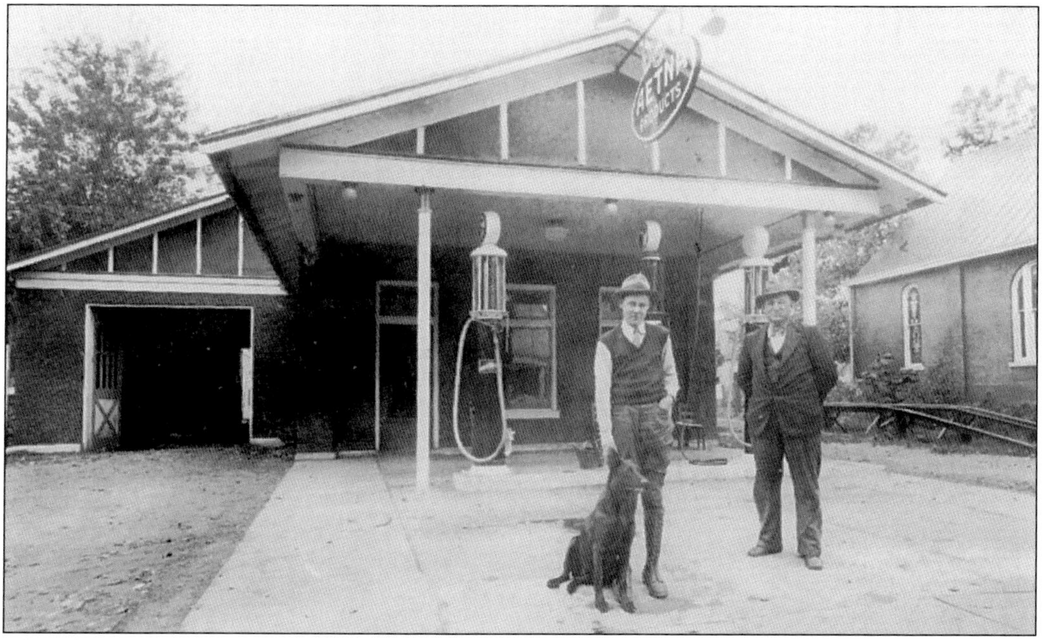

This filling station, built by R.H. Edelen, replaced the old livery stable (lot 35) on the east side of North Third Street. In this 1924 picture, Hugh Cox Dickerson is standing by "Chickie" and the manager, Robert Morgan.

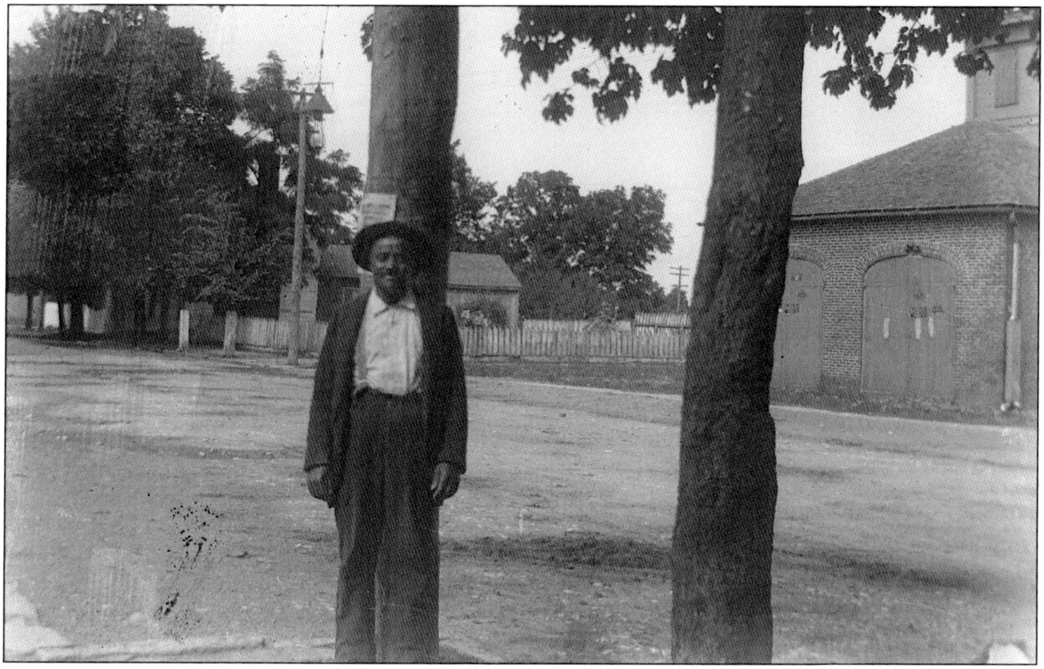

Photographer William F. Monfort took many pictures of Bardstown between 1890 and 1920. This 1910 picture shows a brick firehouse on the right. It was located in the center of the street, at the intersection of East Broadway and Main Street. The building housed the hand-drawn pumper, hose carts, ladders, and buckets used by the Bardstown Volunteer Fire Department. Behind the unidentified man is the Inn of Seven Stars.

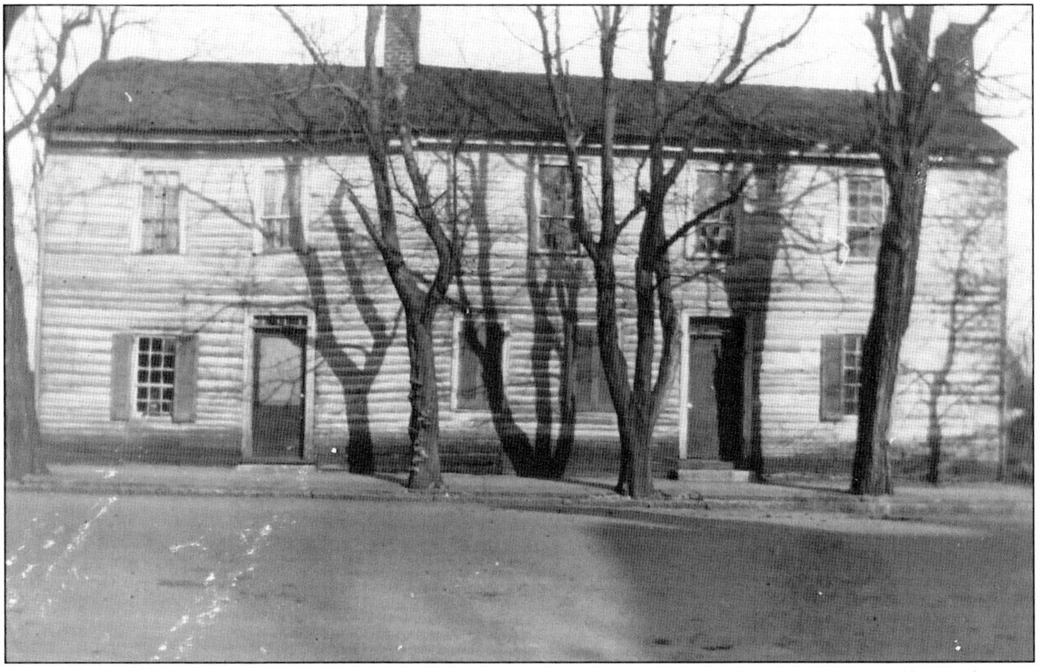

The Inn of Seven Stars, a clapboarded log building located on North Main Street (lot 21), was torn down in 1926. Christian Hahn obtained the title to this lot in 1799, and his family is given credit for its erection. The building's placement directly on the sidewalk indicates that it was built in the early 1800s. Folklore gives the origin of its name to 1861 and the Civil War. As the seven southern states seceded, seven stars were placed on the original Confederate flag. The Seven Stars represented Southern sympathy.

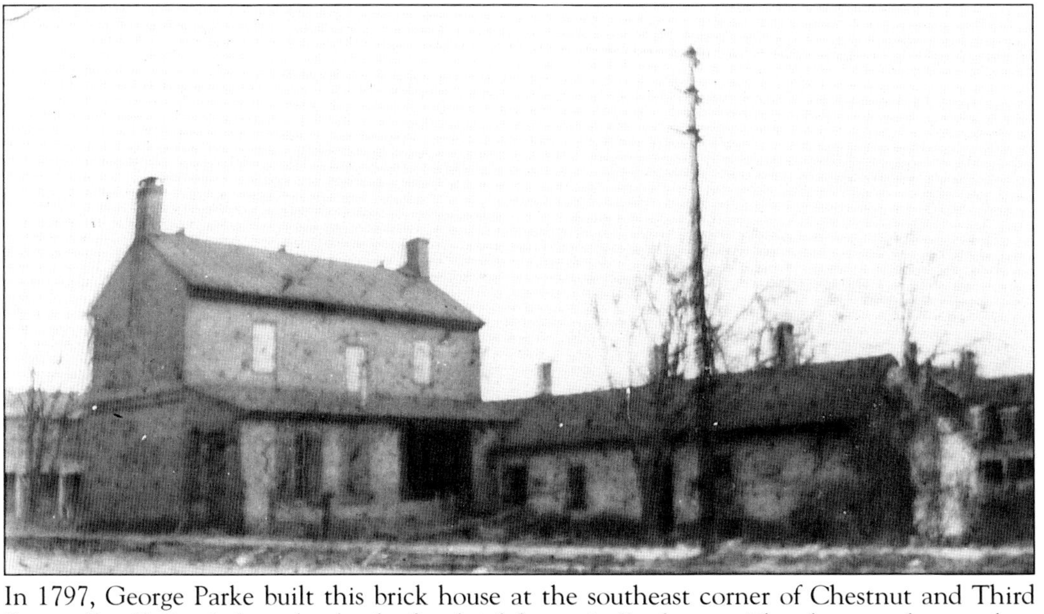

In 1797, George Parke built this brick house at the southeast corner of Chestnut and Third Streets (lot 8). It is believed to be the first brick house in Bardstown. The photograph was taken shortly before the house was torn down in 1926 to make room for a service station. First Federal Savings and Loan Bank of Elizabethtown presently owns the lot.

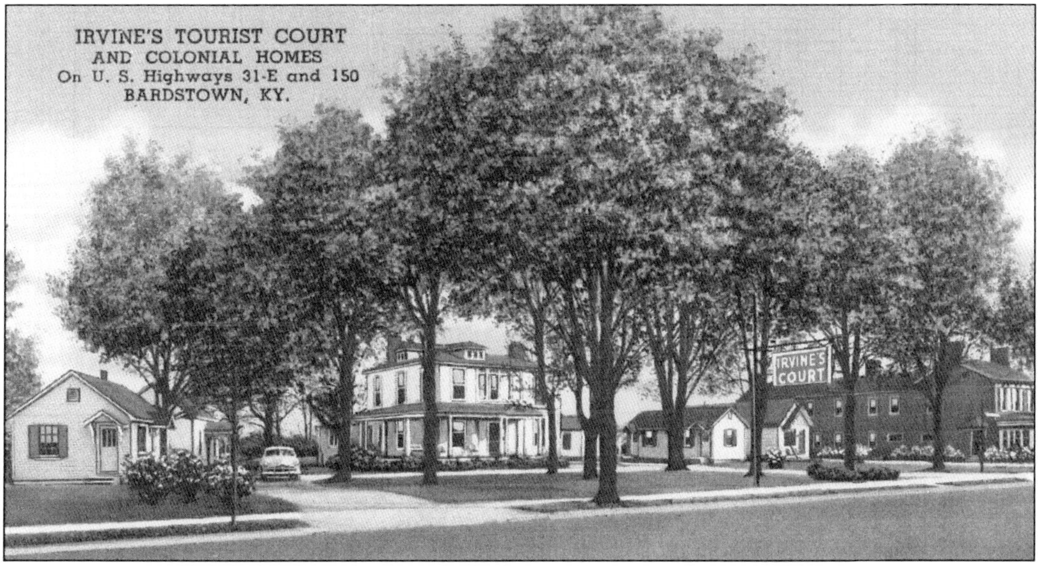

The caption on the back of this 1950s postcard view reads as follows: "Irvine's Tourist Court and Colonial Homes, 521–529 North Third Street, Bardstown, Ky. Phone 390. Twenty-two modern air-conditioned and heated cottages with tile baths. Located in a shaded residential section in the heart of the second oldest city in the state. Near 'My Old Kentucky Home' and Lincoln's Cabin on route to Mammoth Cave."

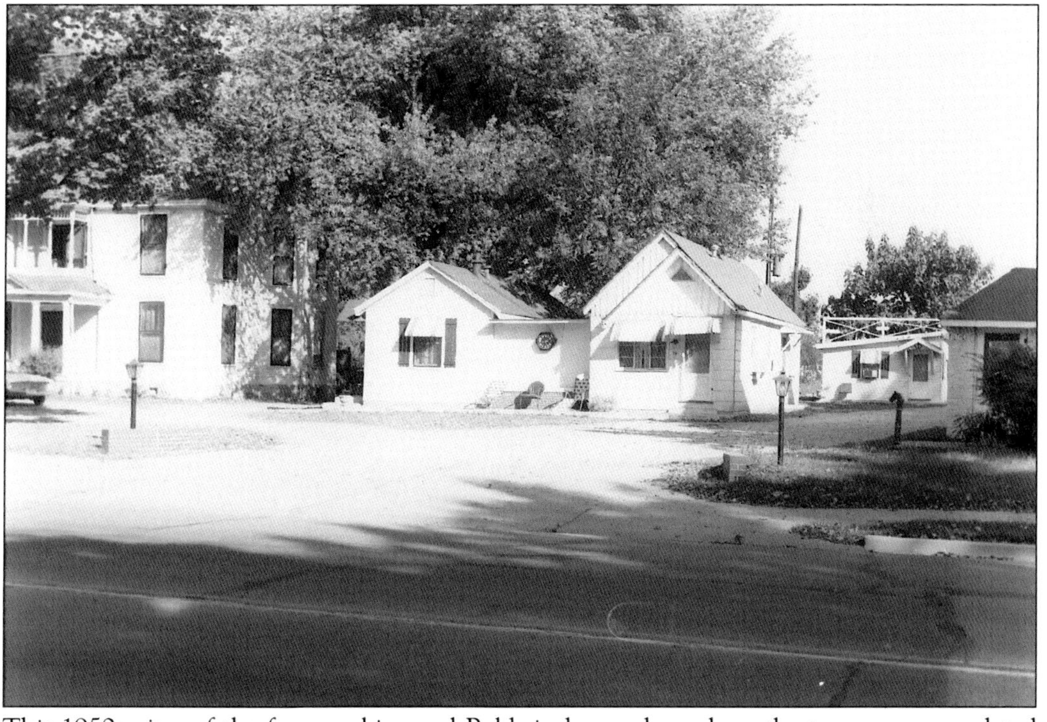

This 1950s view of the frame cabins and Baldwin home shows how the town accommodated the influx of tourists after My Old Kentucky Home opened to the public in 1923. The negative impact of Prohibition on the local whisky economy drove many to open their homes and to build tourist cabins in the 1920s and 1930s. This is the same site as the above picture.

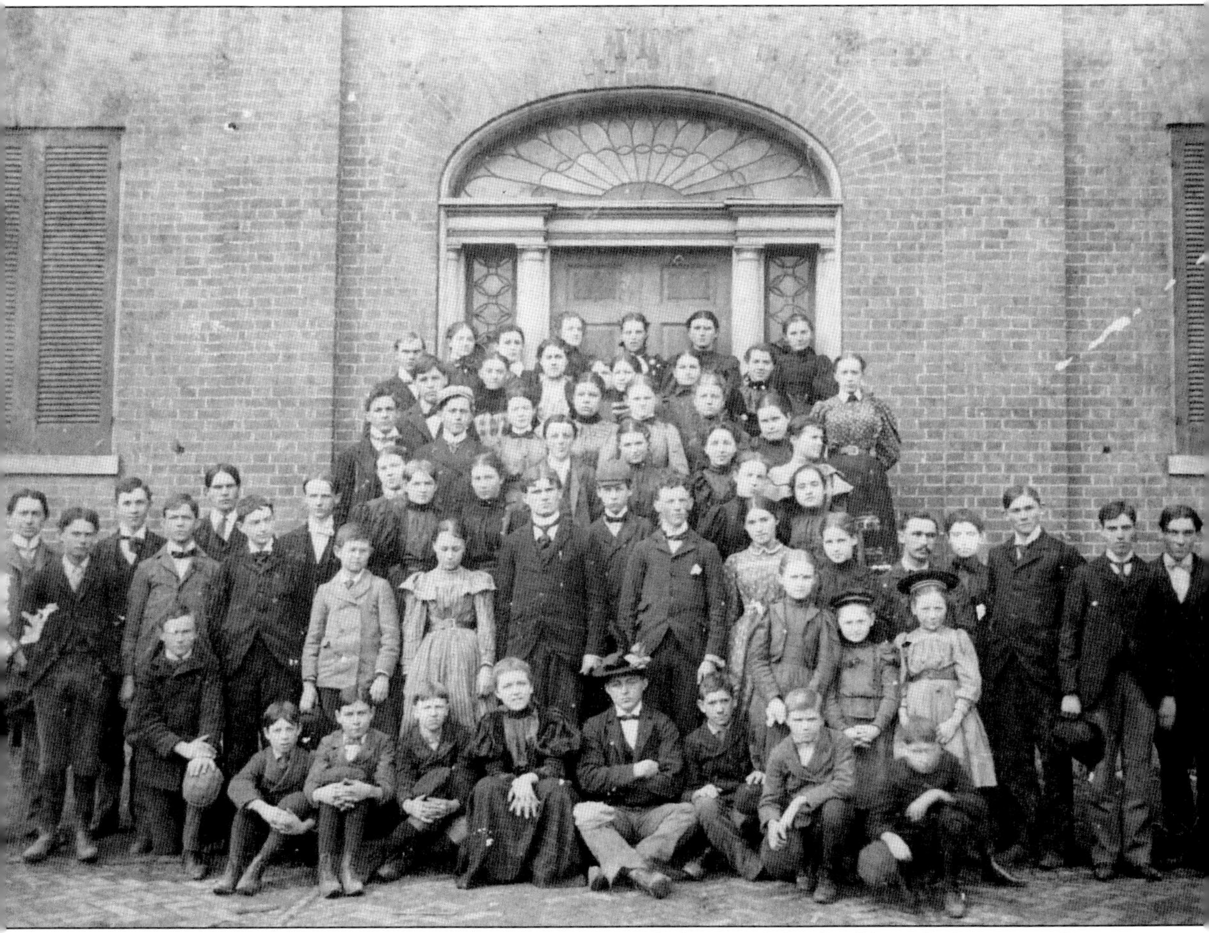

John Rogers, the architect for St. Joseph Cathedral, designed this building for James M. Browne as a residence (c. 1820) on outlot 3. He sold it to the trustees of Bardstown Female College in 1830. A curving stairway with beautifully carved woodwork leads to the third floor. A private school for girls, the college was operated by the Methodists and in 1836, by the Presbyterians. Noted educators Rev. Nathan L. Rice and Rev. Vernon Cosby were in charge of the school. Cosby named it Roseland Academy and was the most remembered of its presidents. It was rented by the Nelson Normal School in the 1890s. Pictured is Professor Edgar Crawford with his students c. 1895. It was purchased by James B. Beam in 1910 and was his home until his death in 1947. It remains in the family—Beam's grandson, Booker Noe, resides here to this day.

This 1886 map indicates the north wings of the school and how the rooms were used. These wings were two-story brick with a wooden porch that connected the rooms with the main building. The circle on the left is a smokehouse, which still remains on the property. The wings were removed after 1910.

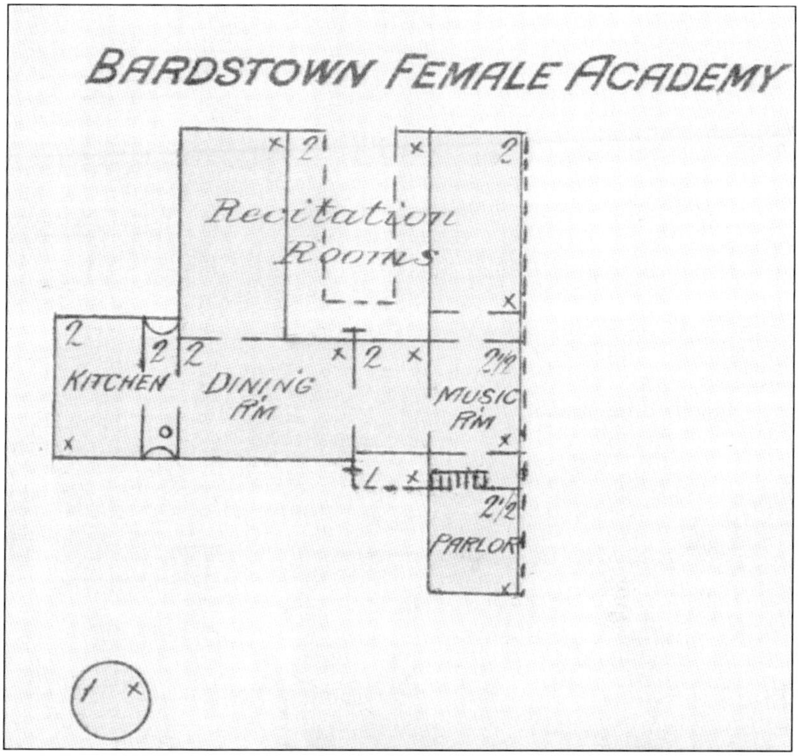

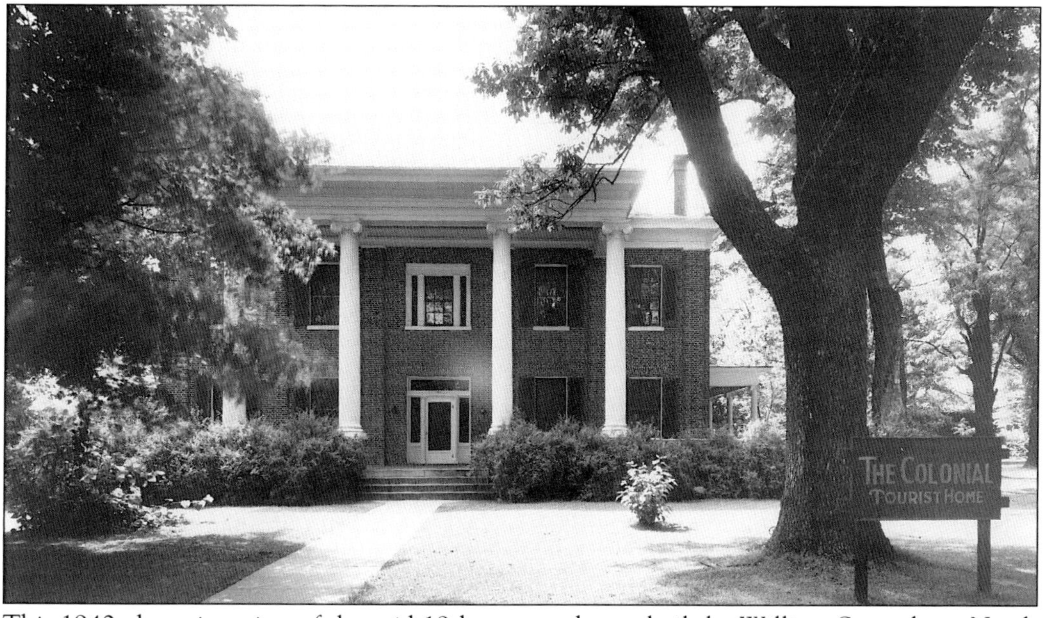

This 1940 photo is a view of the mid-19th-century house built by William Samuels on North Main Street (outlot 3). Leslie B. Samuels operated the T.W. Samuels Distillery at Deatsville and lived here while he served as mayor of Bardstown from 1935 to 1936. He had been on the city council for 35 years. The distiller's home was one of four located on "Distillers Row" beside the home of Jim Beam and across from John H. Beam and John Shaunty. Sold in 1938, it was used as both a funeral home and a tourist home before it was torn down in the 1960s.

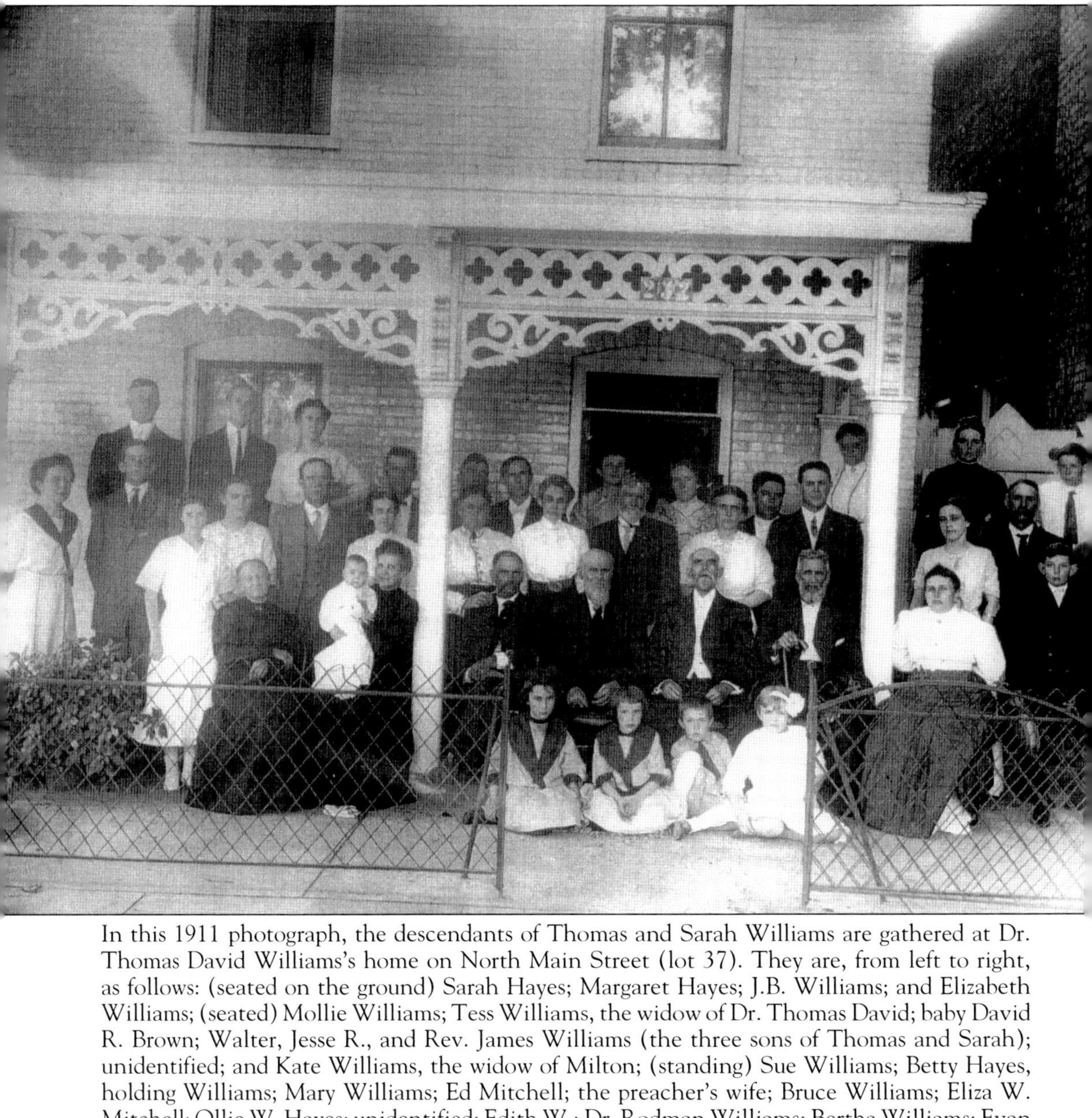

In this 1911 photograph, the descendants of Thomas and Sarah Williams are gathered at Dr. Thomas David Williams's home on North Main Street (lot 37). They are, from left to right, as follows: (seated on the ground) Sarah Hayes; Margaret Hayes; J.B. Williams; and Elizabeth Williams; (seated) Mollie Williams; Tess Williams, the widow of Dr. Thomas David; baby David R. Brown; Walter, Jesse R., and Rev. James Williams (the three sons of Thomas and Sarah); unidentified; and Kate Williams, the widow of Milton; (standing) Sue Williams; Betty Hayes, holding Williams; Mary Williams; Ed Mitchell; the preacher's wife; Bruce Williams; Eliza W. Mitchell; Ollie W. Hayes; unidentified; Edith W.; Dr. Rodman Williams; Bertha Williams; Evan Sales; an unidentified boy; and Jim Rodman; (back row) an unidentified Methodist preacher; Wallace Brown; Nancy Williams Brown; unidentified; unidentified; Sally Mae Williams; Irene Williams, wife of Charlie Williams; unidentified; unidentified; Jesse W. Sales; and Dawson Williams. The names have been copied from the handwritten notes on the back of photo. The building pictured here was known as the Wallace Brown House.

In 1850, James Carothers built a Greek Revival mansion facing Main Street. Directly behind his home was this two-story brick structure. It was attached to the larger house by a walkway and was probably used as a summer kitchen or servants' quarters. In 1835, Charles Nourse purchased the 2-acre lot for $800. It is unknown whether he or the Carothers built the house. It was located on outlot 3, facing Chestnut Street, and was torn down in 1992.

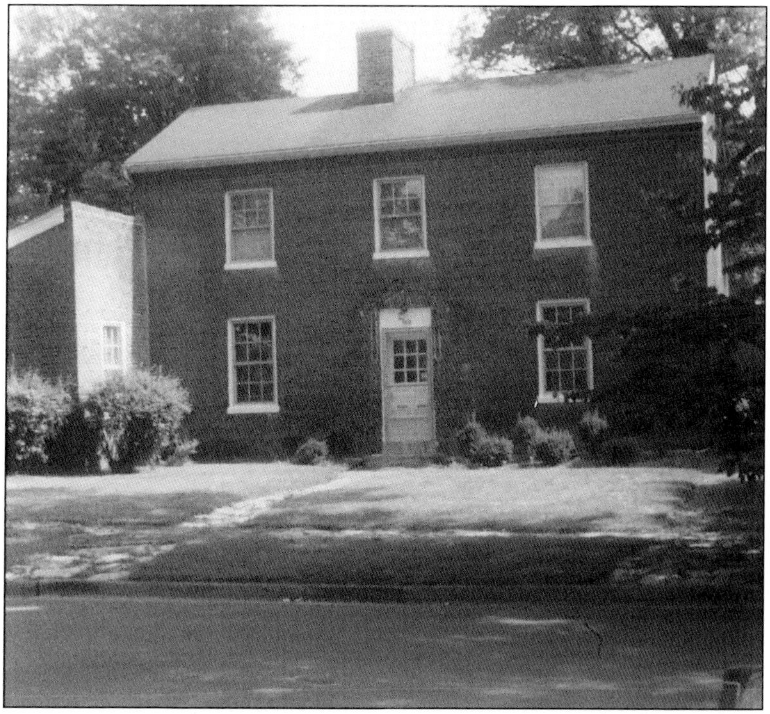

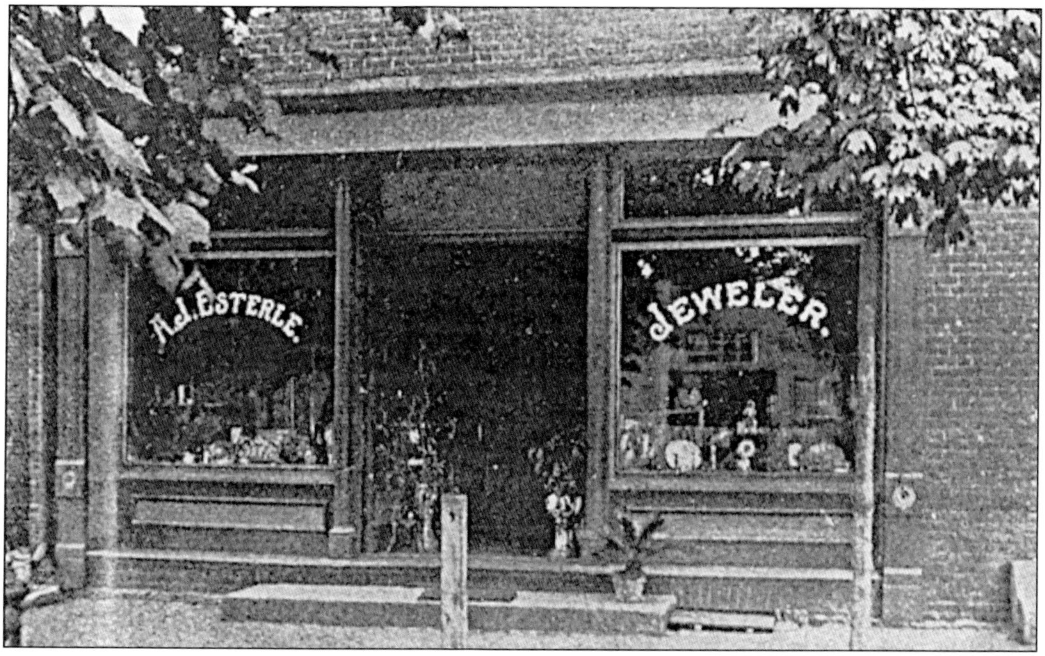

South of Wallace Brown's house on the same lot (number 37) is Esterle's Jewelry Store. As early as 1897, Mr. Esterle operated this business but after his death in 1900 it was operated by his wife. This 1904 view shows that the store front has obviously replaced two windows of one side of a dwelling. The entrance to the residence is at the right of the picture. This building was demolished by the Duval Masonic Lodge in the early 1950s in order to build a new lodge building.

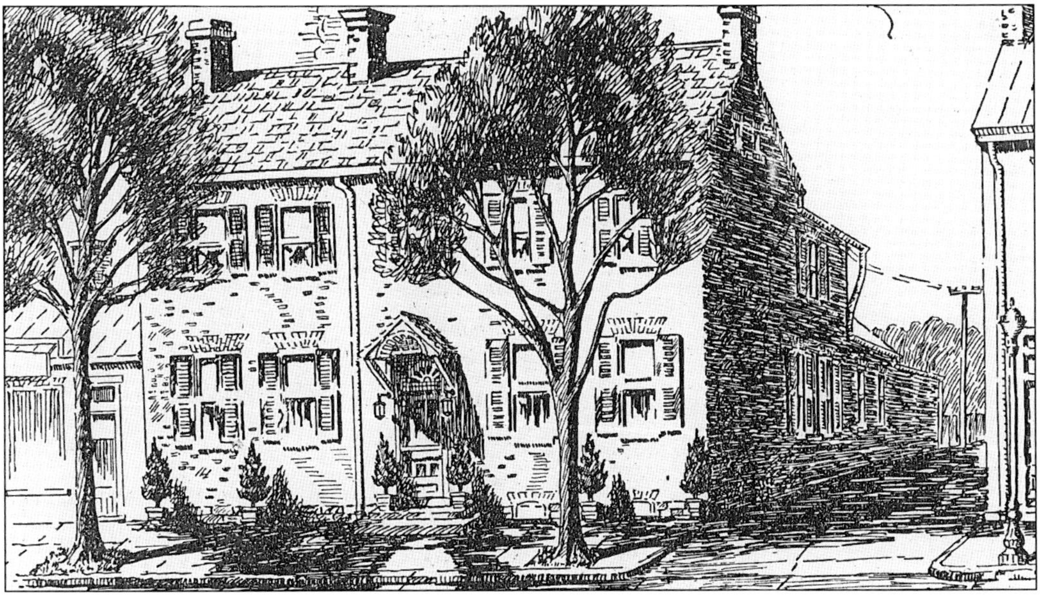

Pictured in this 1941 sketch is the William Kelly house, located on North Main Street (lot 47). In December 1863, Dr. Arch Cox was called upon to treat the Confederate Colonel Basil Duke, who was the brother-in-law of Gen. John Hunt Morgan. Wounded by mortar fire at the ford on the Rolling Fork River at Boston, Colonel Duke was brought to this house and treated in the upstairs bedroom. With his head wound bandaged, he traveled the next day on a feather-bedded wagon. The southern half of this building was torn down in 1941 to build the Arco theater.

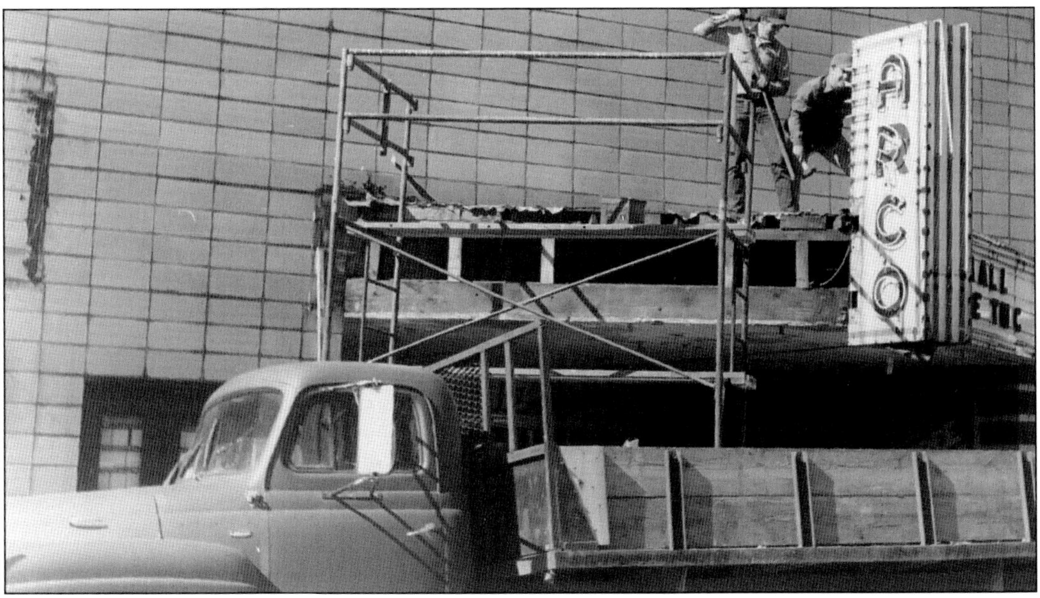

A partnership of C.D. Arnold and Pope Sisco gave the theater its name. The new Melody Theater opened in December 1948. The competition of television and other amusements drove the theaters out of business. The Melody closed in 1953 and the Arco followed, closing in 1965. This photo shows the marquee being dismantled so that a new front can be erected for Hall Electric.

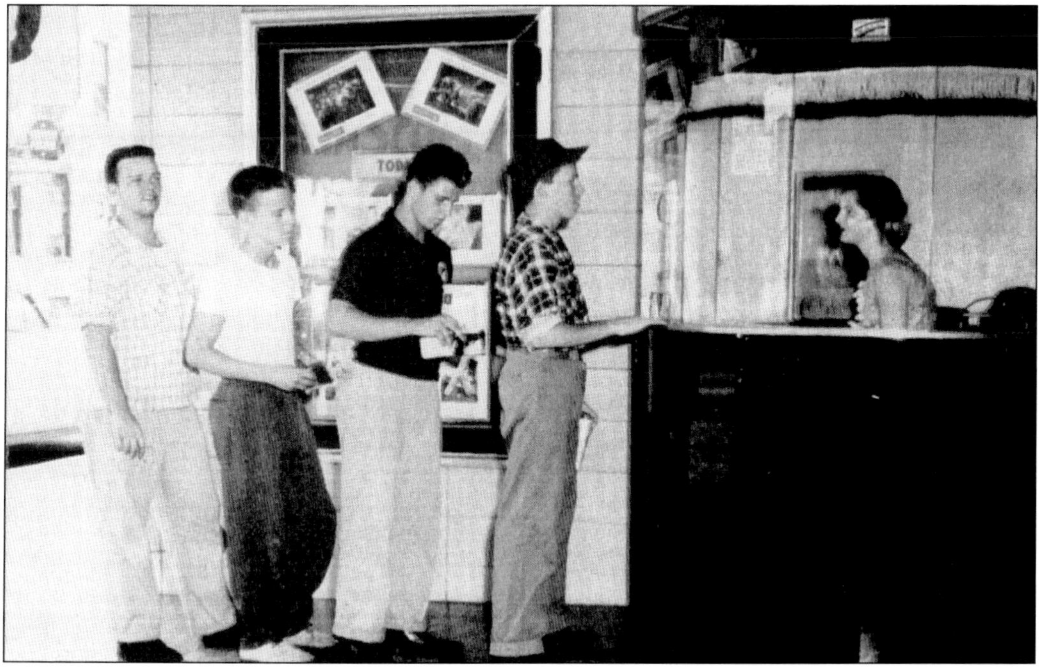

St. Joe Prep students are lined up at the ticket booth at the Arco Theater. The girls from Nazareth College were often bused in to see the matinees on Saturday and Sunday. After the show, they stopped for a Coke or soda at either the "B and B" or the drugstore.

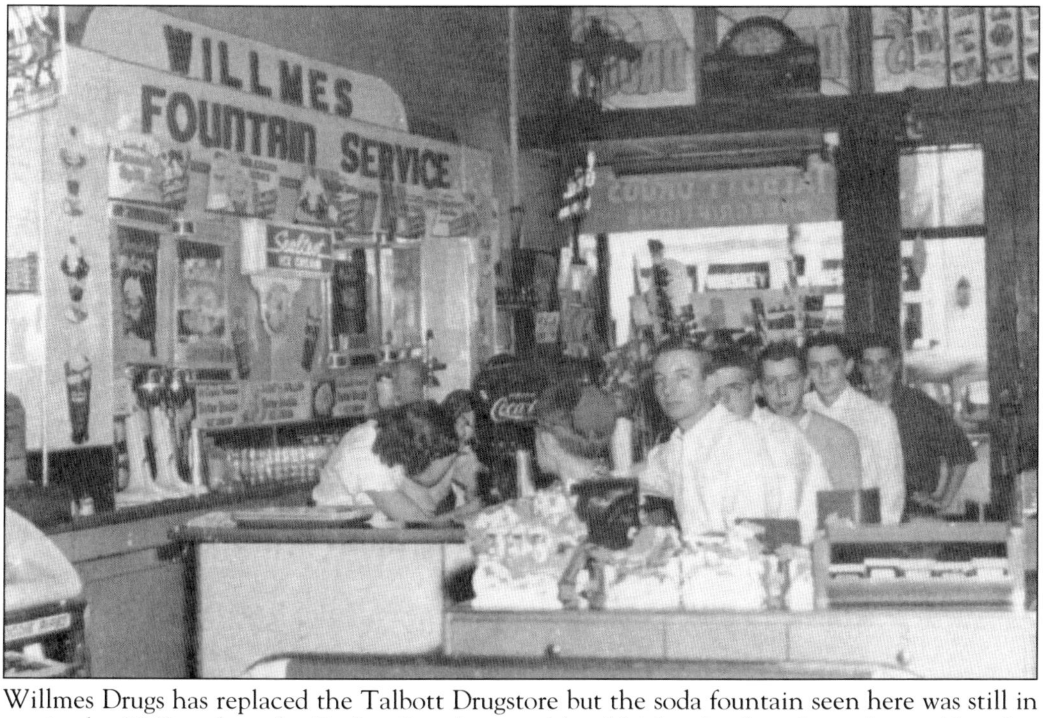

Willmes Drugs has replaced the Talbott Drugstore but the soda fountain seen here was still in use in the 1950s, when the St. Joe Prep boys and local high school students dropped by after school or the movies. Cherry Cokes or purple cows were the treat of the day.

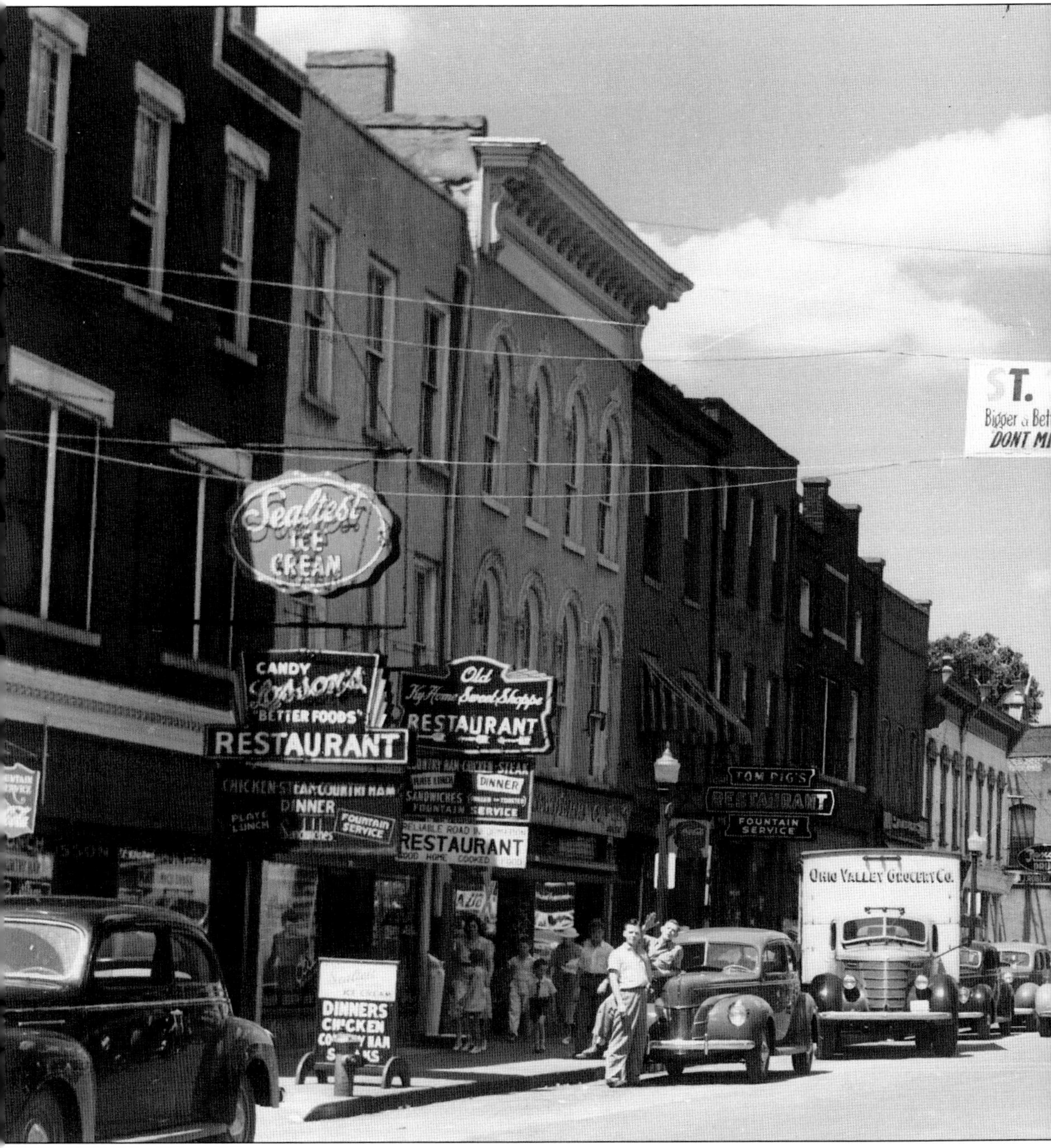

An August day in 1940 was captured in this photograph. Looking north, the business signs on the west side of Main Street show the following businesses: the Losson Restaurant, which operated in different locations for 77 years; The Old Kentucky Home Sweet Shoppe Restaurant, the site of chamber of commerce meetings, a luncheon for guests at the John Fitch monument unveiling, DAR antique shows, and private parties throughout the 1920s and 1930s; Tom Pig's Restaurant, which operated here since 1927; and, at the end of the block, the Rexall Drug store, where different pharmacists have dispensed drugs since 1840. On the same August day in 1940,

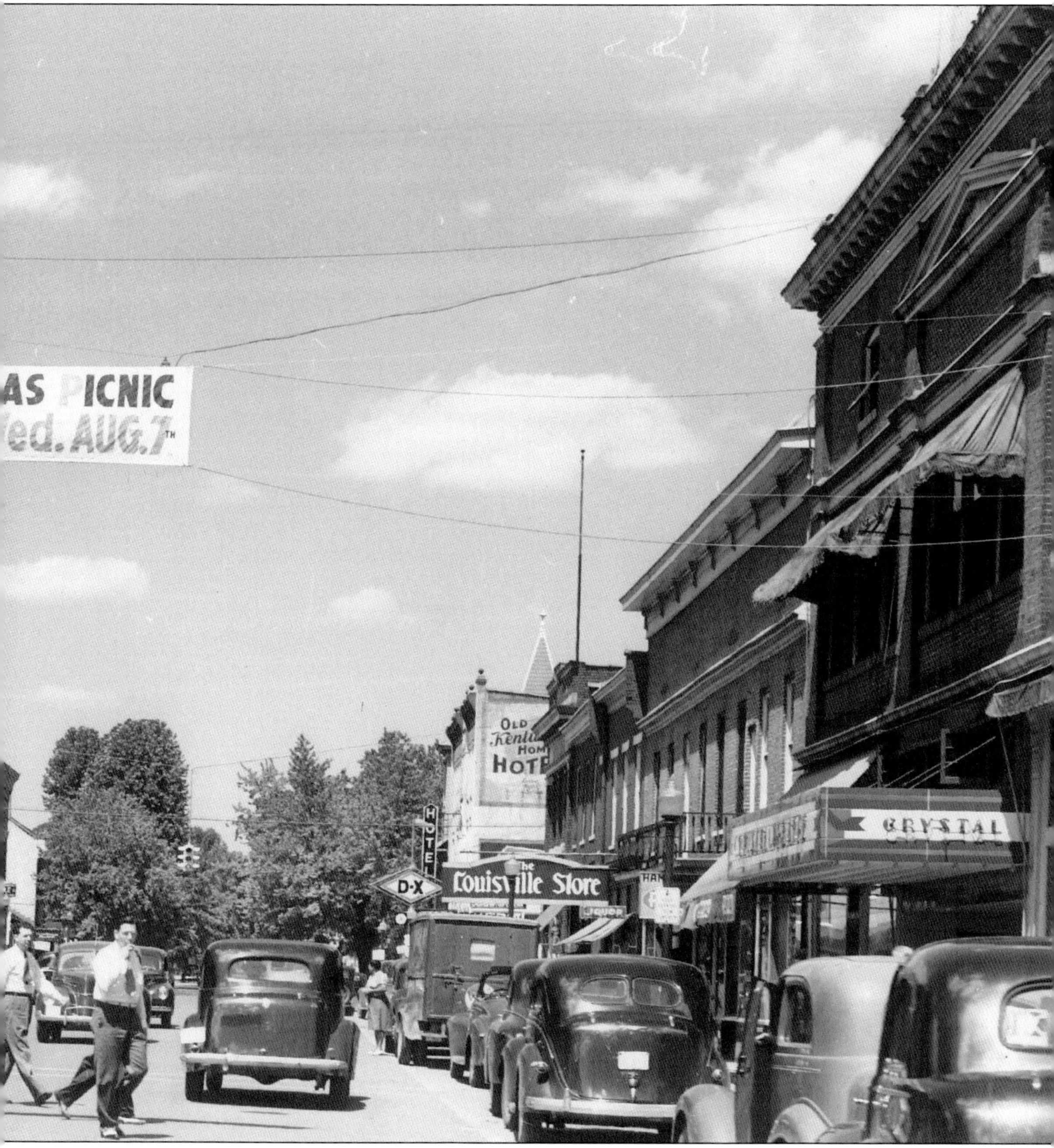

this view of the east side of Main Street shows the Crystal Theater, the "motion-picture show place." The 1910 building housed the silent pictures with Mary B. Crume pounding the keys of the piano as the action demanded. Going north you will see the iron balcony that supplied the second-floor apartments with a hallway and a porch. The Louisville Store is a department store operated by the Shapira family of Louisville. The DX sign can be seen in front of the service station that was built in 1934 on the site of Wigginton and Boone's building. Next is My Old Kentucky Home Hotel, which later became the Stephen Foster Hotel.

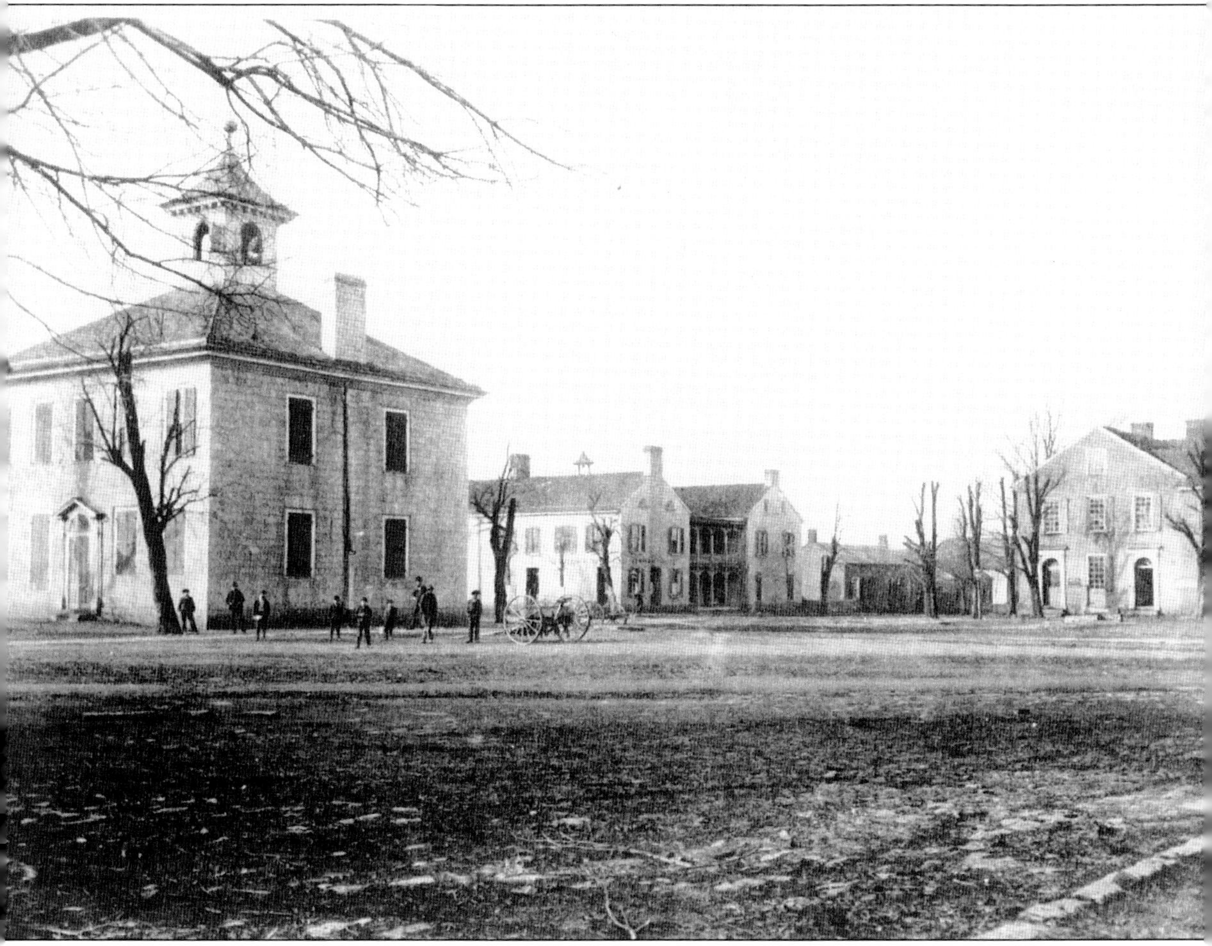

This Georgian-style, stone courthouse (built between 1788 and 1800) resounded with the oratory talents of such men as Henry Clay, John Rowan, Ben Hardin, Charles A. Wickliffe, John Hays, and Felix Grundy. It was the scene of far-reaching decisions of land ownership. Political and religious differences were debated within these walls by representatives of differing factions. The building was removed in 1892 to make room for a larger structure, but the court directed that the stones were to be used in the foundation of the new building. Its shuttered windows indicate court was not being held. Located on the southwest corner of Market Square is the Newman House, later called Talbott Tavern. The brick buildings next door were county offices, handy to Lawyer's Row on the opposite corner. A mounting block is visible in the front. New kerosene street lamps can be seen at the corner of Market Street and the Square. Fifty of these lamps were installed along the streets in 1882.

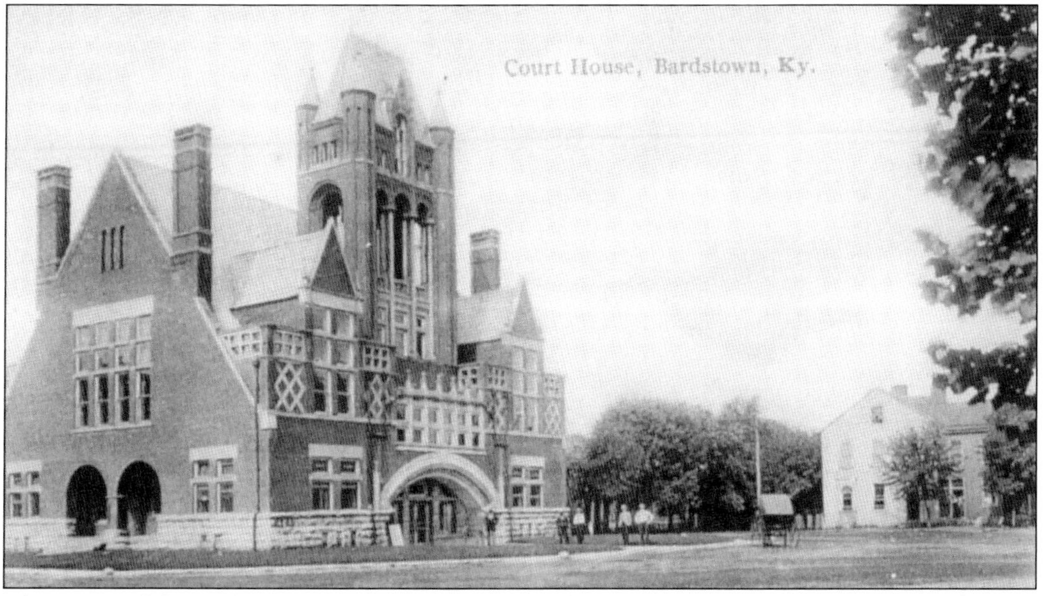

This postcard shows the new courthouse, constructed in 1892. It was the result of an architectural contest offered by the Fiscal Court members. This design was chosen from the entries. It was designed to accommodate all the county offices and the courtroom in one building. To the right is the Brashear House or Lawyers Row.

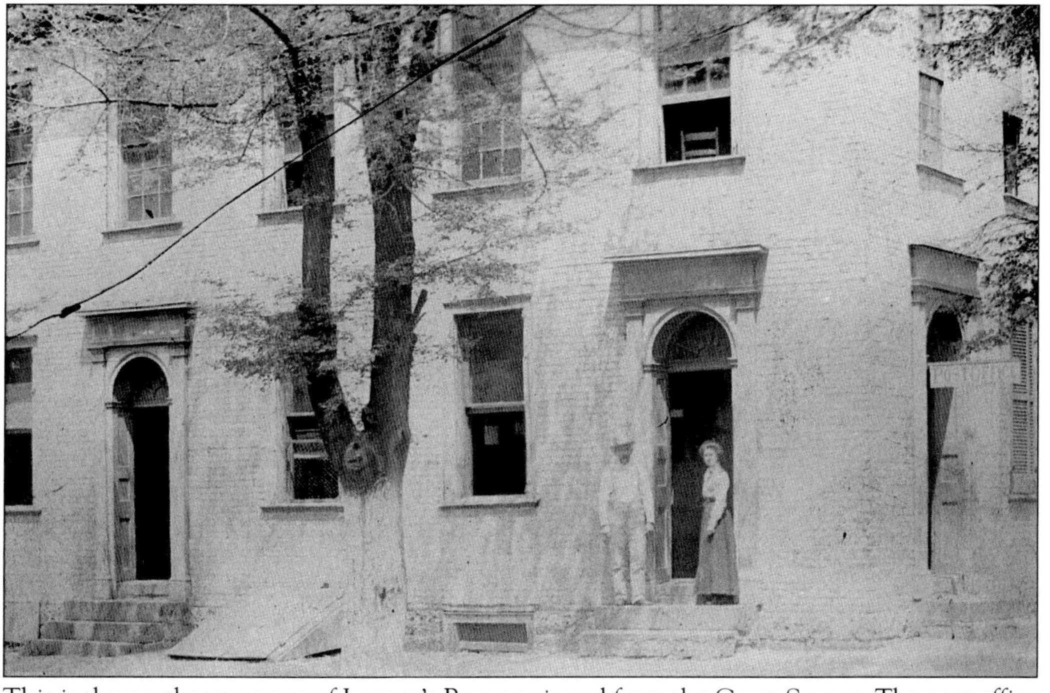

This is the northeast corner of Lawyer's Row as viewed from the Court Square. The post office was located here. George M. Talbott was appointed postmaster in 1895 and Miss Beatrice Mann (on the right) was appointed assistant postmaster in 1893. They used this convenient site to handle all the official duties of a United States Post Office. The building was removed and the new, larger post office was constructed in 1914.

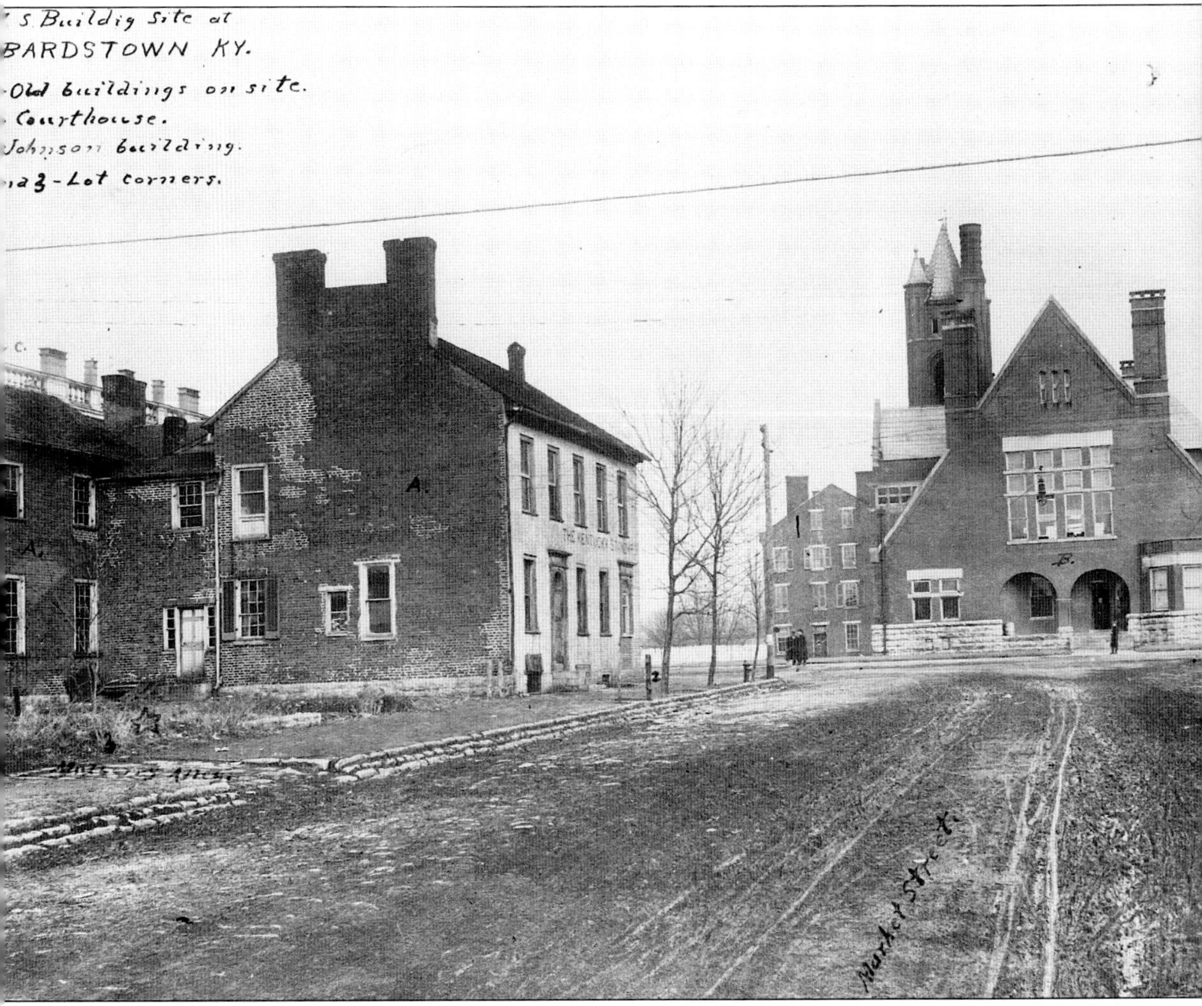

This 1911 view, looking east on Market Street, shows the large brick building (left) built by Dr. Walter Brashear before 1810 as a residence on lot 80. He is best known for his medical history making hip-joint amputation in 1806. The building was used in 1827 by Charles Holloway as Washington Hall, a "tavern and house of public entertainment." At this time it was called Lawyer's Row because the five offices were rented by attorneys Allen McKay, C.T. Atkinson, John D. Wickliffe, Judge John A. Fulton, Judge John S. Kelley, and R.C. Cherry. Note the sign on the front brick wall that reads "The Kentucky Standard." The printing office of this newspaper, started in 1900, occupied the second floor of the building. It was torn down in 1914 to build the new post office.

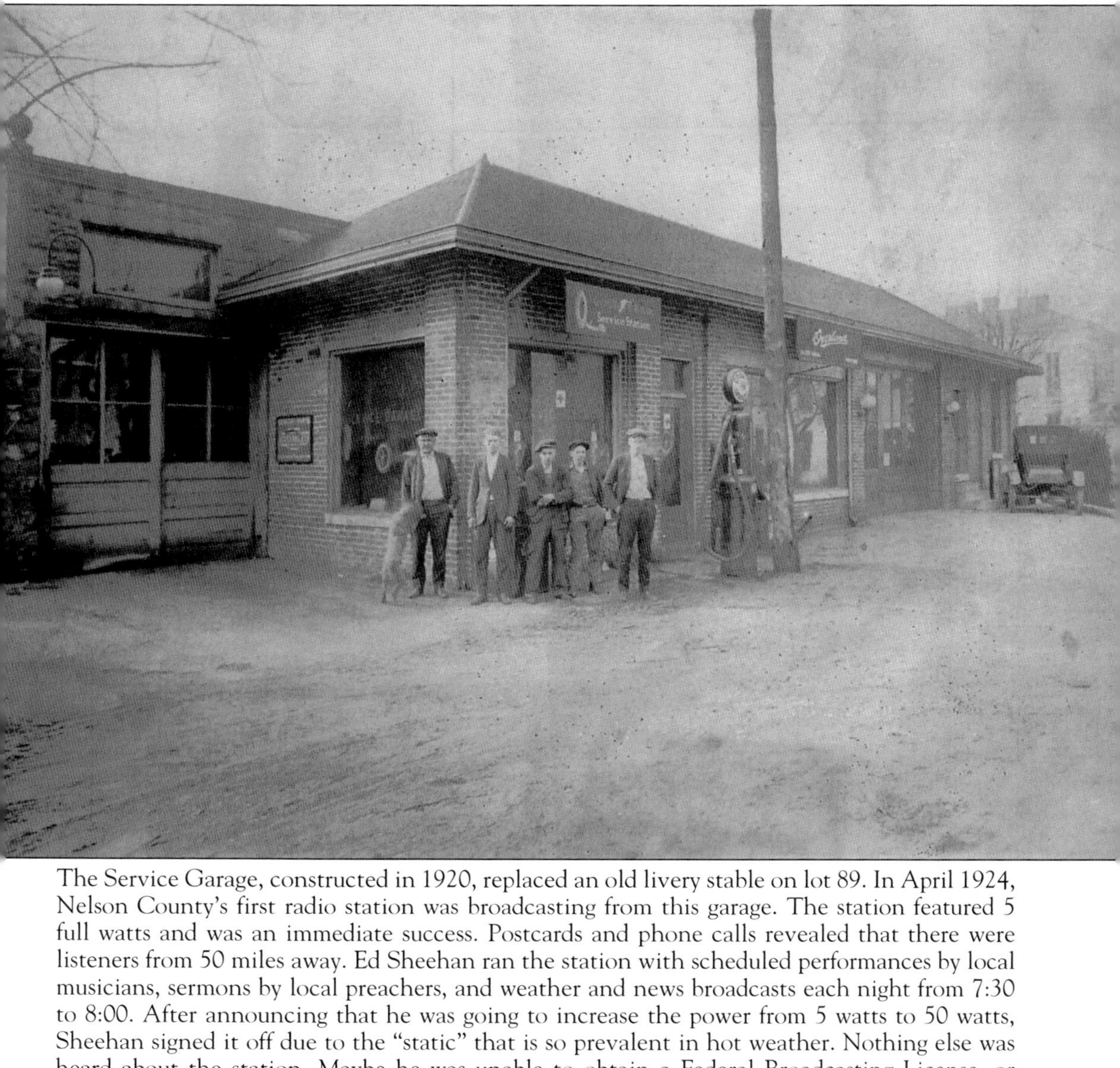

The Service Garage, constructed in 1920, replaced an old livery stable on lot 89. In April 1924, Nelson County's first radio station was broadcasting from this garage. The station featured 5 full watts and was an immediate success. Postcards and phone calls revealed that there were listeners from 50 miles away. Ed Sheehan ran the station with scheduled performances by local musicians, sermons by local preachers, and weather and news broadcasts each night from 7:30 to 8:00. After announcing that he was going to increase the power from 5 watts to 50 watts, Sheehan signed it off due to the "static" that is so prevalent in hot weather. Nothing else was heard about the station. Maybe he was unable to obtain a Federal Broadcasting License, or maybe the cost of broadcasting programs without commercials brought about its demise.

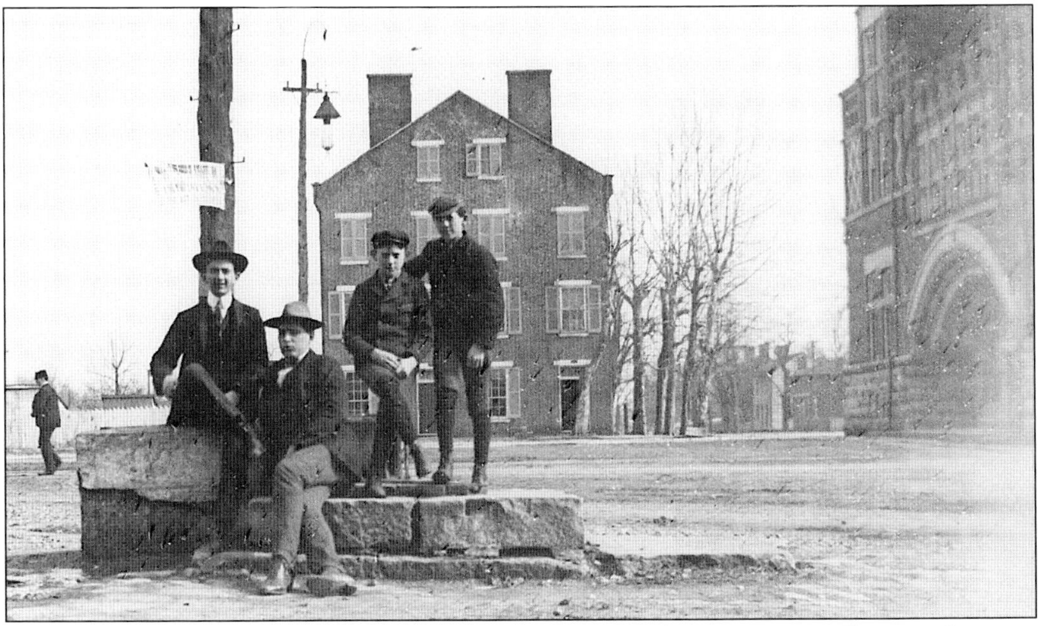

Looking east from the mounting block (shown earlier) is this 1920 view. The courthouse is on the right. The large brick structure in the background is the Hite-Boone building. It was built by Thomas Hite by 1816 and used as a residence and a store. It was removed in 1927 and replaced with Conway Motor Company. The electric street light hanging behind the people replaced the old kerosene street lamps.

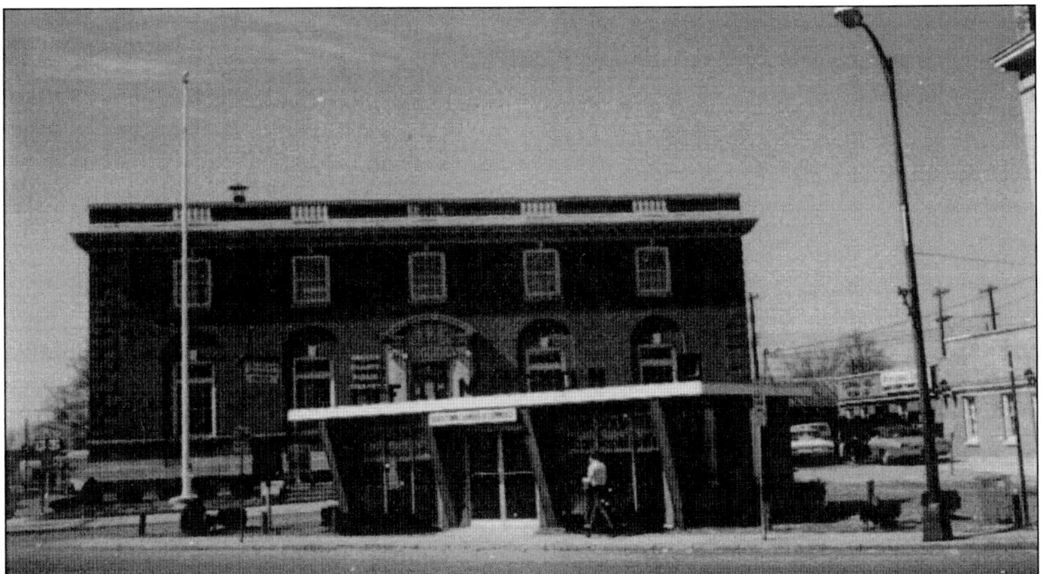

The Bardstown Jaycees erected a small frame building in 1955 to serve as an information center. It was replaced by this building in the spring of 1961. It was to be used as a central ticket office for the Stephen Foster Drama Association during the 10-week season and as an office and general information center year round. Donated labor and materials were used. This building was removed in 1980s, when the information center was moved to 107 East Stephen Foster Avenue.

Two

CHANGES ON OTHER STREETS

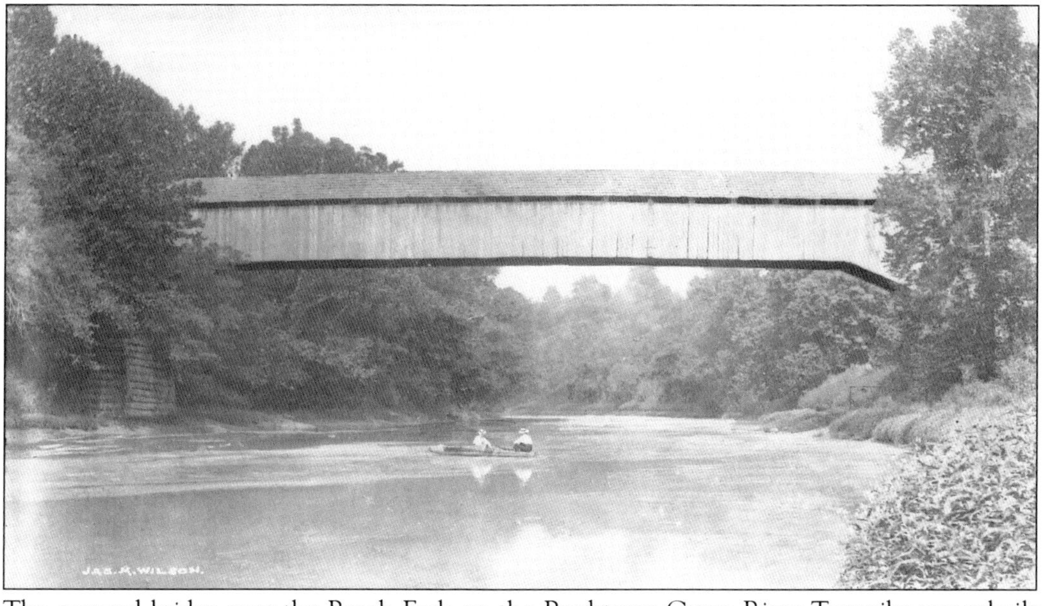

The covered bridge over the Beech Fork on the Bardstown-Green River Turnpike was rebuilt in 1866 after it was destroyed during the Civil War. James Carothers, a noted bridge builder of central Kentucky, built the first one in the 1830s. It was divided by a wooden partition through the middle, separating the traffic. The bridge in this c. 1901 postcard view was rebuilt on the original stone abutments but was not as wide and was not divided. The bridge was used for automobile traffic until 1933, when the new iron bridge was opened. It finally fell into the river in 1938. This was an "out of town" change, but affected every traveler going south on this road.

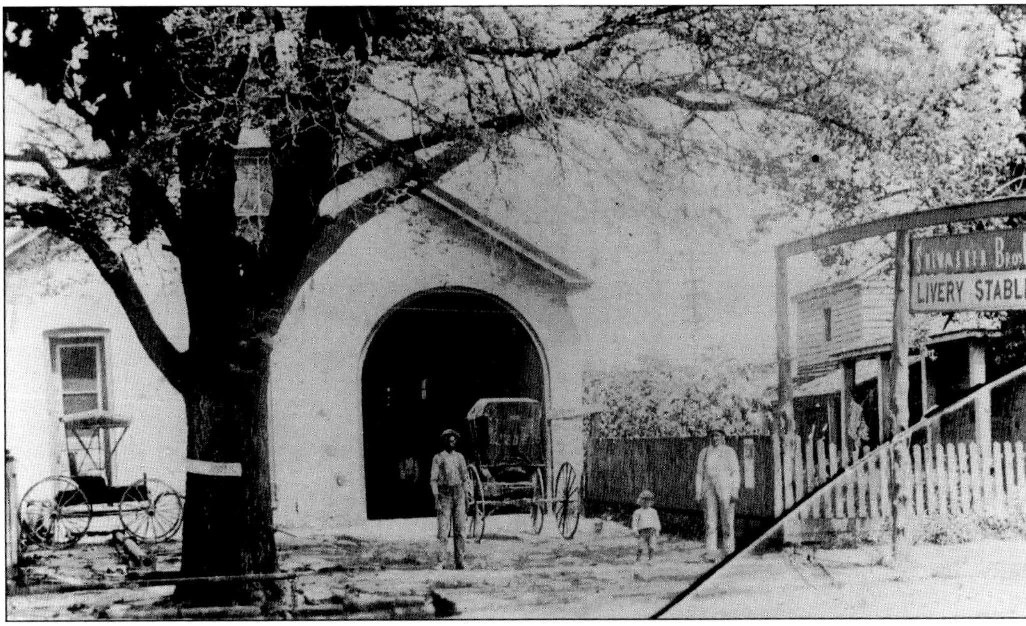

In 1900, Shewmaker Brothers' Livery Stable was located on the north side of West Market Street (lot 81). The small boy seen in this picture is Earl Shewmaker at age three. Jim Shewmaker is on the left and Harry Shewmaker, Earl's father, is on the right. The Old Stable Restaurant is now located on the site.

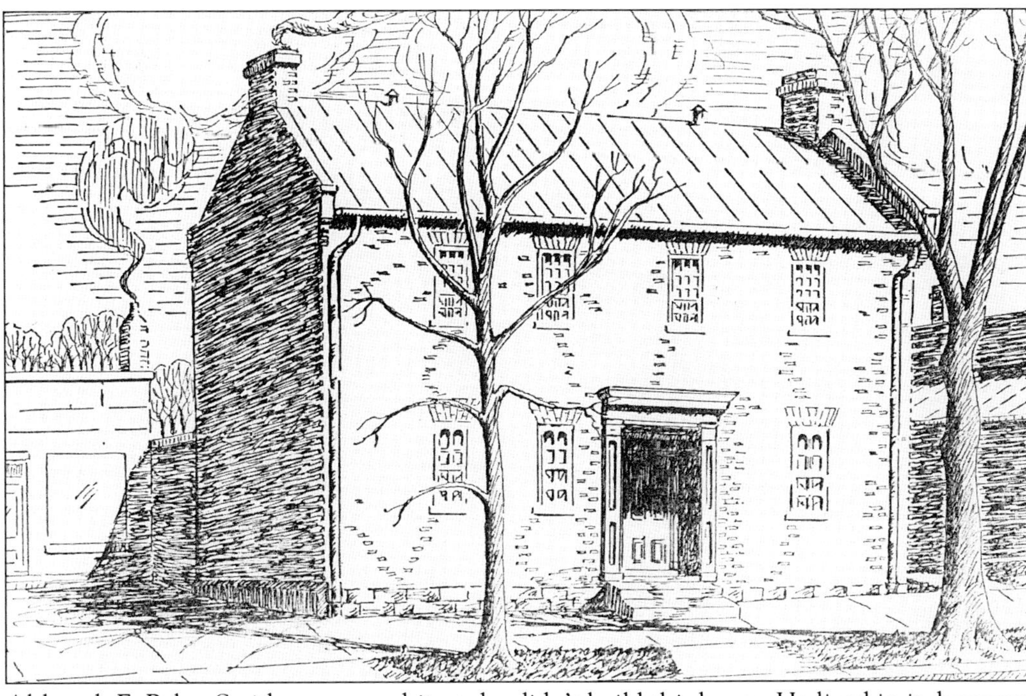

Although E. Baker Smith was an architect, he didn't build this house. He lived in it, however, for more than 60 years. It is an example of the early brick townhouses built with no openings on the end walls. The front doorway doesn't appear to be original. The house was located on West Market Street (lot 82) and was torn down in 1964. The site is now a parking lot.

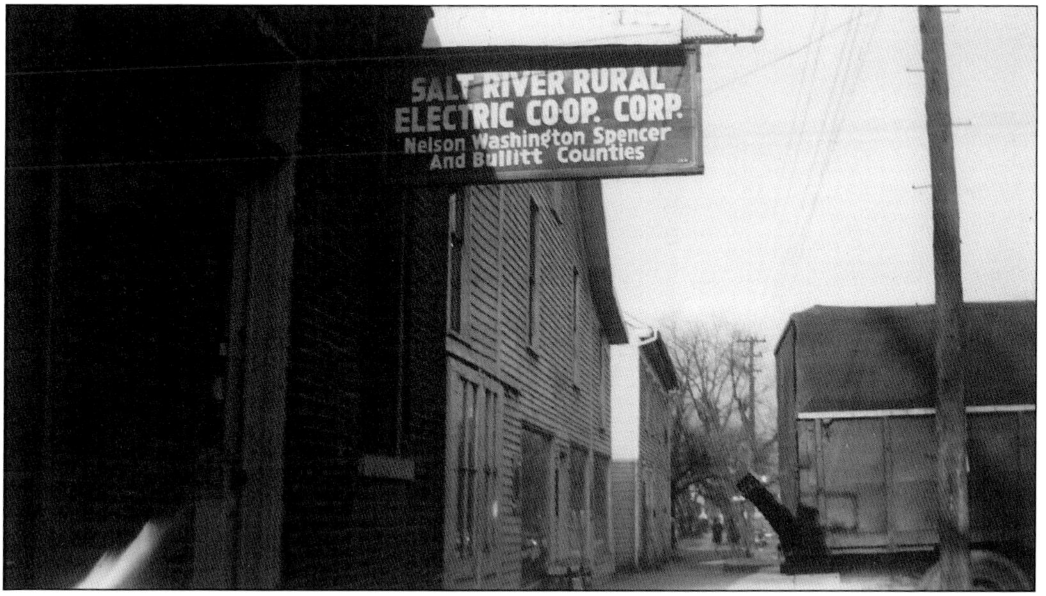

The Boner-Beall law office, located on West Market Street (lot 88) was the office of the Salt River Rural Electric Cooperative Corporation. This picture is undated but it is known that they moved to the present site in 1947. If this picture was made before 1945, the building next door would have been the Rosenham Sisco Carriage Factory, presently Bardstown Auto Sales. If the photo was made after 1945, the building next door would have been a produce business operated by W.A. Ice.

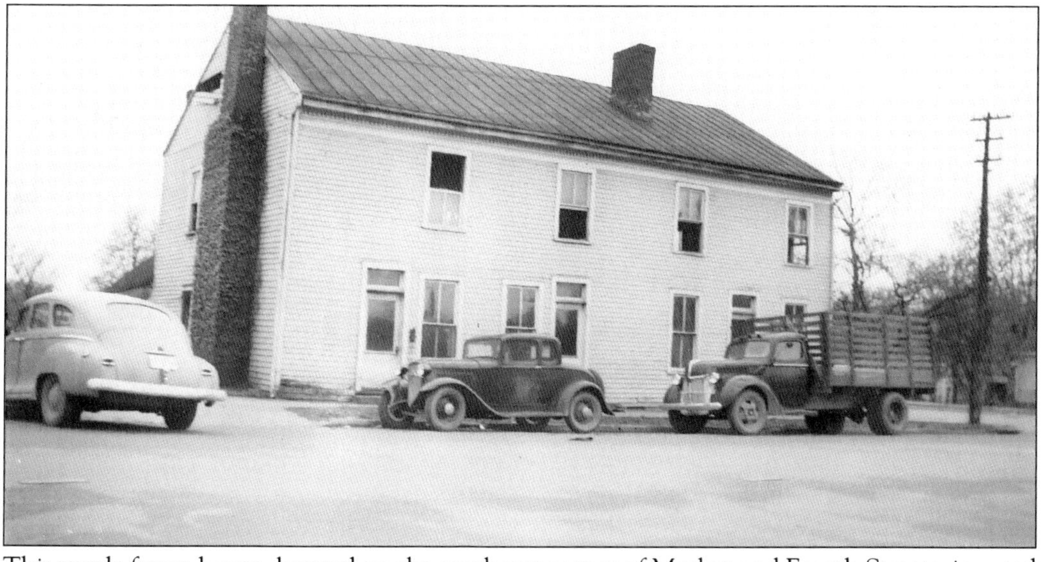

This sturdy frame house, located on the southeast corner of Market and Fourth Streets, is noted on the Atlas Map of 1882. It was the residence of Felix Rogers in 1843. This picture was made in 1948, before it was torn down.

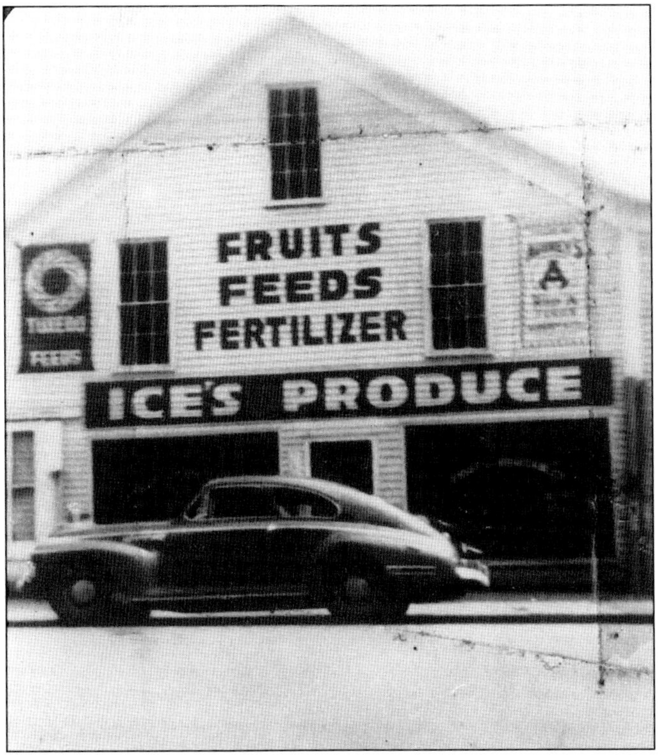

Pictured is Ice's Produce in the 1950s. It was used in the 1880s by Sisco and Rosenham as a carriage business in the front and a blacksmith shop in back and was located on West Market Street (lot 87). At the time of the 1963 fire, old surrey tops were still stored upstairs. In later years, the shop served as a Chevrolet dealership. Sympson and Samuels Motor Company sold cars here until their new building was constructed across the street in 1937. It was then used as Bardstown Auto Sales. W.A. Ice purchased the building in 1945. He and his son, W.A. Jr., were in the produce business together until W.A. Jr.'s son, Jimmy Ice, bought the business in 1956.

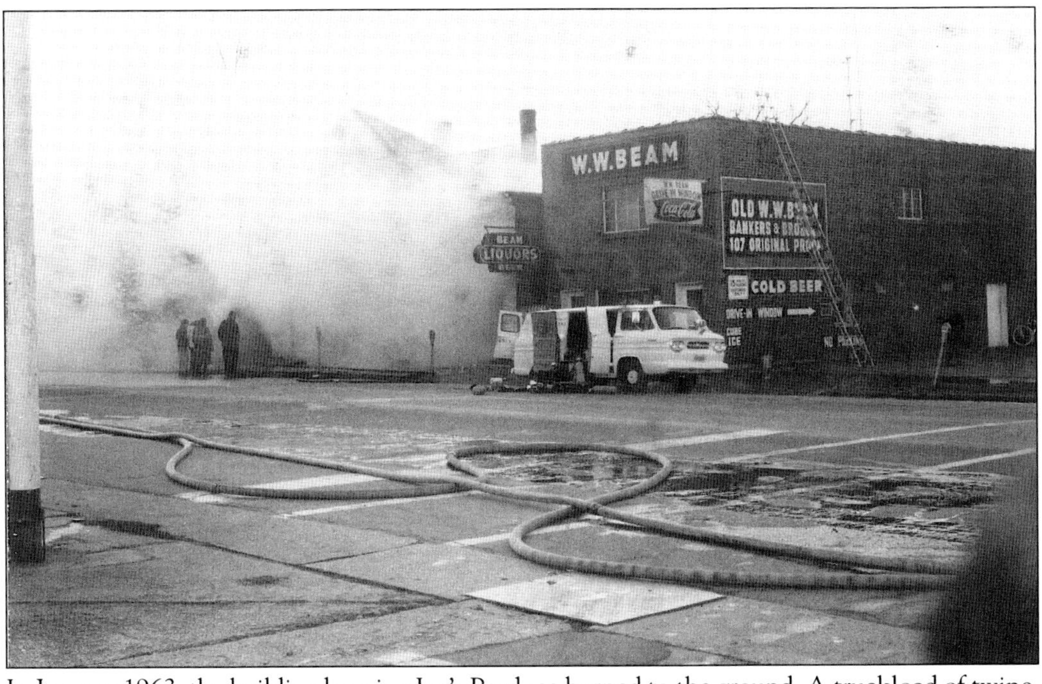

In January 1963, the building housing Ice's Produce burned to the ground. A truckload of twine, fertilizer, and corn added to the flames. Jimmy and Aline Ice and their family salvaged vehicles they used in their trucking operation and were back in business selling out of the back of a truck until they could rebuild.

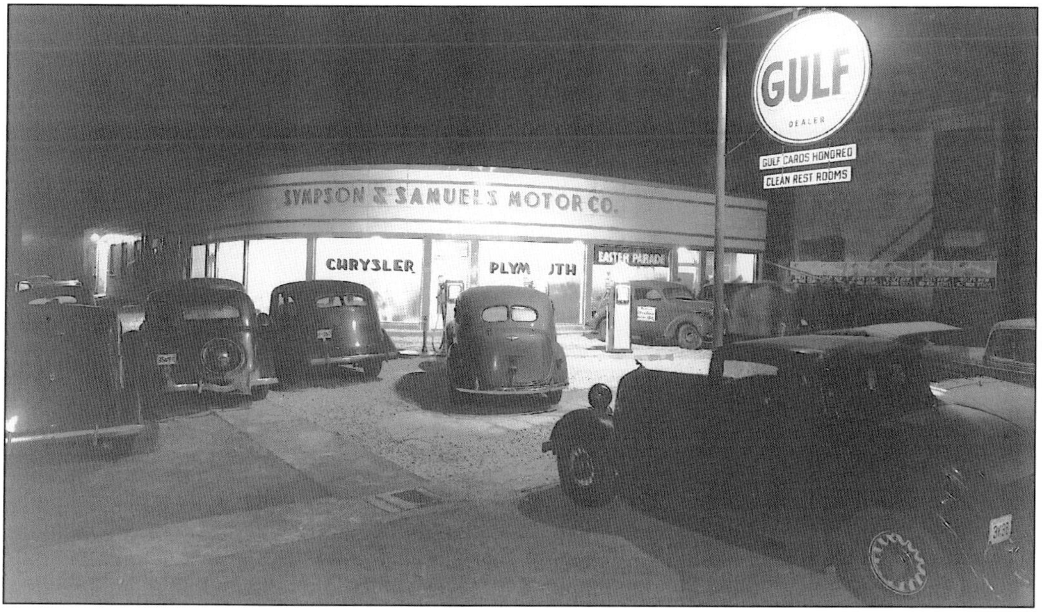

This new building was described in the newspaper as "a gigantic mirror, the front containing 900 square feet of glass." The 1937 grand opening of the Sympson and Samuels Motor Company, located on the corner of Fourth and Market Streets (lot 82), was attended by 5,000 people, according to *The Kentucky Standard*. The spacious showroom displayed Chrysler and Plymouth automobiles, radios, electric refrigerators, and Westinghouse electric appliances. After a parade of cars led by the Old Star Band, the program was held in the showroom and garage area. This scene shows the crowd enjoying a picture show, vaudeville acts, and old-fashioned and modern dancing to the tunes of the Paul Barry orchestra. This building was remodeled in 1978, and part of the original structure was retained in the present Market Place.

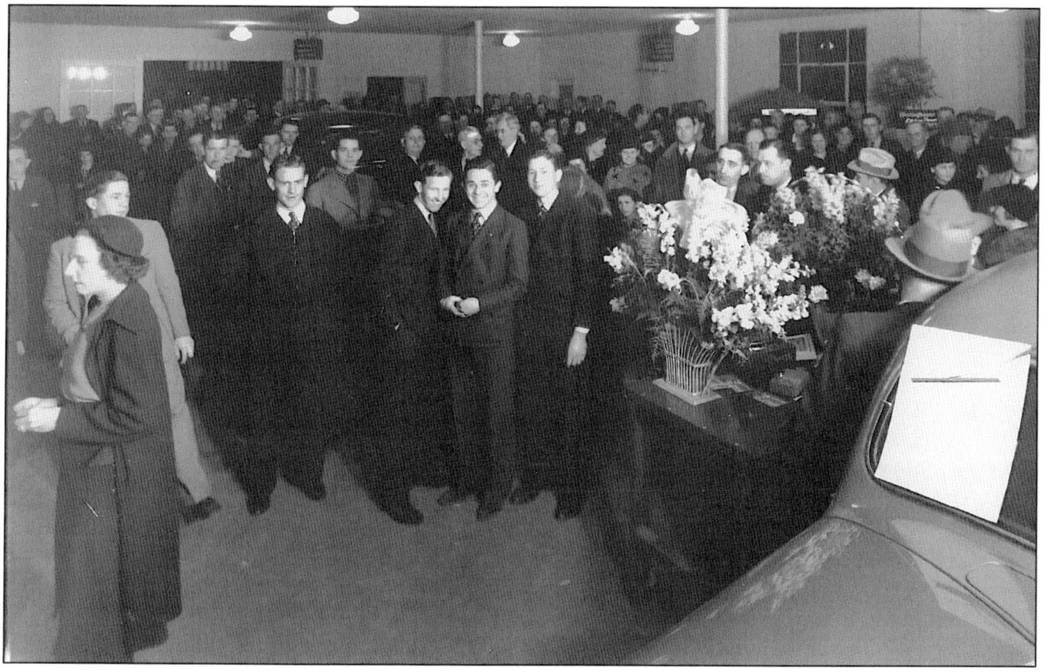

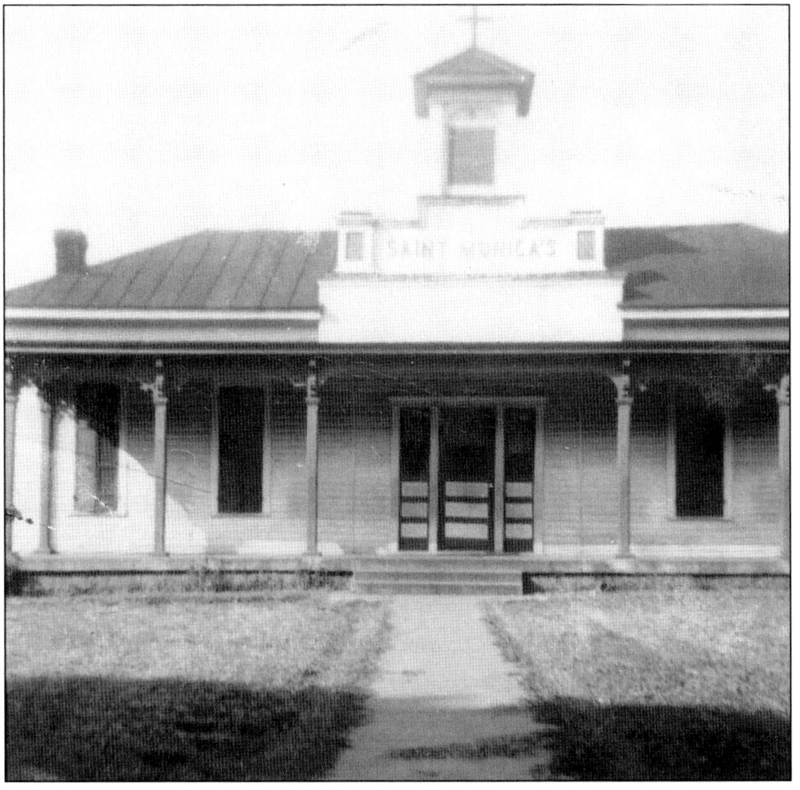

St. Monica's School building was located on West Stephen Foster Street (lot 84). First called St. Martha's, it is noted on the Atlas Map of 1882. The Sisters of Charity operated the school, which was attended by African-American Catholics. The building was also used for church services until the new church was constructed on South Third Street in 1955. It was torn down in 1957.

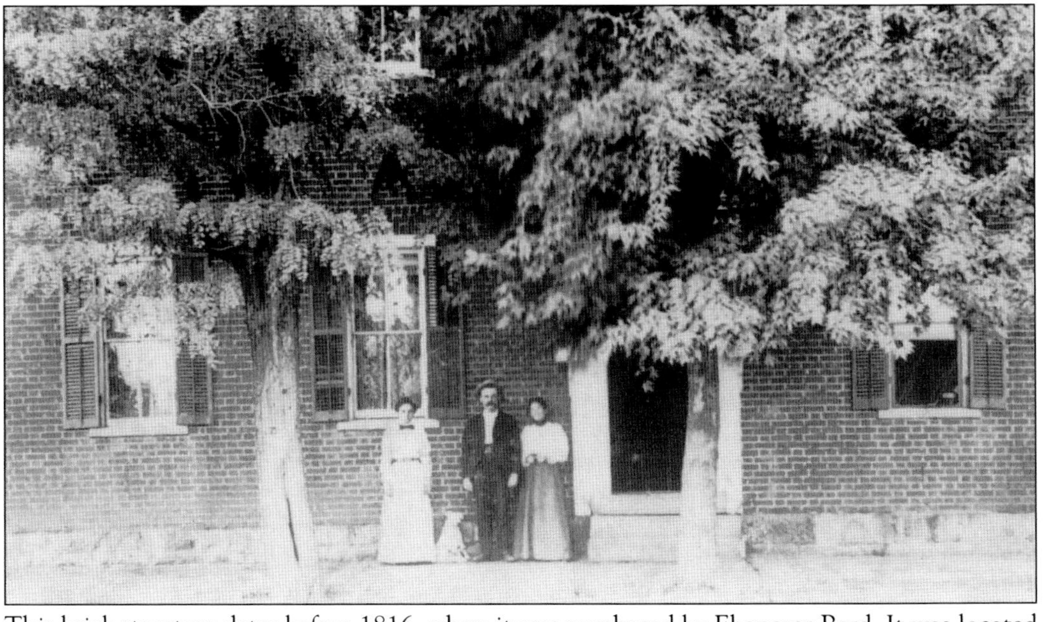

This brick structure dates before 1816, when it was purchased by Ebenezer Bard. It was located on the north side of West Market Street (outlot 7). Bard mortgaged this house along with his "coppersmith shop" in 1820 for $4,240. The T.A. Spalding family resided here in the early 1900s. After the construction of their new home, this one was demolished and the bricks were used to construct the building presently there.

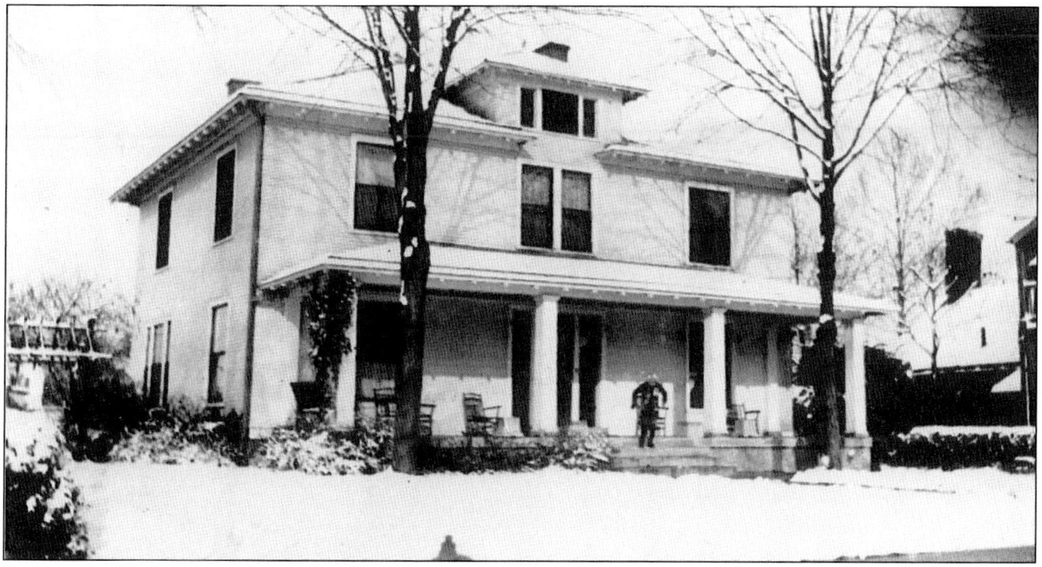

In 1911, Thomas A. Spalding (of the Spalding and Sons Dry Goods family) built this house on the northeast corner of West Market and Fifth Streets for his residence. He lived next door while constructing it. It was used from 1951 to 1953 as a funeral home by his daughter, Mrs. Josephine Smith. It was sold to the Mitchell Oil Company in 1961 and razed.

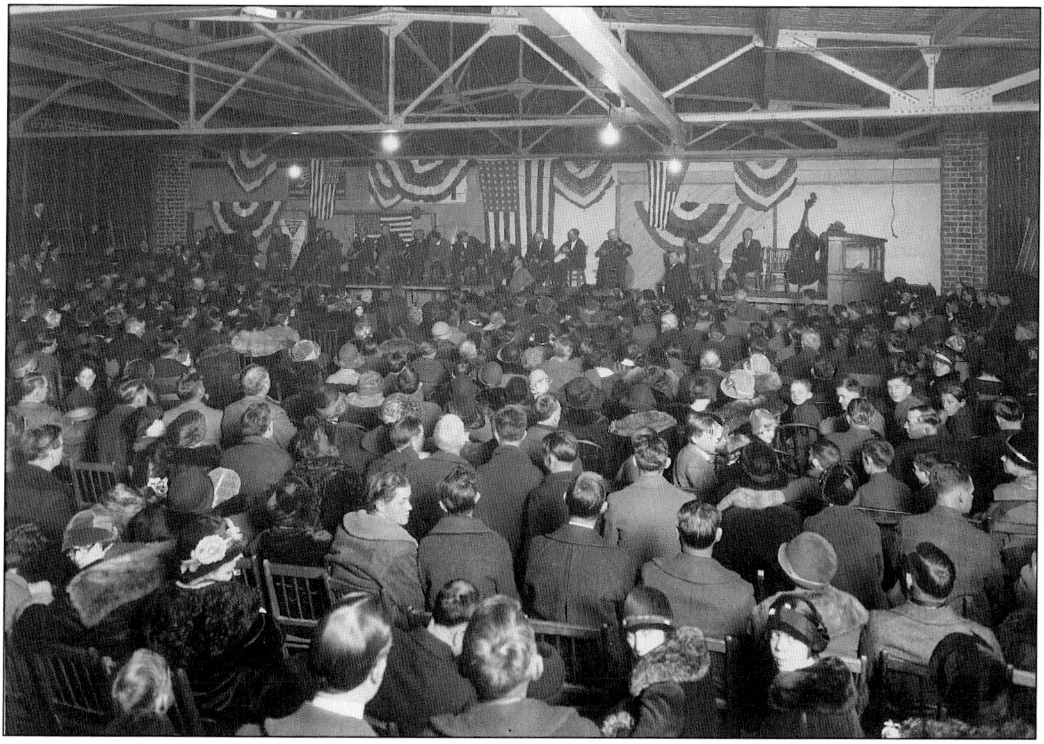

J.F. Conway liked to use the service area in his garage on West Market Street to host community events. This photo taken c. 1925 shows a fiddler's contest. The flat bed of a Ford truck provided a platform for the bass fiddle and guitar players on the right. The other platform has 13 fiddlers warming up to perform. Each performer had his fans to cheer him on.

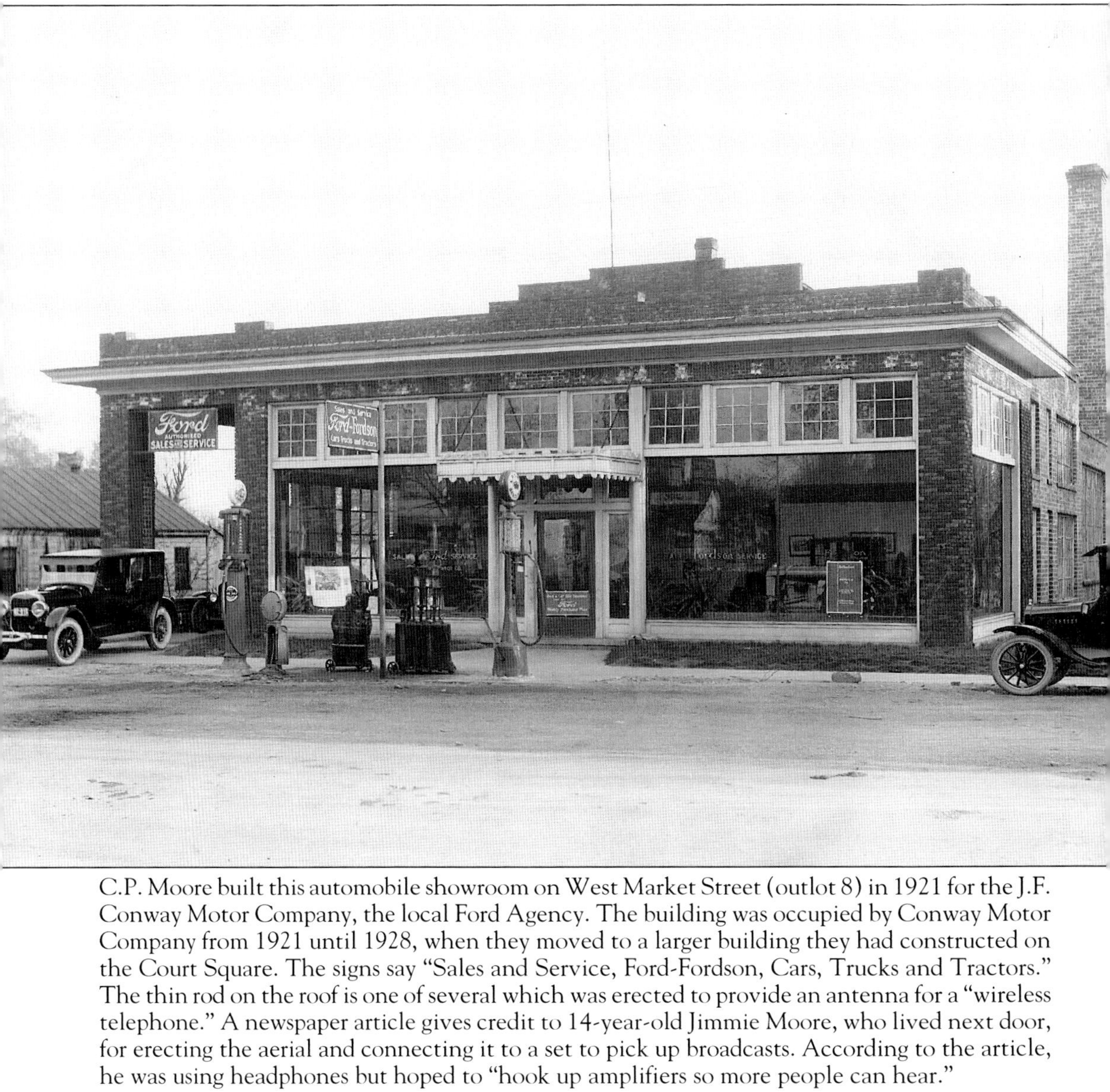

C.P. Moore built this automobile showroom on West Market Street (outlot 8) in 1921 for the J.F. Conway Motor Company, the local Ford Agency. The building was occupied by Conway Motor Company from 1921 until 1928, when they moved to a larger building they had constructed on the Court Square. The signs say "Sales and Service, Ford-Fordson, Cars, Trucks and Tractors." The thin rod on the roof is one of several which was erected to provide an antenna for a "wireless telephone." A newspaper article gives credit to 14-year-old Jimmie Moore, who lived next door, for erecting the aerial and connecting it to a set to pick up broadcasts. According to the article, he was using headphones but hoped to "hook up amplifiers so more people can hear."

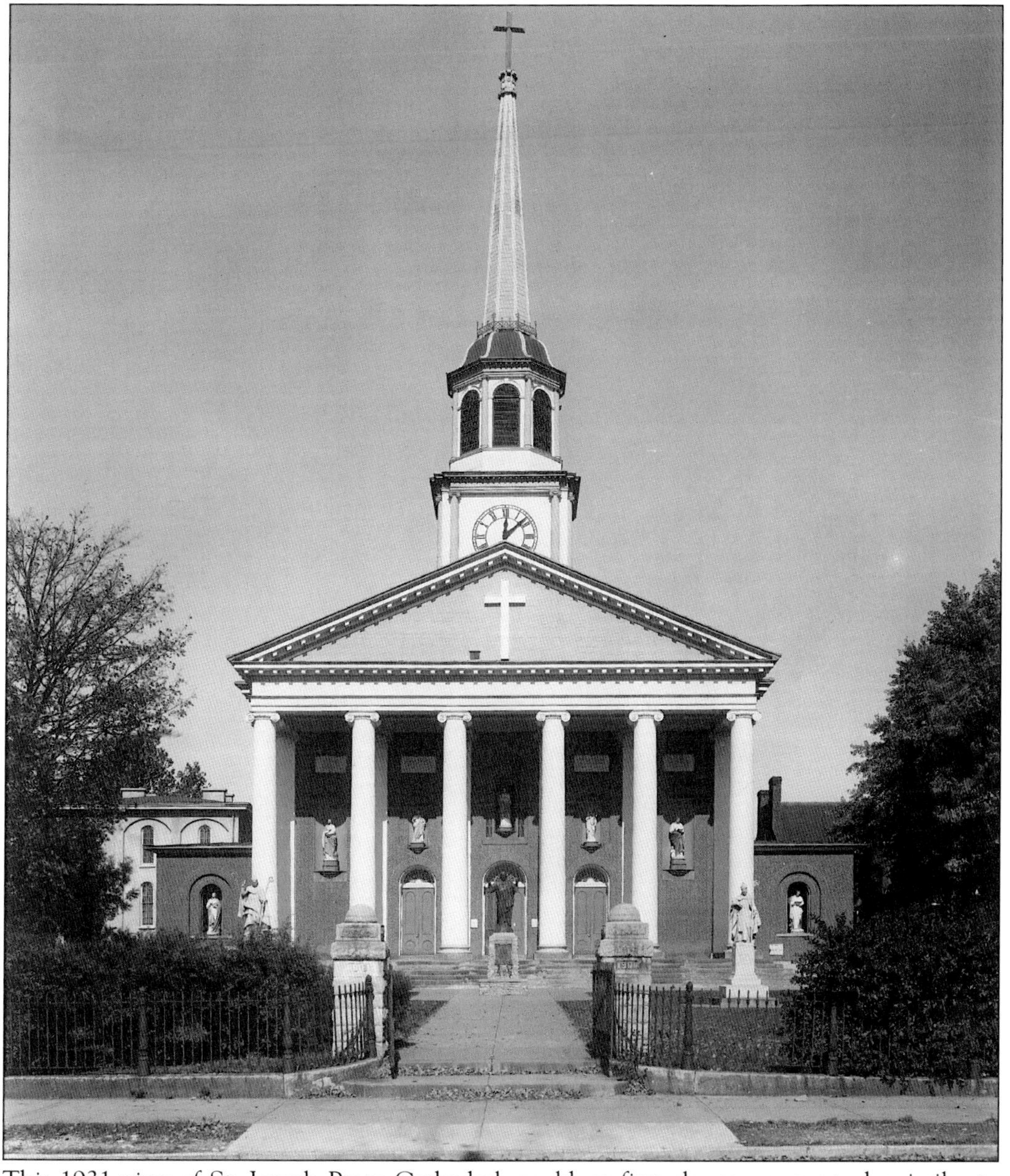

This 1931 view of St. Joseph Proto-Cathedral would, at first glance, appear to be similar to the view today, but a closer look at this 1816 structure shows additional details that have been removed. At the base of the steeple is a fine tracery of wrought-iron railing. The pediment columns on the steeple and trim around the bell tower are painted in contrasting colors. In the niches, in the side rooms, are statues. The stone pillars and iron fence which continued into a stonewall not pictured have all been replaced. The statue of St. Joseph in the middle of the walk has been removed to the Catholic cemetery on North Third Street. The wooden plaques mounted above the windows on each side are carved with the Ten Commandments. These were replaced in 1950 with porcelain plaques.

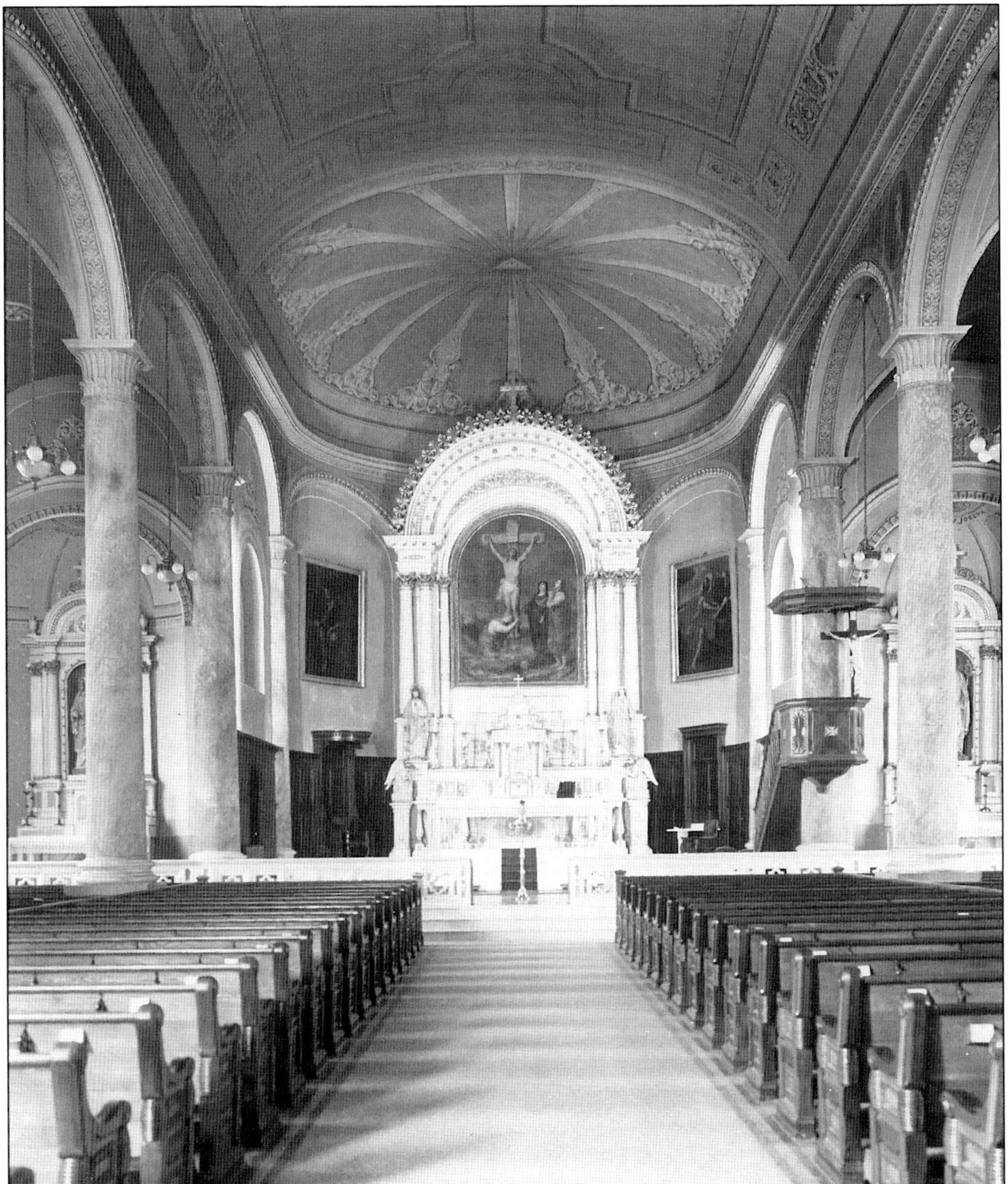

The interior of St. Joseph Cathedral has undergone many changes since its construction in 1816. The first major change was the renovation of 1879. This 1934 view shows the ceiling painting and the elaborate wooden altar. Carved trim and wooden urns frame the painting *The Crucifixion* and the statues on each side altar. The Bishop's throne on the left of the sanctuary and the elevated pulpit (right) were retained from the earlier church. The original stone altar was replaced by dropping the 3,000 pound, 10-foot-long stone below the floor of the sanctuary. In 1903, F.O. Raab was hired to clean and restore the paintings. Electric lights were installed in 1910, replacing kerosene lamps. The marble altar rail was also installed in the early 1900s. The pulpit, wooden altar surroundings, and wooden paneling in the sanctuary were removed in 1960.

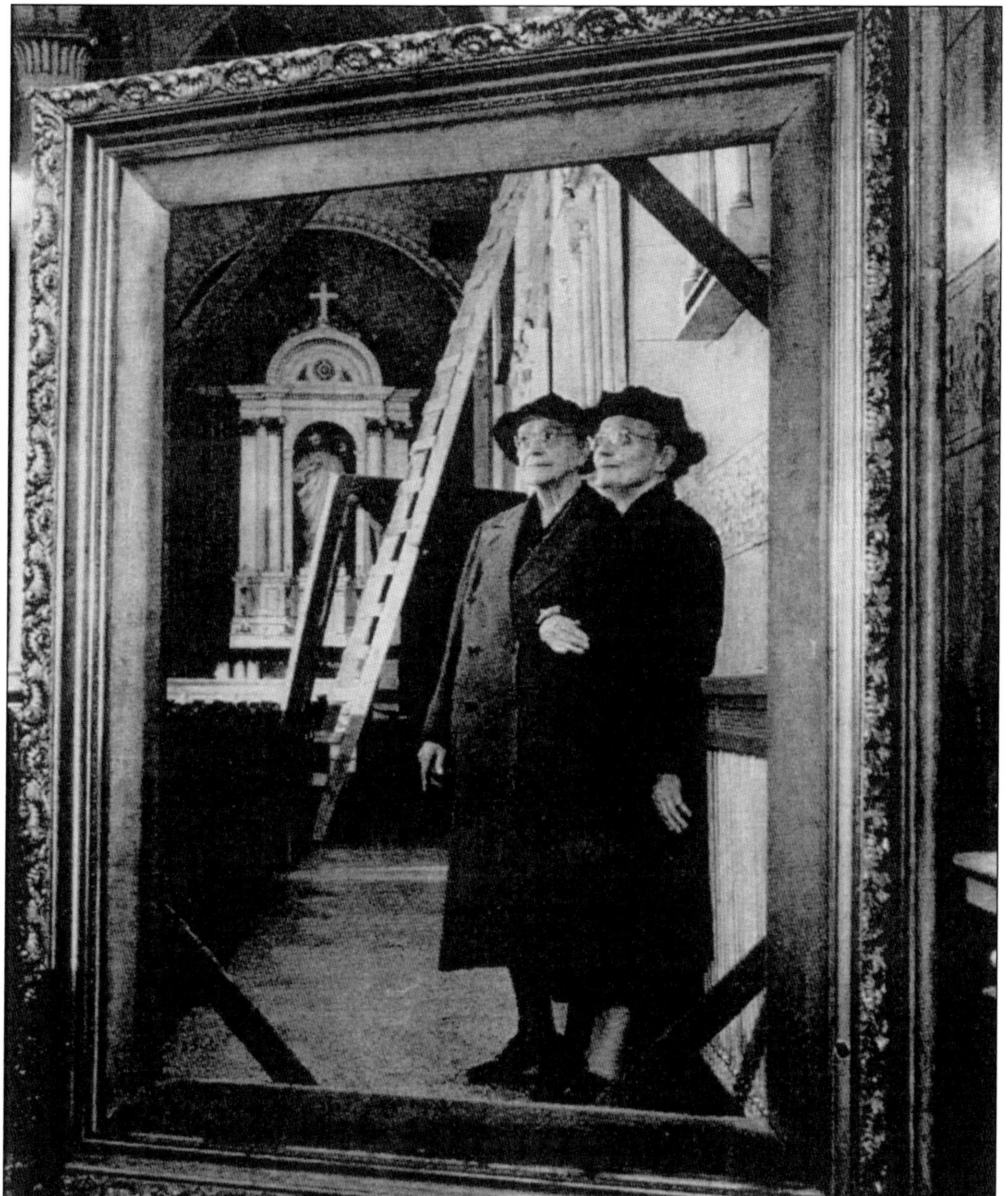

On November 12, 1952, church members arriving early for Mass frightened thieves away from St. Joseph Cathedral. They took ladders from the school construction site next door and climbed the walls to cut the paintings from their frames. The paintings, gifts of King Francis I of Sicily and Pope Leo XII, had been in the church since the late 1820s. Pictured are the Misses Reynolds, who discovered the theft and also served as guides for visitors. The thieves escaped with nine paintings. The thieves were not caught, but the paintings were discovered six months later in the Chicago area. After extensive repair and restoration, they were returned to the church at Easter 1955. The stations of the cross paintings have been removed to other churches since 1960. The others are still hanging.

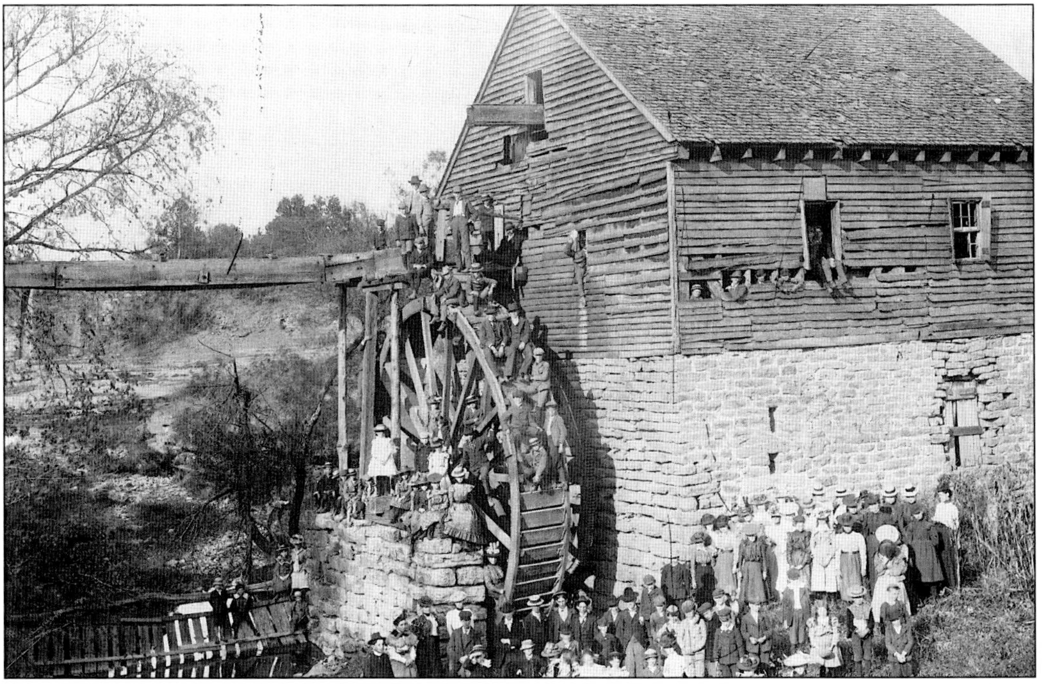

The Old Mill on Town Creek, directly below First Street, was the gathering spot for many school groups and community picnics. Built before 1800 by Nehemiah Webb as a grist mill, it was later called Brown's Mill. By 1890, it was called Doran's Mill. The overshot wheel withstood many floods but could not survive progress. As this photo indicates, many people visited the mill site. All pictures date before 1901, when the mill was removed by the City.

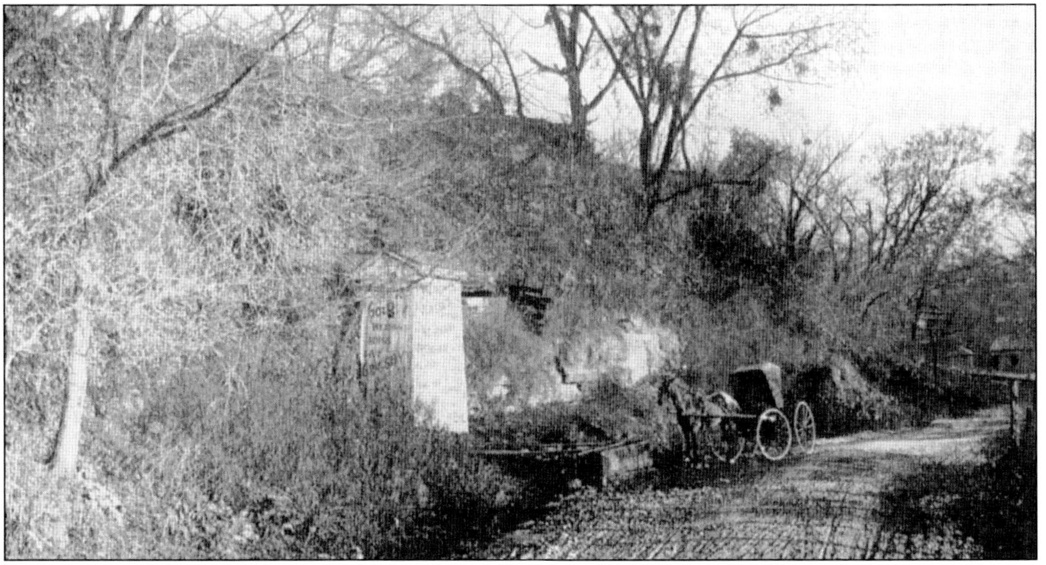

"Lovers Leap" is the caption under this old photo of the "long hill" stretch of the Bloomfield-Springfield Turnpike just below First Street. An abrupt drop-off right above this road gave the site its name. The stone watering trough was placed to catch spring water to provide refreshment to the horses. Advertising signs cover the small building, along with one that indicates that the water is not for humans.

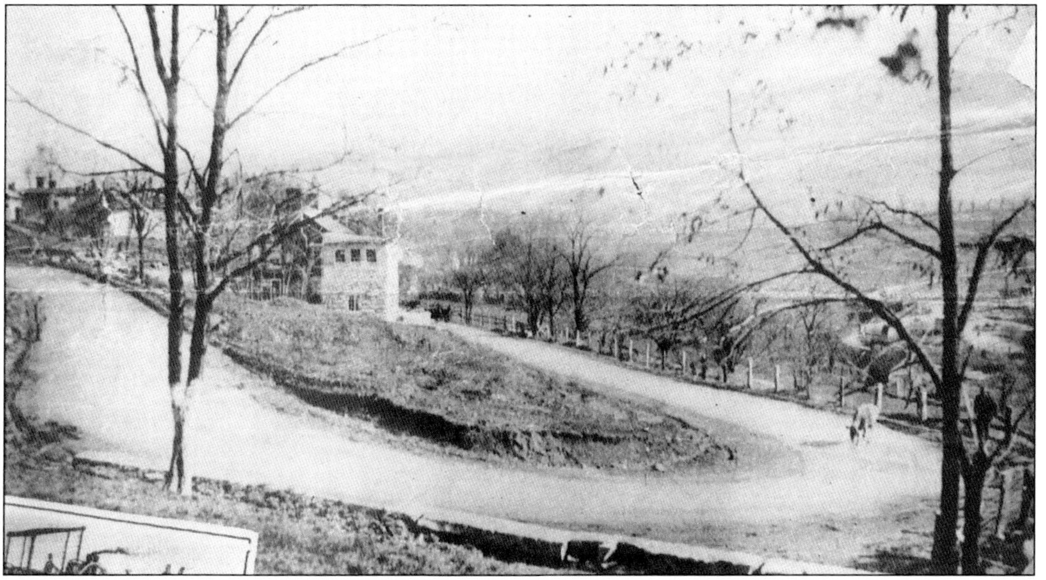

Continuing along the turnpike, you will come to the curve pictured here. This road was used by all visitors to My Old Kentucky Home coming from the west. This was the main (eastern) entrance into town until 1933, when "The Fill" was constructed. It extended East Stephen Foster to meet Springfield Road. The curve is still visible today as you leave the top of the hill going east. The house in the background still stands.

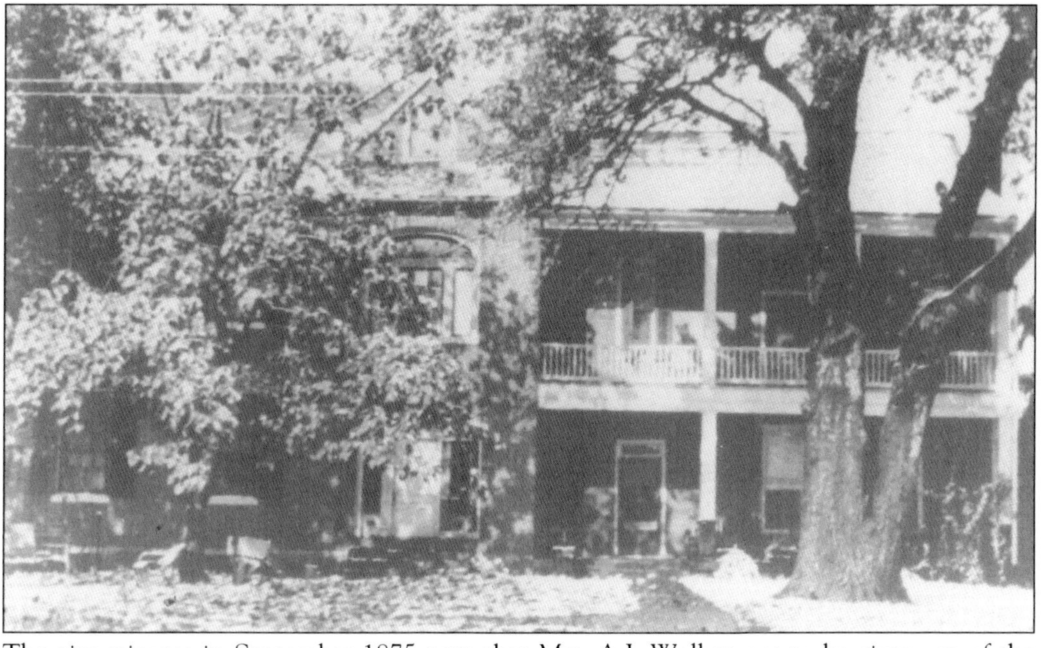

The city minutes in September 1875 note that Mrs. A.J. Walker was to be given use of the school furniture belonging to the town of Bardstown, consisting of desks, stove, etc. for the 1875 school year. The building was located on East Market Street (lot 71). The Samuel C. Crume family occupied the east half as a residence (1907–1934), until this wing was torn down in order to build another residence. The remaining structure is still occupied as a residence.

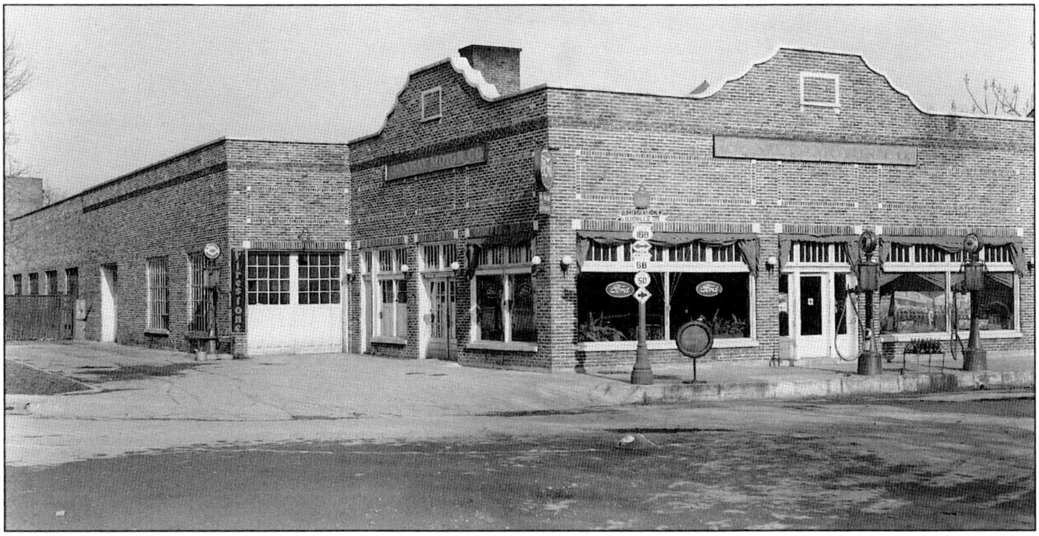

This 1930s photo shows the Conway Motor Company (lot 77) on the east corner of the Court Square. This was designed and built in 1928 for J.F. Conway's Ford Agency. From 1919 to 1921, a small building on Main Street (lot 47) served as the first business location. In 1921, the business was moved to the large garage on West Stephen Foster (outlot 8). By 1969, the business had grown and was moved into a new building north of town. Shortly after, this building was demolished to make room for a parking lot for Wilson and Muir Bank.

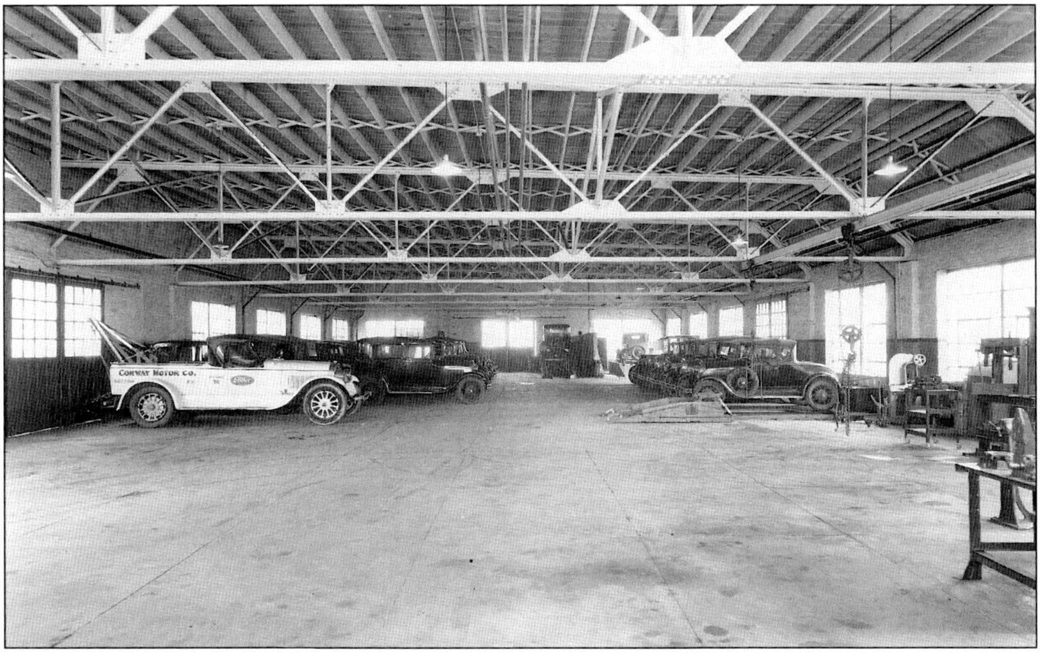

The new service area of the Conway Motor Company has a Lincoln wrecker (left) and a row of new coupes ready for delivery. Owner J.F. Conway said in later years that to sell an automobile in the 1920s they had to promise to teach the customer how to drive first. He was quoted as having said that it was "a nerve-wracking business." In 1919, when he began to sell cars, a Ford five-passenger touring car sold for $510.

Bardstown's reputation for having examples of early Kentucky architecture is depicted in this view of East Market Street in 1920. Unfortunately, only two of these buildings remain in 1998. The two removed in this picture are as follows: (left) the Jonathan Simpson home on lot 93, the present site of the Sutherland Building or Court House Annex; (right) the two-story frame building in front of the Chapeze House, presently the yard of the Tourist Information Center. Simpson was a silversmith-metal worker who also made surveying instruments and clocks. Dr. Chapeze's building was constructed in 1813.

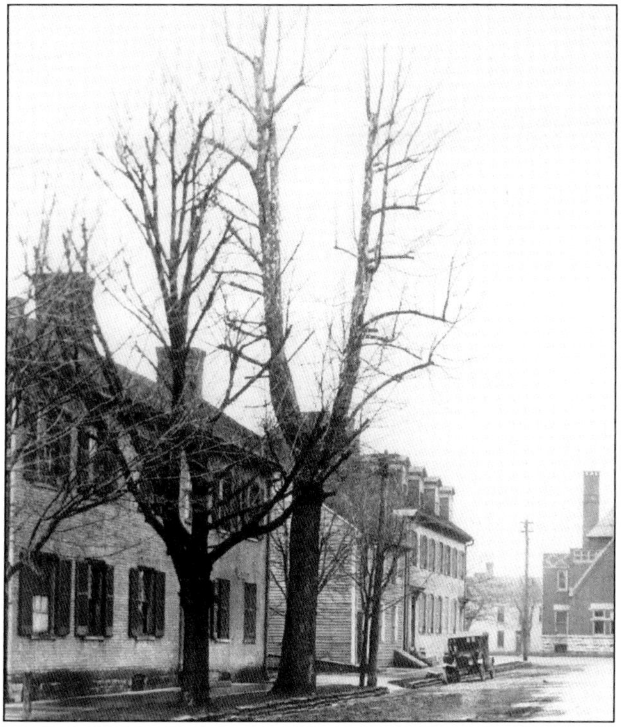

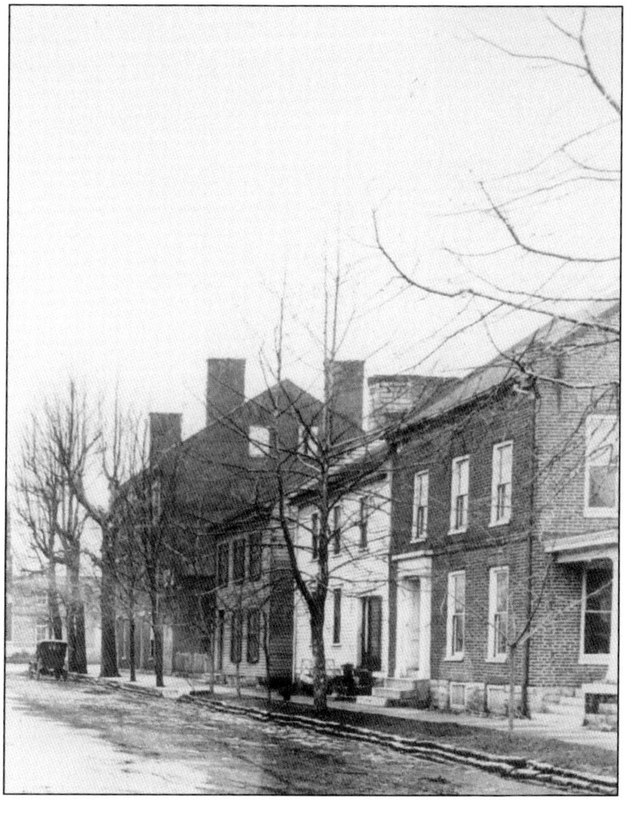

Pictured in this 1920 view is the three-story Hite-Boone Building, torn down in 1927 for the construction of the Conway Motor Ford Garage. It was located on the north side of East Market Street (lot 77). The two-story, log and frame dwelling was the home of John Weller in 1802. It was demolished in 1950 to enlarge the Conway sales area. The entire lot is now a parking lot for Wilson and Muir Bank. The two remaining buildings are the Adam Anthony coppersmith shop and brick residence. He purchased these buildings in 1809 for "3,000 gallons of whiskey." He made copper stills for local farmer distillers and they paid him with their product.

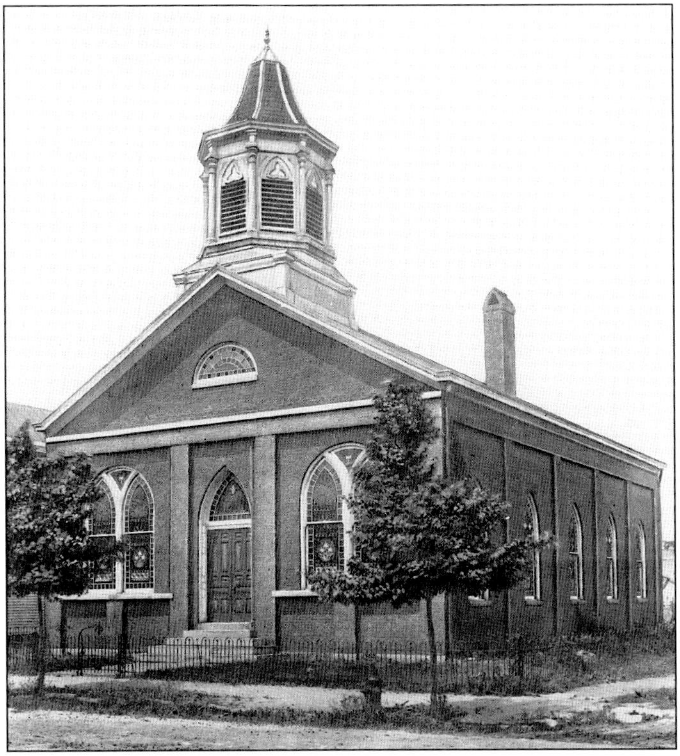

The Bardstown Methodist Church on the northwest corner of Second and Arch Streets (lot 52) was constructed after the Bardstown Fire of 1856. The fire started on the Southwest corner of Second and Market Streets and raged north along both sides of Second Street. It burned the previous church that was located on lot 58.

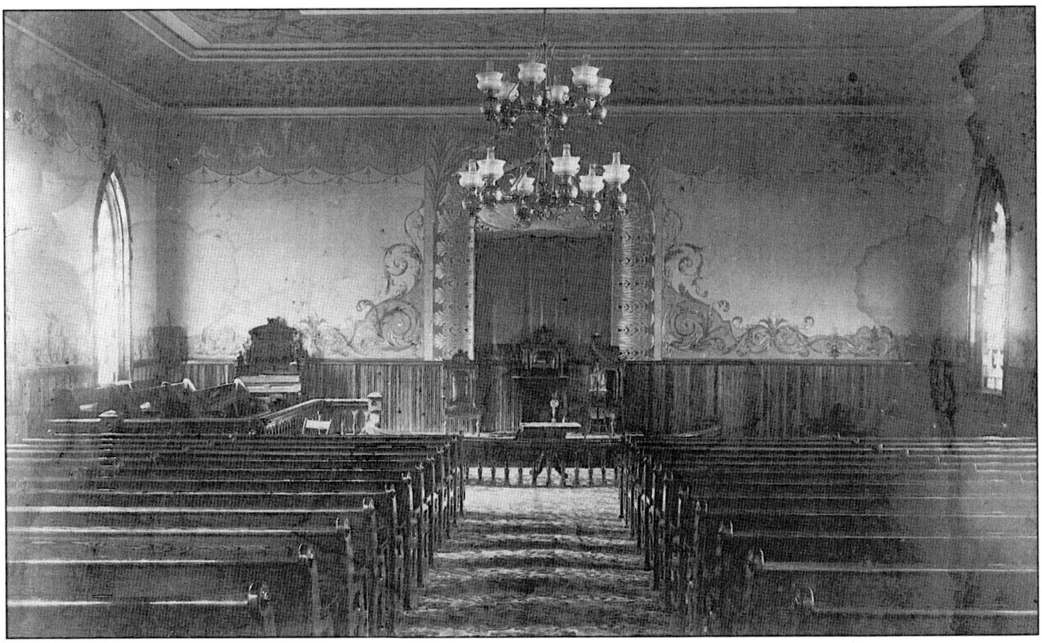

Pictured is the interior of the Bardstown Methodist Church *c.* 1900. The elaborate paper designs on the ceiling and wide borders above the wainscoting reflect the decorating style of the times. The Gothic-style, stained-glass windows were installed in the building in 1893. No one seems to know when the wonderful chandelier was replaced or what happened to it. It appears that these same pews are in use today.

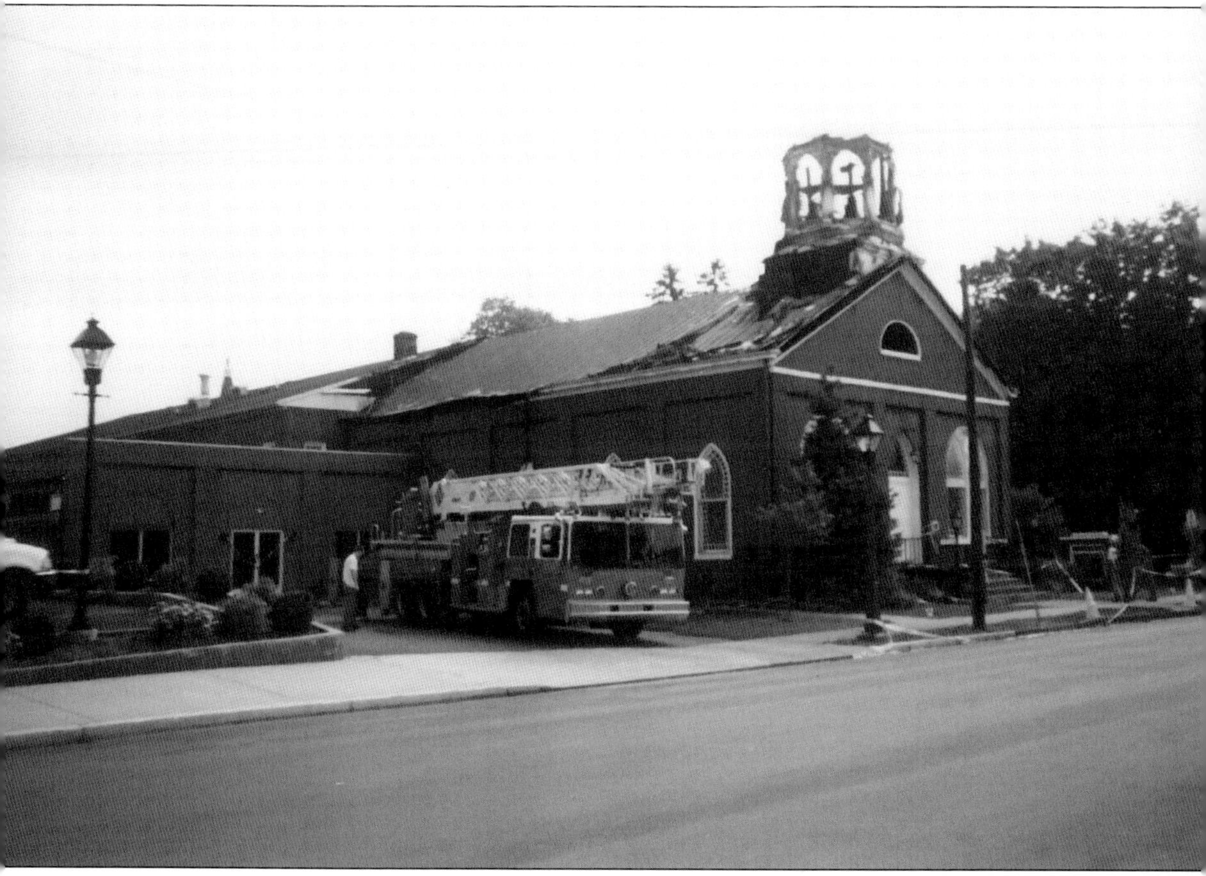

Lightning struck the tower on this church on May 24, 1998, during a violent thunderstorm in the early morning hours. It smoldered undiscovered for several hours until an alert policeman called the alarm. Great damage was done to the interior. Miraculously, the stained-glass windows remained unbroken, except for the round one over the main doors. It was totally destroyed, along with the steeple and bell.

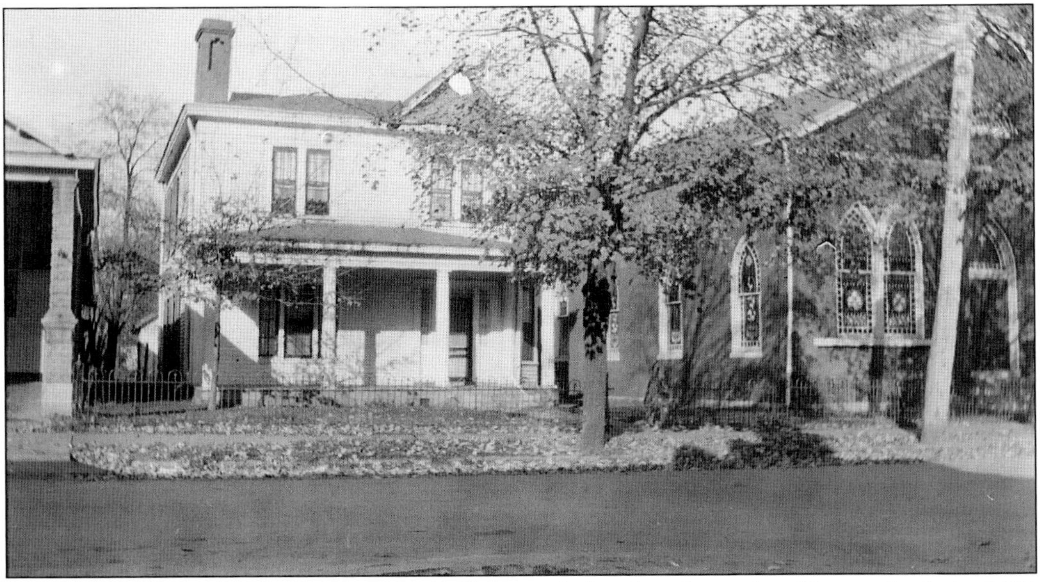

The Methodist church parsonage, located west of the church on lot 52, was built in 1886 according to the Insurance Map. It was used until 1960, when it was sold to the Wilson Brothers' Garage to make more space for their automobile agency.

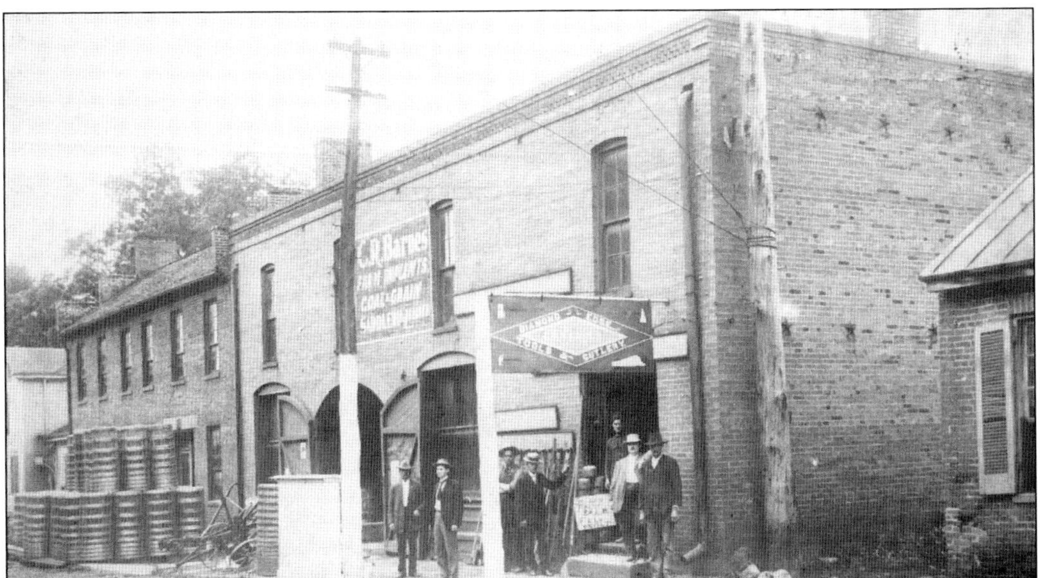

The sign reads: "C.R. Barnes Farm Implements, Coal, Grain, Saddlery, and Lumber." This brick warehouse building dates from 1896, when Mr. Barnes built it on lot 62 to adjoin the building to the east. This turn-of-the-century photo shows rolls of wire fencing stacked in front. Mr. Barnes kept four teams of horses to deliver goods. Another barn was used as a feedlot for mules. He bought 60 mules in the fall, fed them, and then shipped them to Atlanta in the spring. He operated a similar business across the street until a 1904 fire burned his warehouse full of lumber, lime cement, doors, and window sashes.

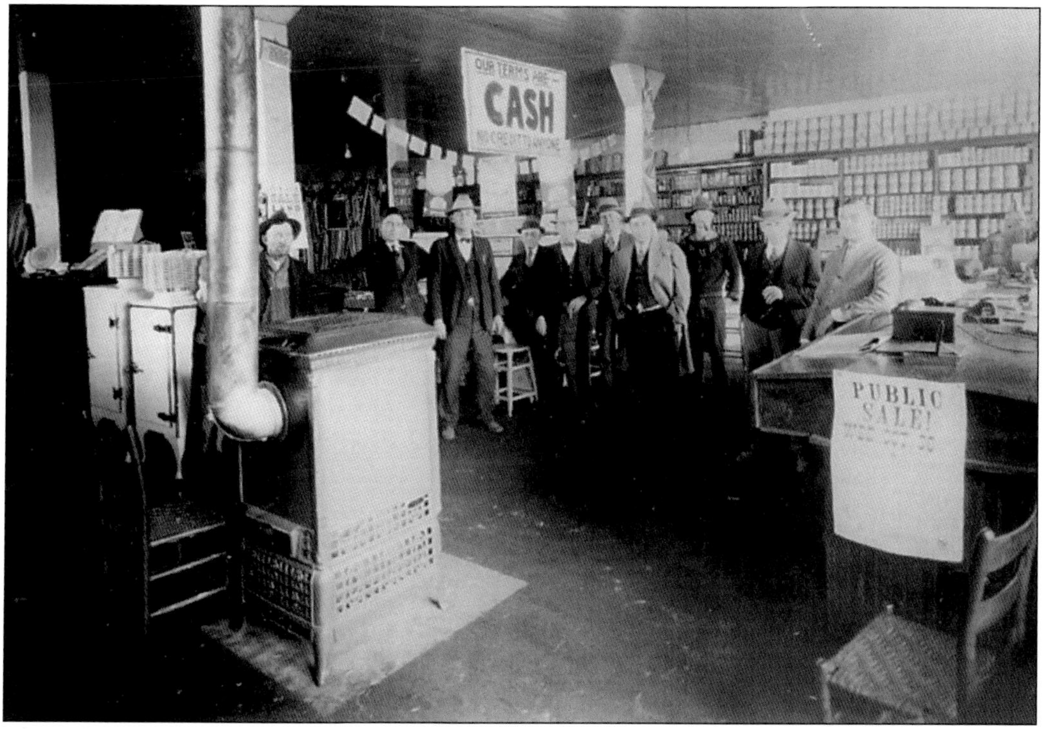

The C.R. Barnes Company became Connor and Haydon. These customers don't seem to be buying much. The hardware store sold farm implements, coal, grain, buggies, lumber, and anything else one might need in a farming endeavor in the 1930s. The business later became known as Jewell and Haydon. This brick storehouse, located on the south side of East Arch Street (lot 62), was torn down in 1979.

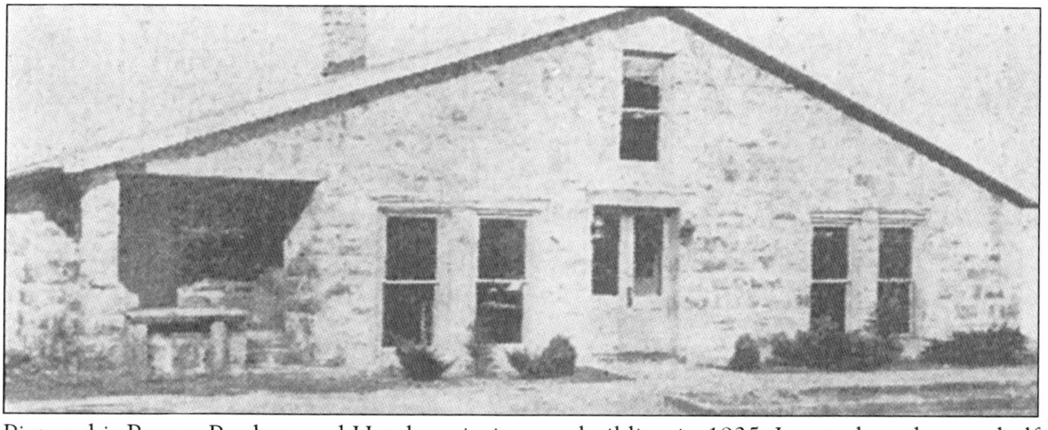

Pictured is Barnes Produce and Hatchery in its new building in 1935. Located on the east half of lot 49 on Flaget Avenue, the shop advertised that they "buy and sell country ham, eggs, poultry, furs, and hides." The business continued to operate at this site until 1960, when Wilson Brothers' Garage bought it to use as a parking lot.

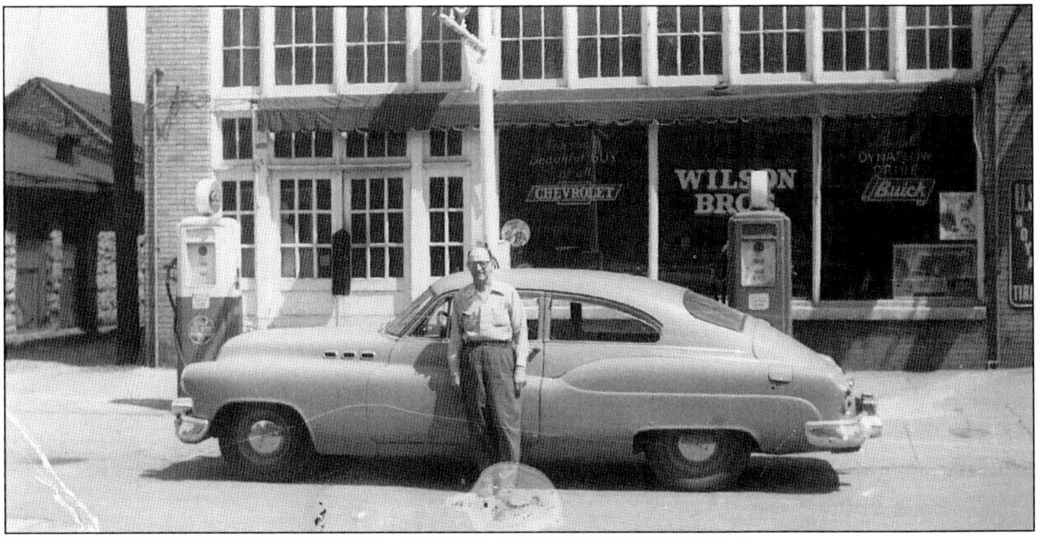

Pictured in this c. 1955 view is Wilson Brothers' Garage (lot 51) on East Flaget Avenue. Frank and Cameron Wilson were partners in the Chevrolet dealership located on West Stephen Foster (in the old Sisco-Rosenham Carriage building). Note the stone wall of the Barnes Produce Hatchery building (left). Tom Rodman stands in the foreground. The business was located here from the late 1920s on.

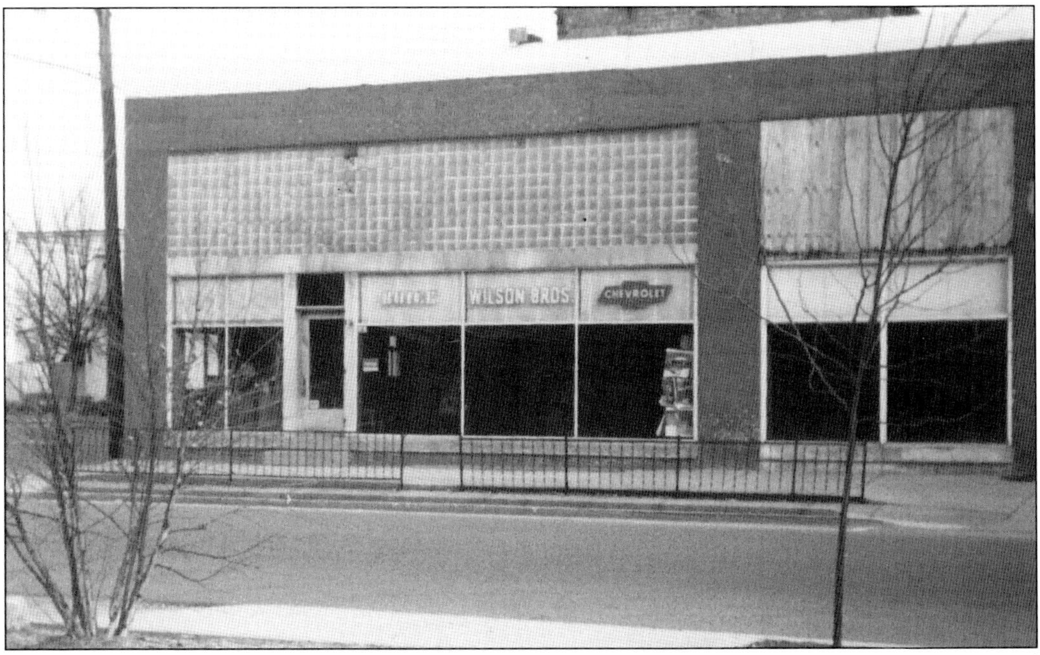

This is the same building as it looked in 1993, when the Chevrolet-Buick dealership moved north of town on John Rowan Boulevard. The November 1, 1919 start of this business makes it the oldest automobile agency in Bardstown. It is now owned by Guthrie M. Wilson and his son Guffy.

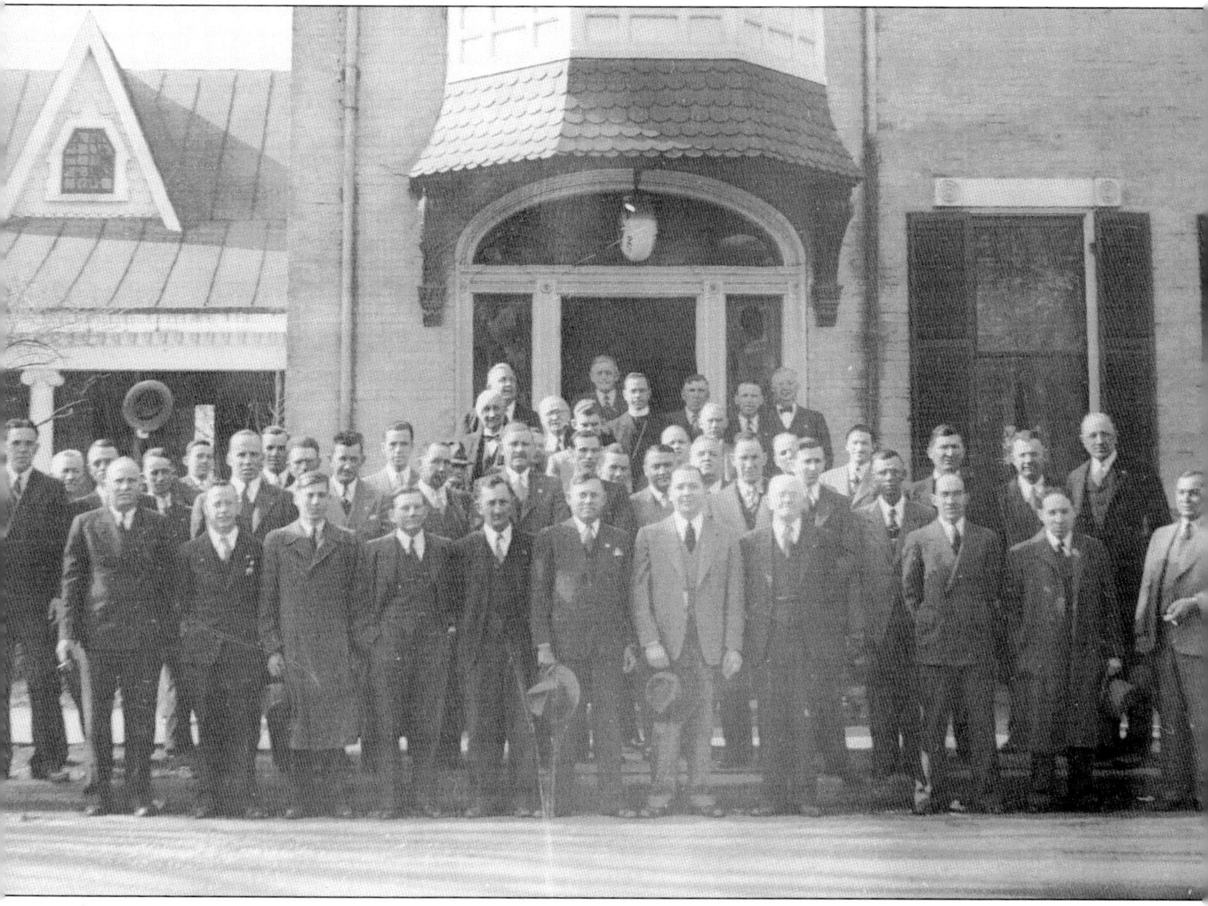

The members of the Bardstown Council Knights of Columbus are attending a breakfast given at the K of C Home on Sunday, March 29, 1942, commemorating the 60th anniversary of the founding of the order. This building was located on the southeast corner of Fourth and Flaget Streets. The Georgian-design residence was remodeled in the late 1800s with the bay window over the front door, and the Gothic dormer on the side wing. The lot was the site of St. Joseph Church picnics, exhibitions, and outdoor community events. Girl Scouts and Boy Scouts used the building for their meetings. It was removed in the late 1950s to provide space for a new K of C Hall.

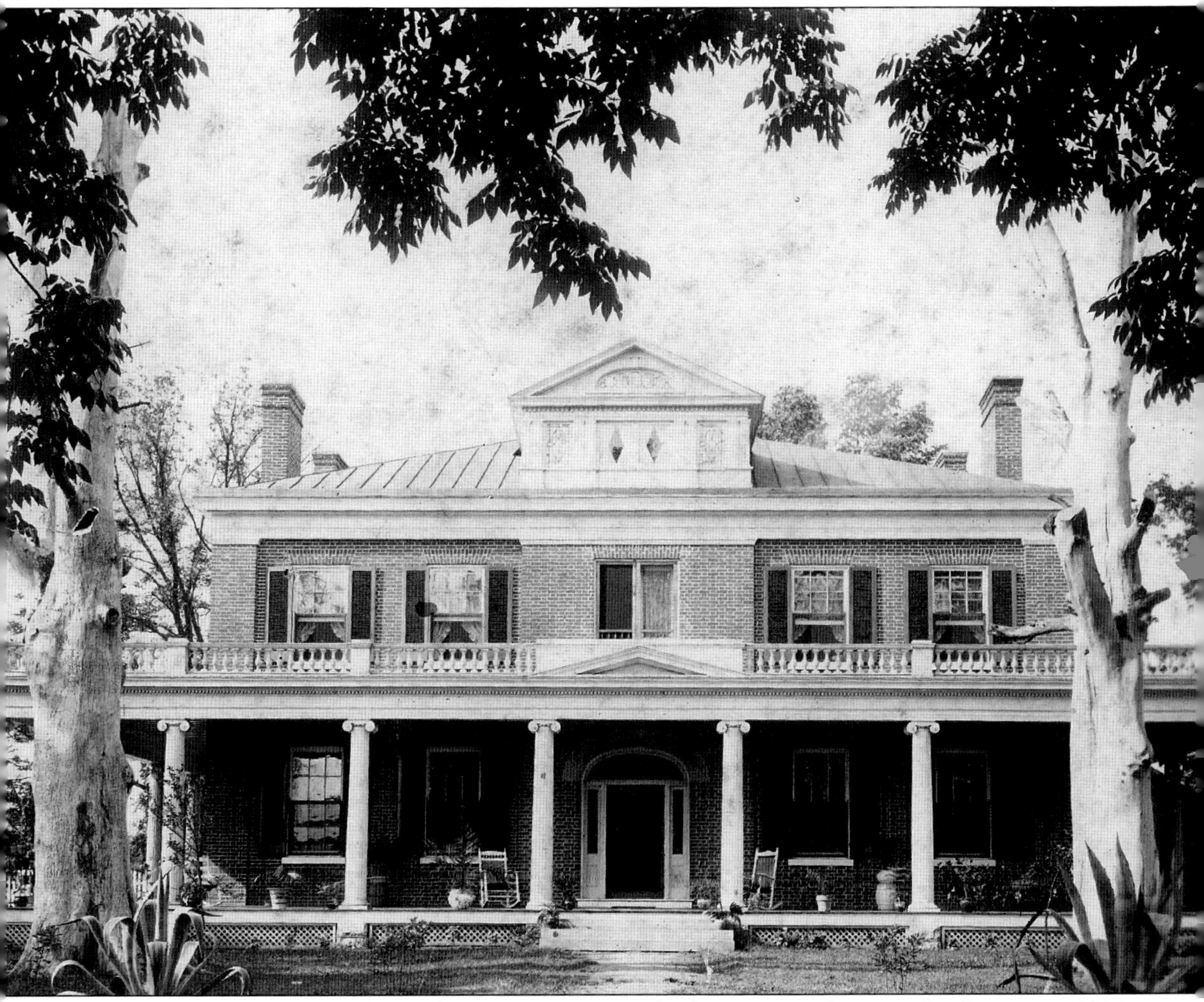

Anatok was the name chosen by James L. Druien for his new residence in Bardstown in 1901. He purchased the large brick house from the Pius Whelan estate and employed an architect to modernize the 1847 building. The architect designed heating, plumbing, and electrical systems for the home. He chose to move the two-story front porch to the back door of the new brick kitchen wing and made it one story. He added the pediment with leaded-glass windows. It was destroyed in a 1935 fire that started in the "cupola" (pediment). Rev. Felix Johnson was saying mass for the Catholic Sisters who lived here at the time. He hurriedly completed the service as the volunteer firefighters used their new equipment to fight the flames. The fire was believed to be caused by defective wiring. The damage to the building was estimated at $4,000.

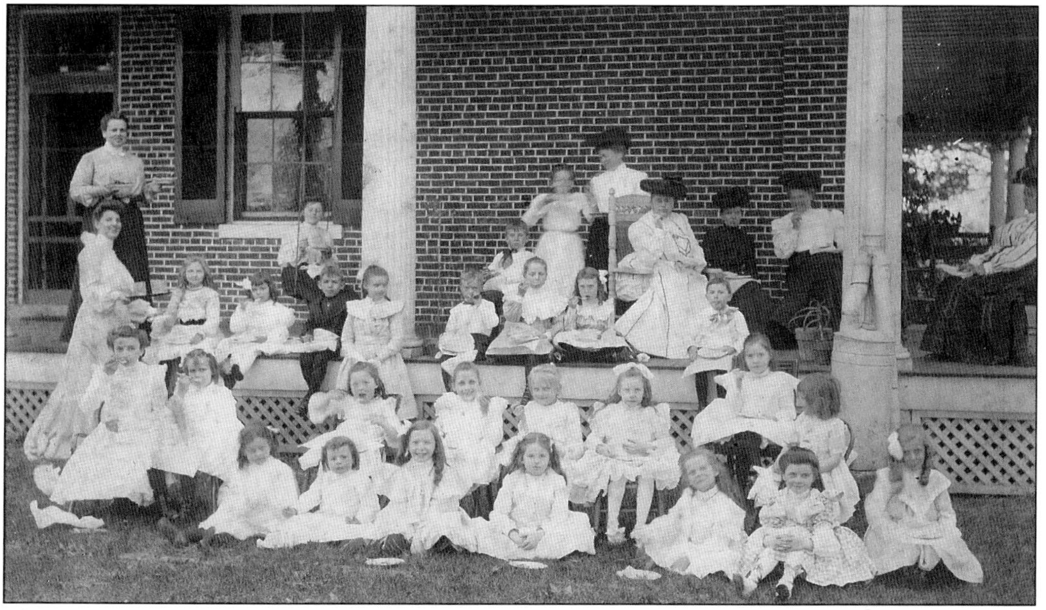

The columned and balustraded porch at Anatok was a spot for entertaining as well as for cooling off. Mildred Druien's birthday party is captured on film with the sons and daughters of the community eating cake and ice cream as their mothers rock and remember on the east porch. Mrs. Druien is on the left, on the porch.

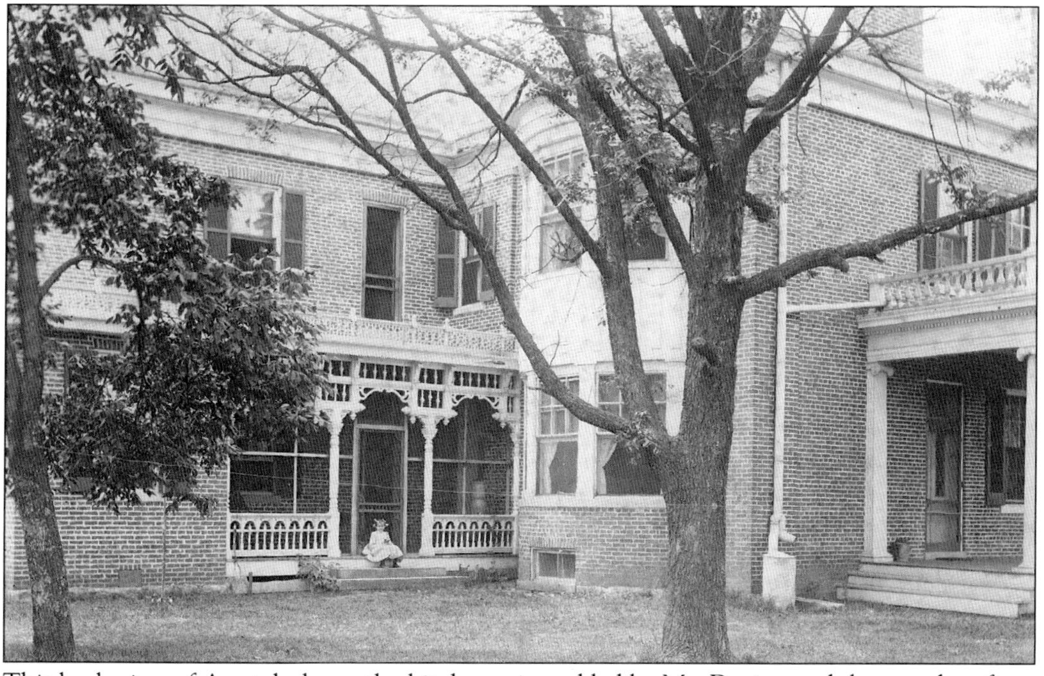

This back view of Anatok shows the kitchen wing added by Mr. Druien and the east door from the kitchen. The bay windows were also added at the 1901 renovation. Margaret Druien is seated on the porch. The elaborate wood trim and balustrade provided a railing for the walk-out porches on both the front and back of the house. This photo shows the downspouts, which caught rainwater and diverted it to a cistern.

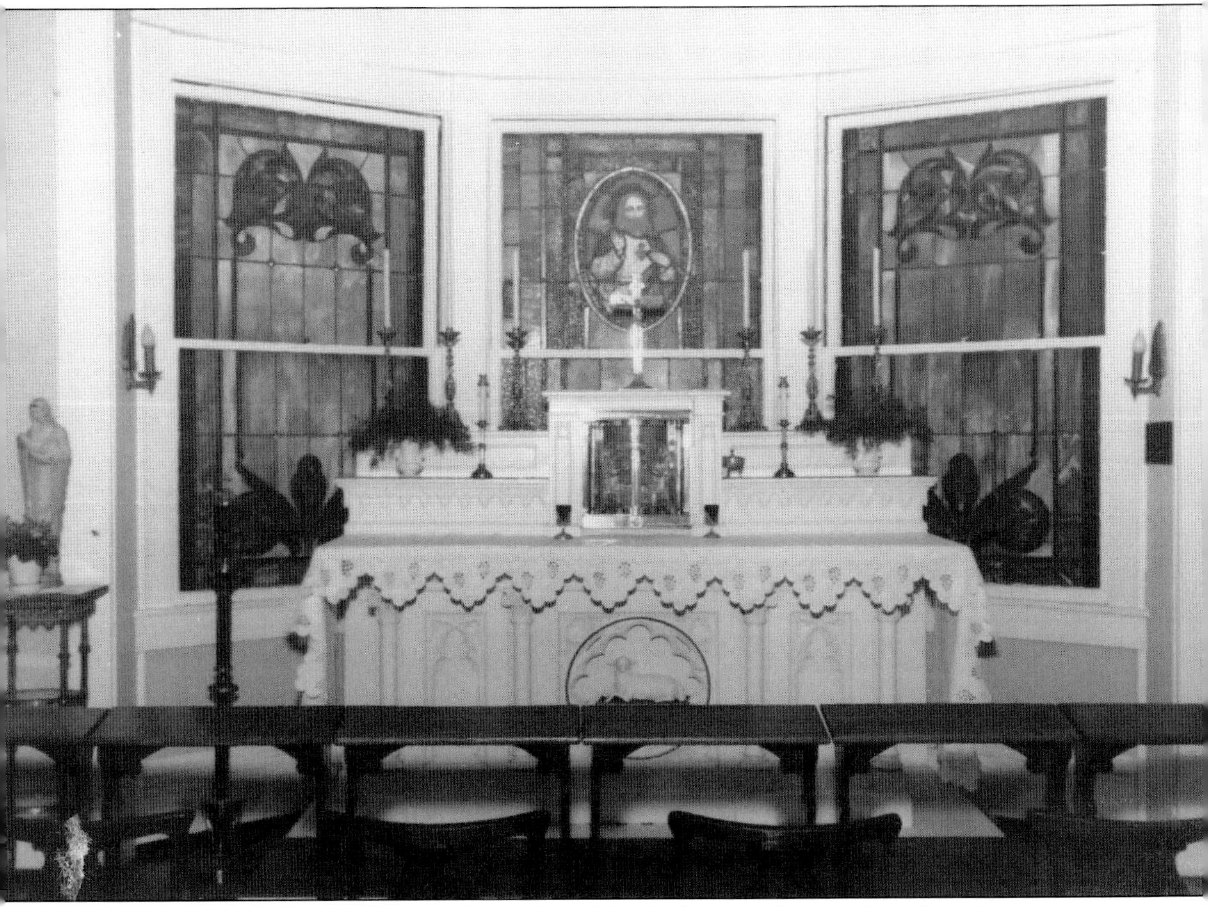

The Sisters of Charity of Nazareth purchased the building and grounds of Anatok at auction in 1929. Since it was located one block from the cathedral and less than a block from Bethlehem Academy, it was very convenient to use as a convent. Used as such from 1930 to 1968, the first-floor room with the bay window was used as a chapel. The stained-glass windows were installed from a legacy from Fr. C.J. O'Connell.

In 1971, it was renovated and used as a private residence by the Franklin Hibbs family until 1988. It is presently utilized as office space by Flaget Hospital.

Located on the southeast corner of Fifth and Graves Streets, Bethlehem Academy was opened by the Sisters of Charity in 1819 on outlot 8. The brick section to the right was the original house, purchased in 1819 by Rev. John David, the founder of The Sisters of Charity. He bought the house from Nehemiah Webb for $800. A later frame addition on the south enlarged the school. Expansion and growth has allowed this school to continue educating in this community.

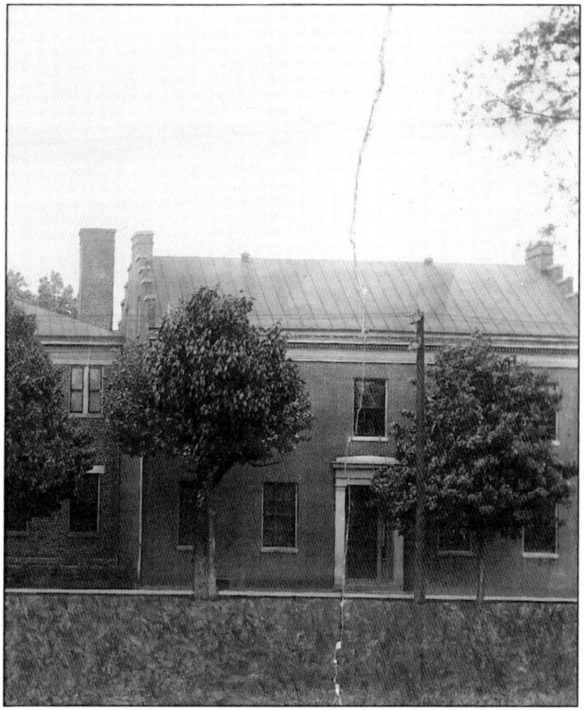

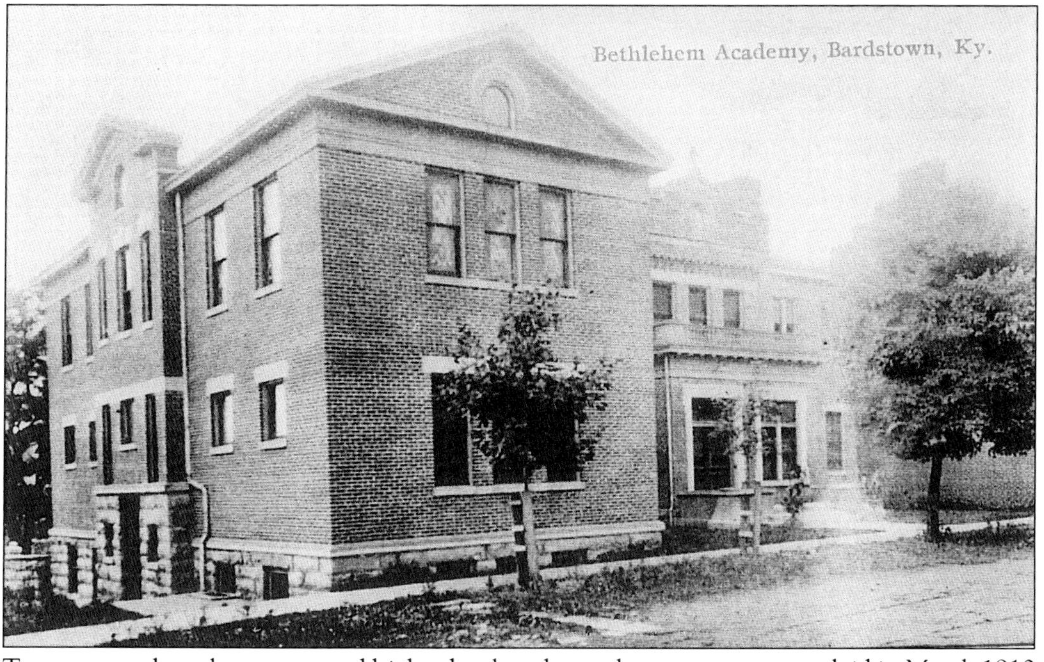

To accommodate elementary and high school students, the cornerstone was laid in March 1910 for a large brick wing to the north. It served as an elementary school and a girls' high school from 1911 until 1953, when the elementary grades moved into the new St. Joseph Parochial School. Bethlehem moved into a new high school building in 1959, and this building was demolished in 1963. The girls' school became coed when St. Joe Prep closed in 1968. The Bardstown Medical Building is presently located on this site.

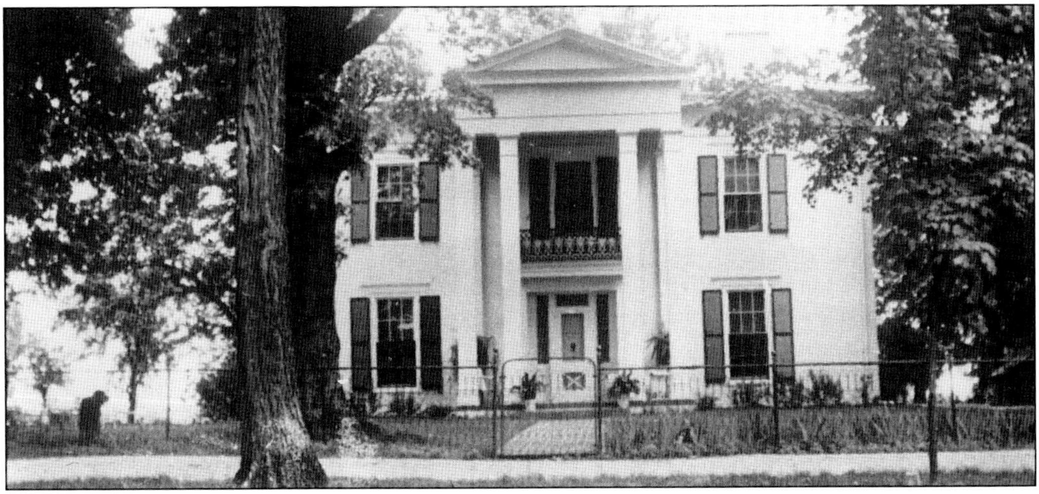

Pictured is Villa Lawn before it was torn down in 1964. It was built by Walter Beall before 1800 and was encircled by a race track. The home has been owned by the Muir family since 1864. Jasper Muir removed many of the original rooms but still had a large house. Henry Muir, Jasper's son, replaced his father's elaborate Victorian-style porches with this columned, two-story porch in 1922. The mansion was located at the end of a long, tree-lined avenue in the southeast section of Bardstown on Duke Street.

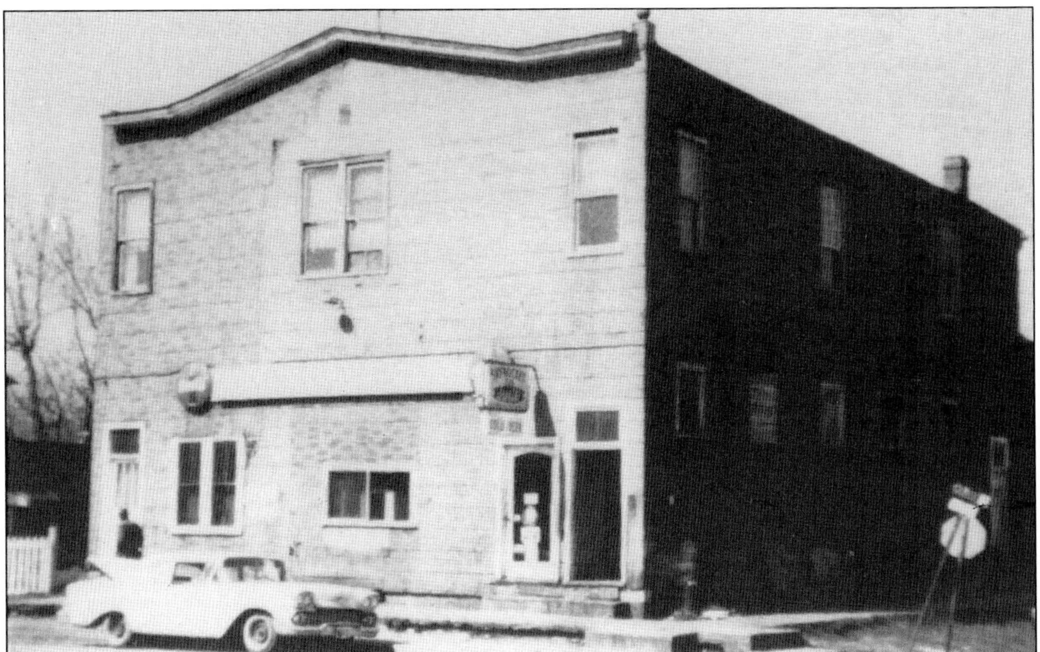

The Skyrocket Club on the southwest corner of Fourth and Brashear Streets was built by E.W. Lewis in 1923 to be used by Euclid Lodge No. 13 as a Masonic hall. Mr. Lewis later took it back. A restaurant and meeting hall were located on the first floor and apartments occupied the second. The hall was used during the 1937 flood to house evacuees from Louisville. In 1932, the Bardstown Training School Commencement was held there. The hall was also used for weekly movies and dances. This 1969 photo shows the building four years before it was torn down to make space for a parking lot.

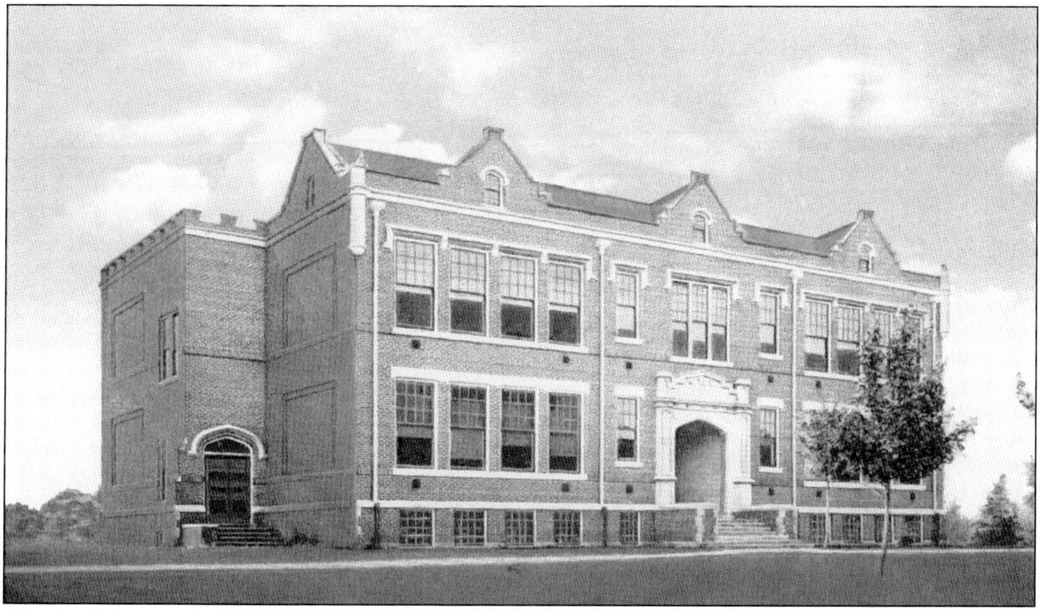

This building is the Bardstown Grade School (lot 24), built in 1908. It was also used for high school classes until a high school building was constructed north of this building in 1927. These were replaced by new buildings in the 1960s.

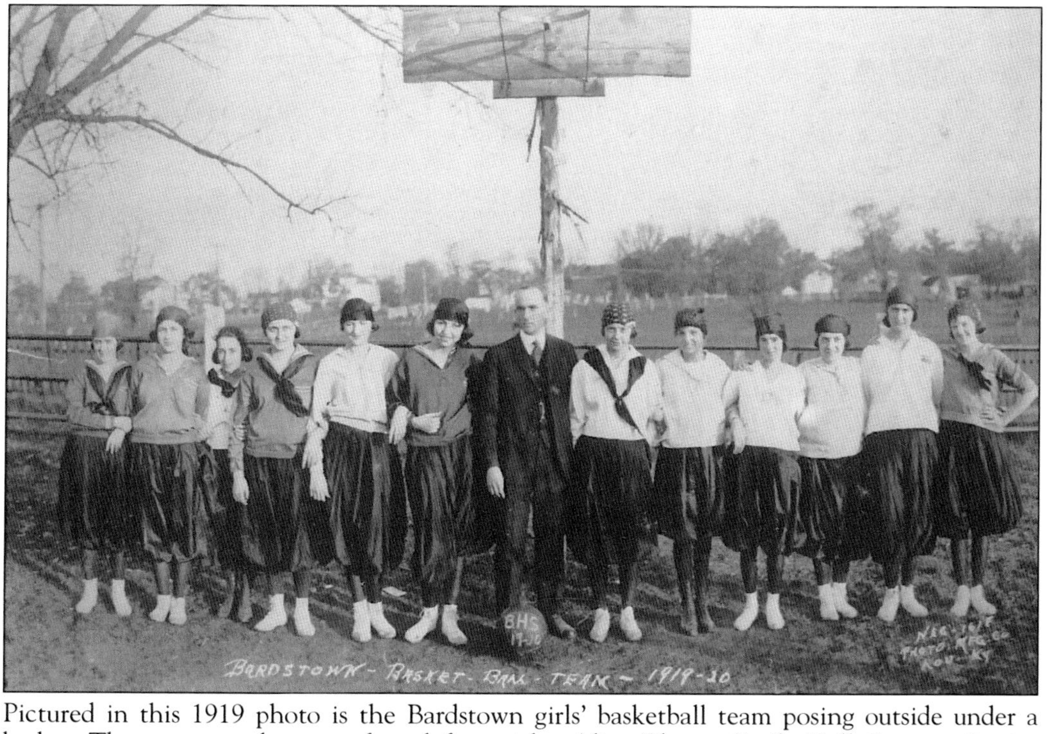

Pictured in this 1919 photo is the Bardstown girls' basketball team posing outside under a basket. The team members are, from left to right, Alice Cherry, Emily Hall Cravens, Louise Beam, Volinda Irvine, Lucy Kendrick Lewis, Beulah Mae Sympson, Prof. Hilliard (coach), Eleanor Arnold, Louise Conrad, Lelia Mann, Emily Carothers, Anna Lee Irvine, and Thelma Bradbury.

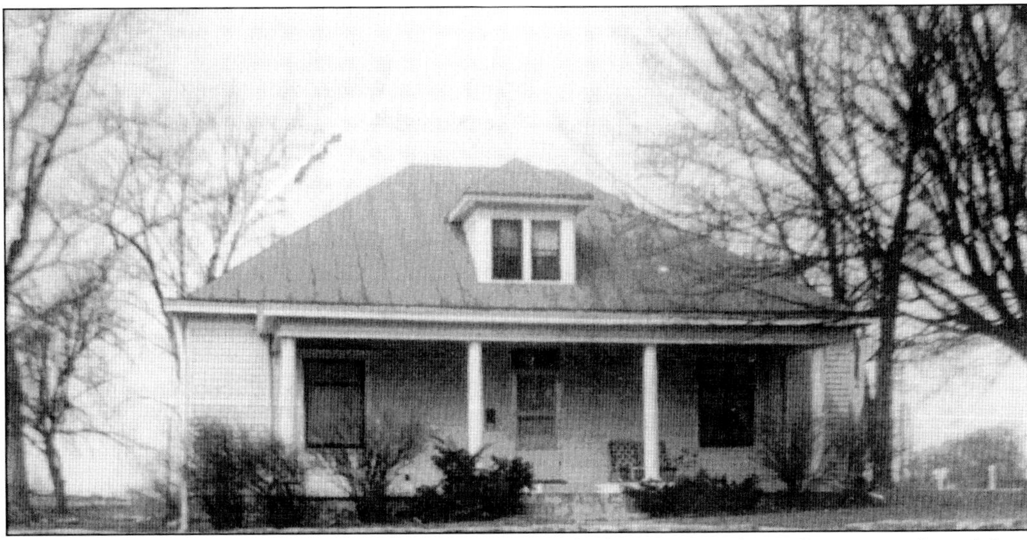

Pictured is the Pius Whelan house located at the end of West Broadway. It was purchased from the Whelan estate by the Bardstown Independent School in 1963. They sold it to the City of Bardstown in 1969 to be removed in order to extend Broadway westward.

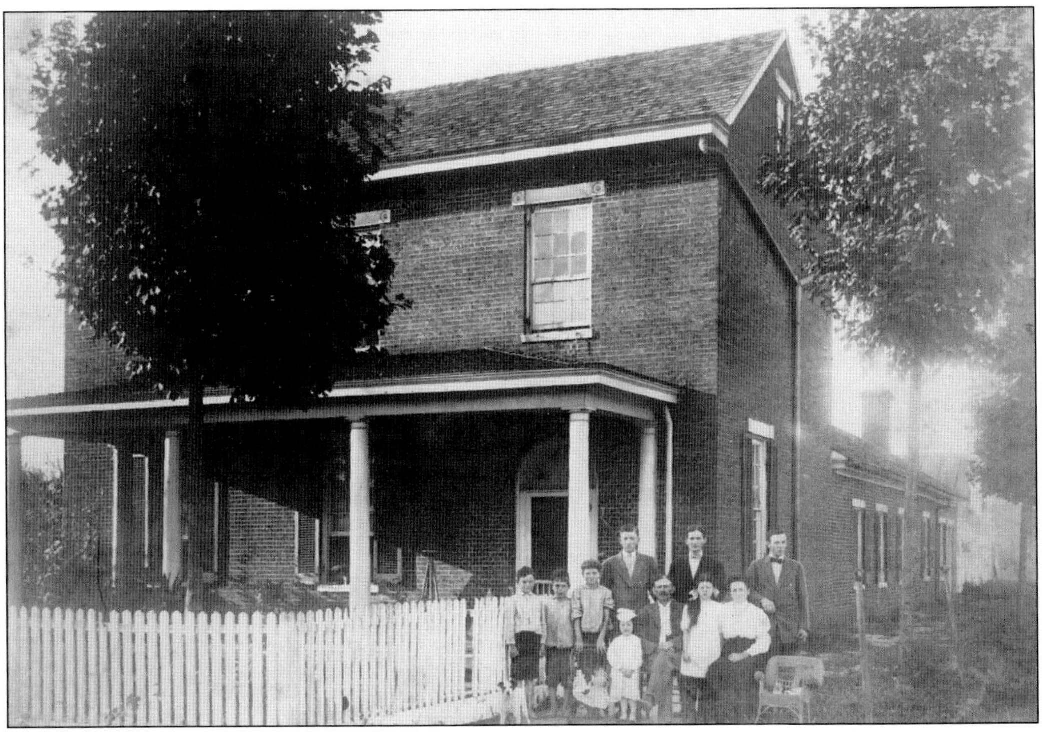

This 1900 family photo was taken at the residence of Columbus Reason Barnes Sr. at the northwest corner of Fourth and Broadway. Known as the McQuillan House, it was purchased by Barnes in 1896. He sold it later to R.W. Haviland. Several Barnes children were born here, including C.R. Jr., J.P., Catherine, and Fannie Cotton Barnes. The house was torn down in 1969 to provide for the expansion of a garage.

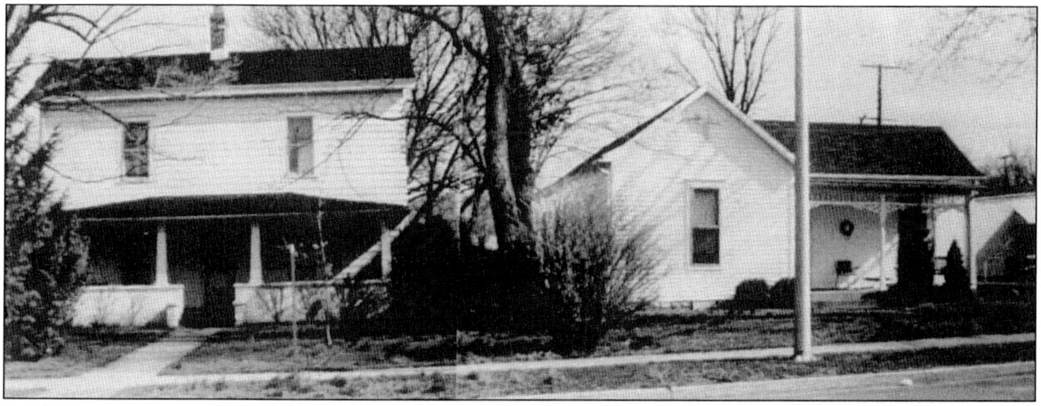

In the 1980s, townhouses became a popular way to utilize the lots on West Broadway. Pictured are two of four houses on the north side of Broadway that were removed. Eight townhouses were built in the same space. The houses belonged to Mrs. Lawrence Ballard and Mr. Bill Mattingly.

Beechland is the name of the James Marshall Brown home, which was located directly across from the cemetery on Louisville Road. Erected c. 1830, it was a plantation home typical of central Kentucky. Brown was a recognized builder/brick mason who worked on many of the large homes in Bardstown. This estate was sold in 1944, and the home was purchased by Gerald Padgett. He intended to restore it for his residence but an automobile accident prevented his wife from climbing stairs. The house was empty for many years. It was removed when the Kentucky Home Square shopping center was built in the 1970s.

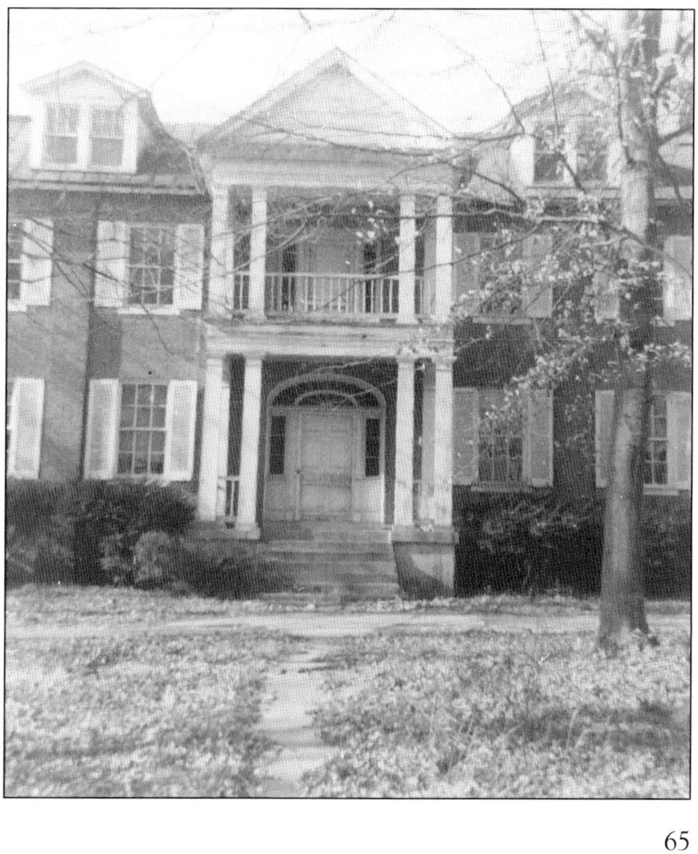

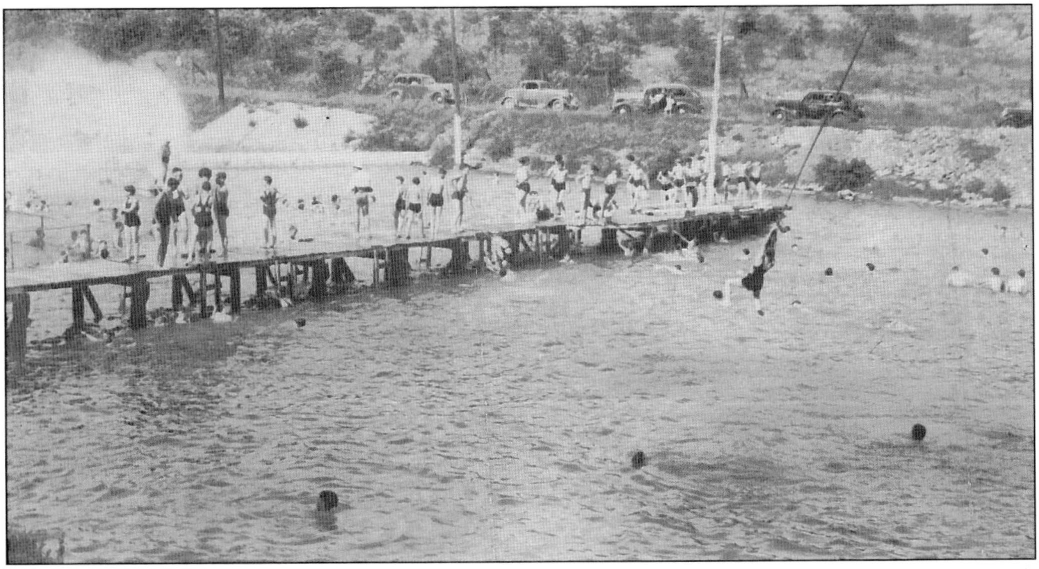

This early 1940s photo shows where the "old swimming hole" became the swimming pool. In the late 1920s, Will Stiles developed the pool where Town Creek flows under the East Broadway bridge. The rope pictured on the right swings out over the water and a fenced area for the non-swimmers can be seen on the left.

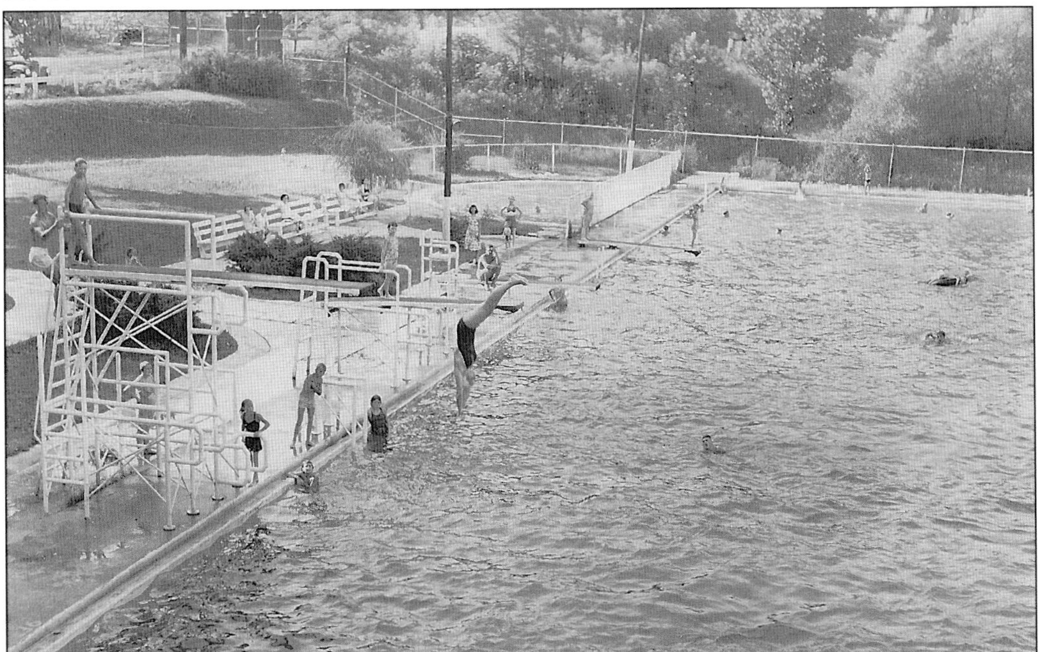

In the 1940s, the City of Bardstown enlarged and improved Stiles's operation and built a stone bathhouse and diving boards. The mayor was happy to announce that there was free admission to the pool. City officials continued to operate the "largest swimming pool in this area" until constant flooding from the creek over which it was built compelled them to built a new pool in the 1970s. It was built on property purchased from St. Joe Preparatory School on West Broadway.

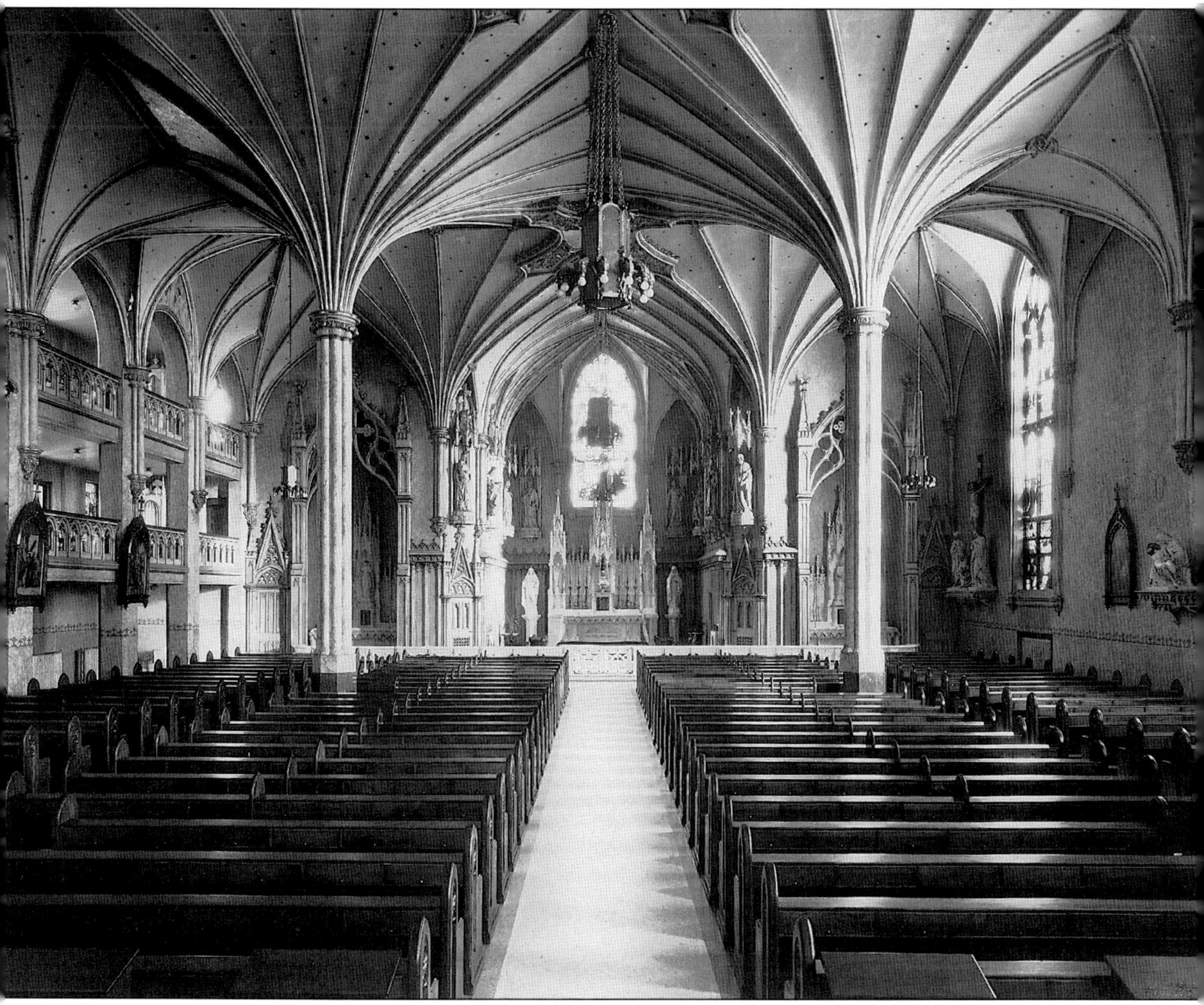

The St. Vincent de Paul Church at Nazareth has undergone many changes since it was first constructed in 1854. The Sisters of Charity of Nazareth Motherhouse and convent have been at this location since 1822. This view of the church (made before the last renovation in 1975) displays the ornate ceiling with its groined arches and fan vaulting. The Gothic spires, altars, and statues were added in the 1924 enlargement. Three hand-carved altars of Carrara marble were purchased in Europe. DaVinci's *Last Supper* is sculptured under the table of the center altar. The balconies to the left were used by the Sisters to attend Mass with direct access from the infirmary and upper floors of the Motherhouse. The stained-glass windows are still in place today but the pews and altar have been rearranged.

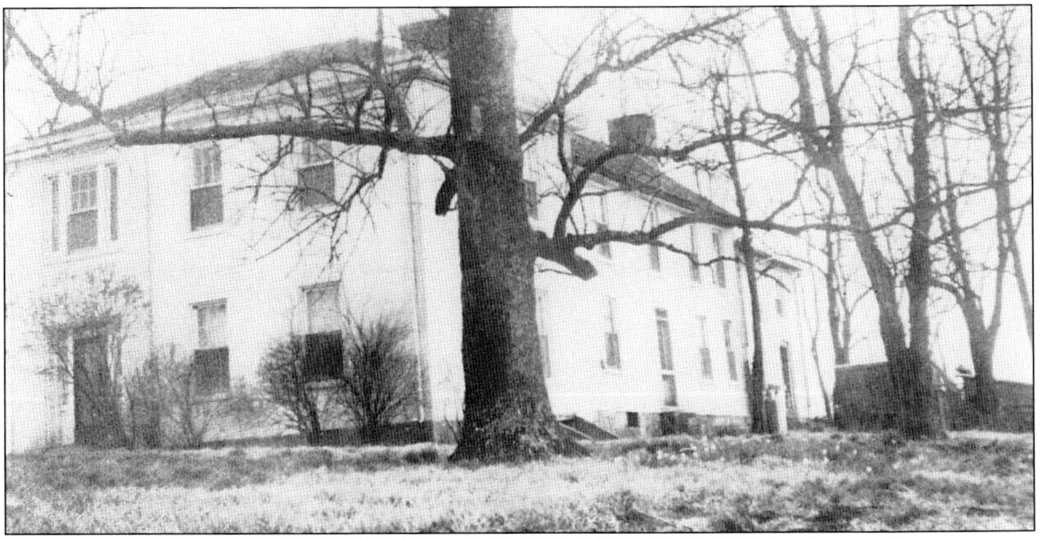

This large brick-and-frame structure was known as the Hynes-Talbott house. The property was owned by Andrew Hynes in the late 1790s. The oldest section (pre-1800), added to by Daniel Talbott, was known as "Old Blue." It was part of the land purchased by the Bardstown Industrial Development Corporation for an industrial park. The building was demolished in the 1970s. Its location was directly west of the railroad and north of the present water tower on Withrow Court.

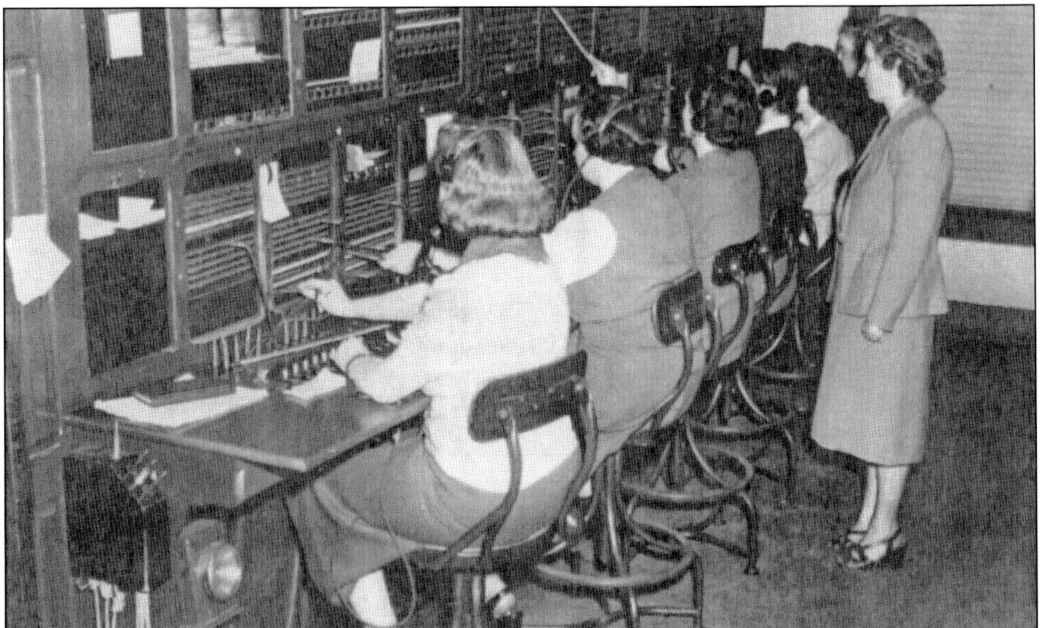

This change was to everyone's advantage. At midnight on Saturday, January 29, 1949, dial service was put in operation at Bardstown. The switchboard operators, from left to right, are Ethel Smith, Mary Frances Coomes, Effie Carney, Catherine Rapier, Betty Godbey, and Kathleen Price. Standing is chief operator Mary Hughes.

Three

My Old Kentucky Home

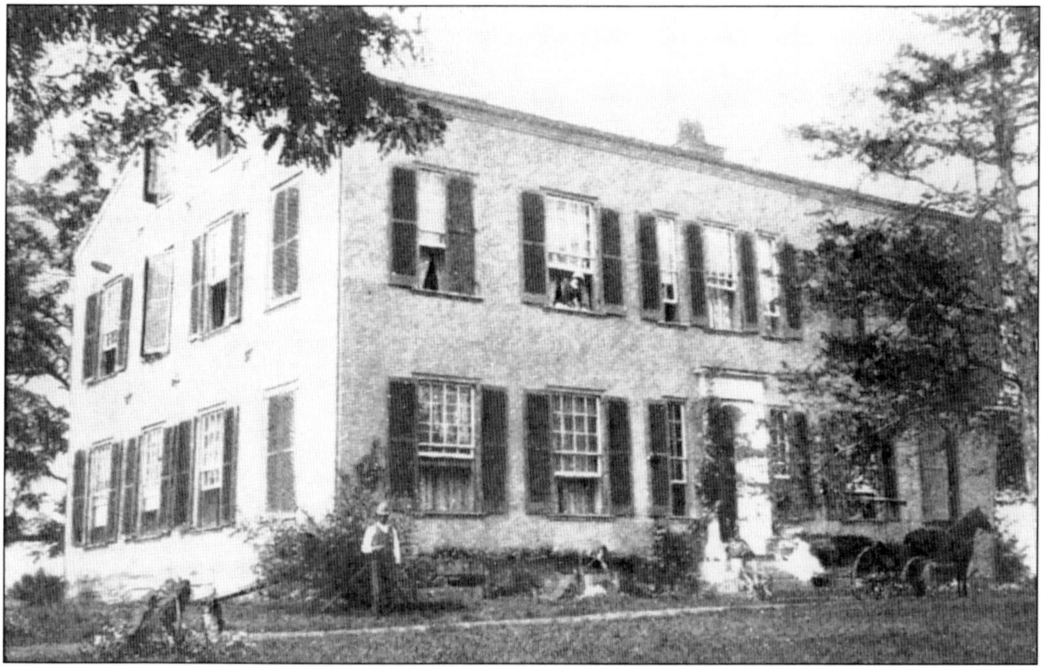

In 1800, Pennsylvanian John Rowan began to build his home on a hill east of Bardstown. A lawyer by profession, John Rowan would be remembered more for his ownership of this home than any of his court cases. The plantation inspired Stephen C. Foster to compose the song "My Old Kentucky Home" in 1852. The Foster and Rowan families were related, and Stephen had heard of his cousin John's plantation from family members who had visited Federal Hill and told glowing tales of its Southern beauty and hospitality.

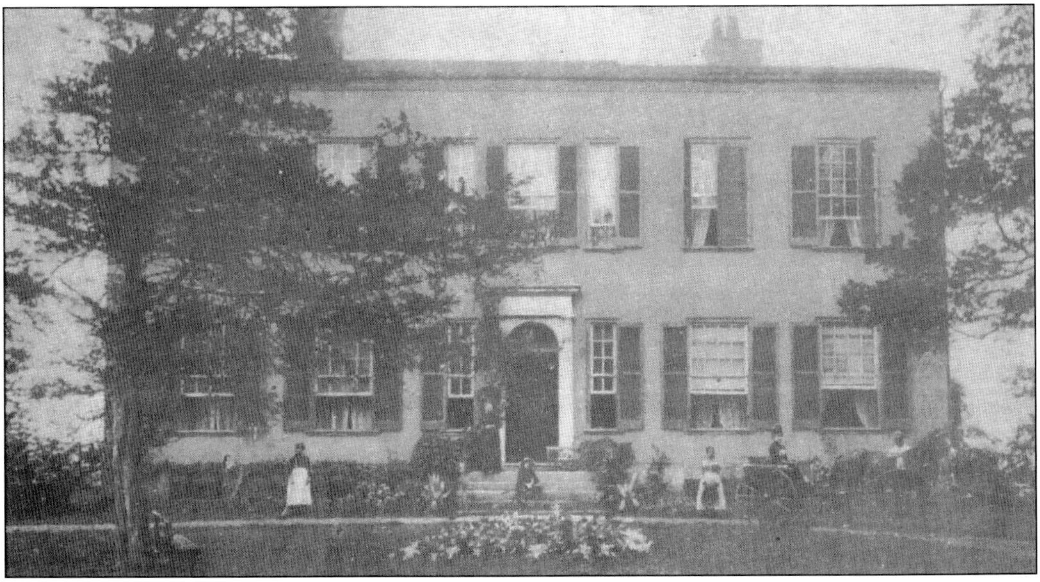

In 1922, the state legislature authorized the organization of The Old Kentucky Home Commission. Eight members, four from each political party, collected public donations to purchase Federal Hill from the owner, Madge Rowan Frost (John's granddaughter). This postcard, sent as a fund-raiser, reads as follows: "My Old Kentucky Home Let's Buy it. Does it Touch Your Heart, Let it Touch your Pocket Book. . ." Pennies from schoolchildren were part of the $65,000 raised to purchase the plantation.

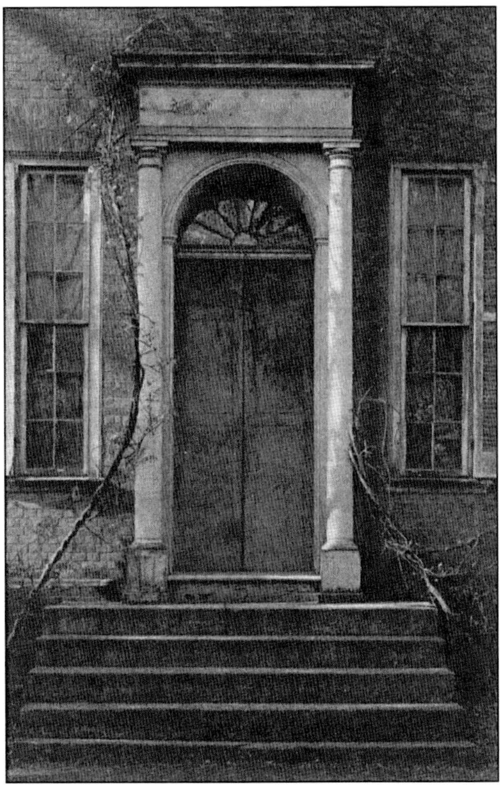

Hospitality of a home begins at the front door, so it is appropriate that the doorway image of Federal Hill is used to promote this historic site. Photographed before the State purchased the home, this view of the double doors with the sunburst transom and side windows reflects the lonely home of a widow who, with limited help and energy, is preserving history. Soon, the vine-covered walls will be cleaned and the walks and drive improved to welcome those who come to view Foster's inspiration.

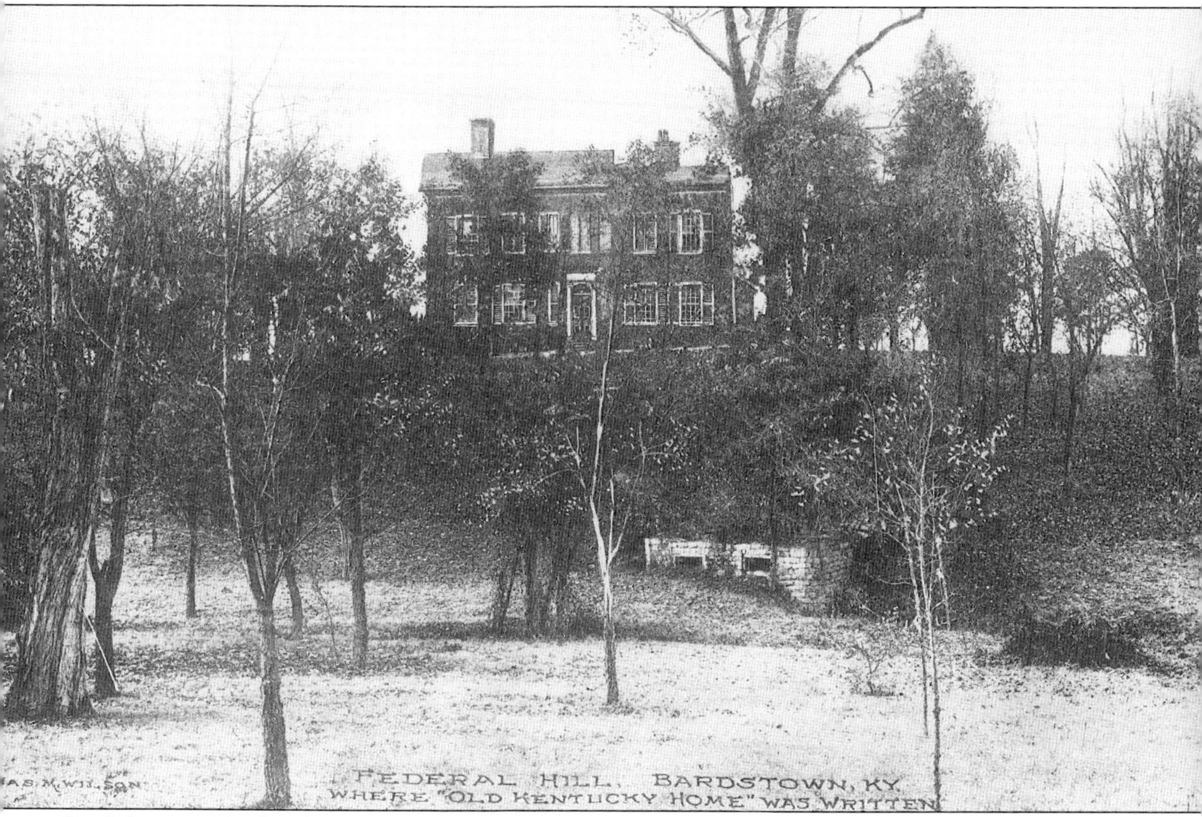

On July 4, 1923, the dedication of My Old Kentucky Home brought a steady stream of traffic into Bardstown. A special train from Louisville carrying 441 people was joined by many who came by car. A select traffic squad of 12 men on motorcycles was sent from the Louisville Police Force to handle the estimated 6,000 cars that day. These diligent law enforcers embarrassed Mayor John Sisco—he was stopped for speeding to the festivities. The natural amphitheater at the front of the house supplied the seating for an estimated 15,000 people. The audience enjoyed the Foster melodies and patriotic airs played by the 10th Infantry Band from Camp Knox. Arch H. Pulliam, vice-chairman of My Old Kentucky Home Commission, presented the estate to Kentucky. A delegation of Foster relatives and dignitaries from Pittsburgh were recognized.

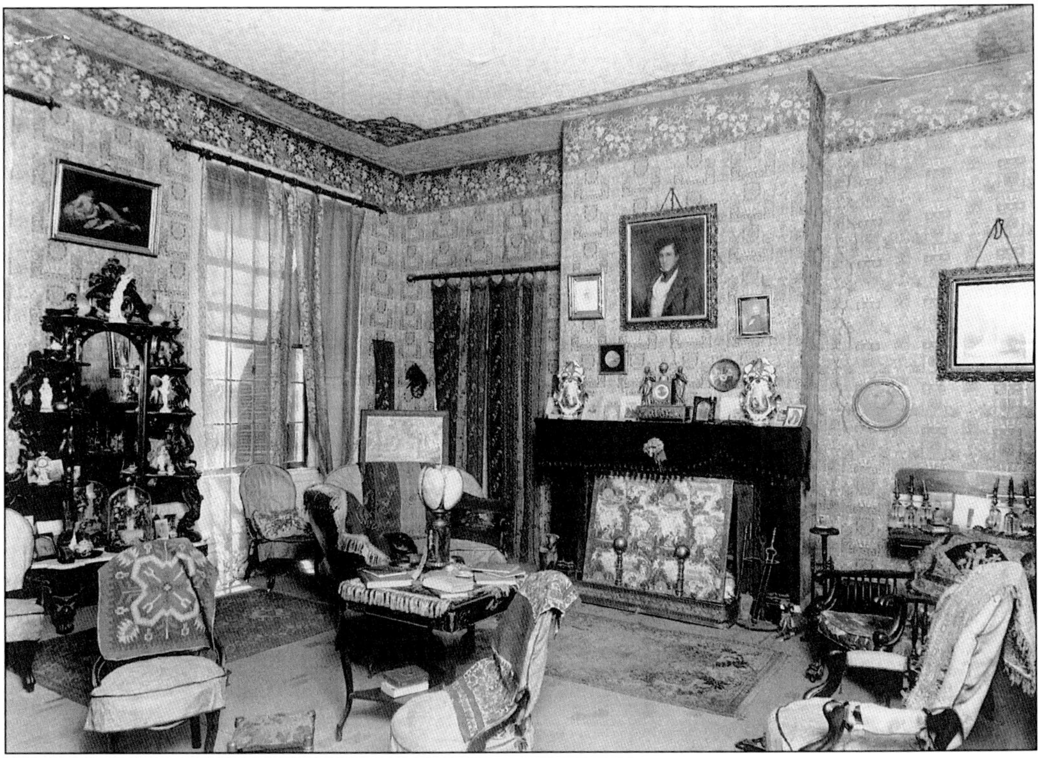

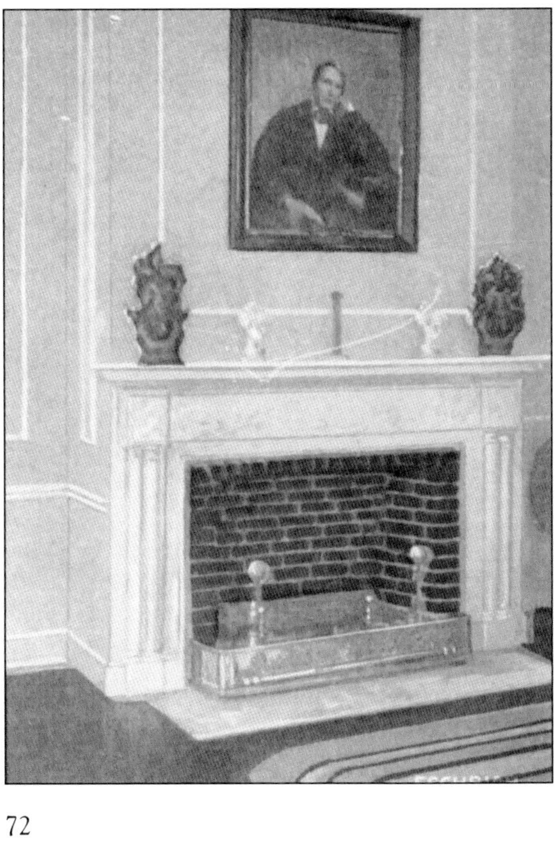

T.B. Duncan and Sons were employed to redecorate the home before opening it to the public. Pictured is the "parlor as we found it before decorating." The overdraped, overpatterened wall and furniture was the style of the 1890–1920s. Souvenirs of Mrs. Frost's travels were displayed on her family furnishings. The fireplaces were used to heat the home. Draped doorways and mixed furniture styles from the Frost and the Rowan family overwhelm the beautiful carved woodwork of the 1820s. The two ornate vases on the mantel are still in the home today.

Pictured is the same parlor and mantel at the 1923 dedication(after redecoration). Notice the same vases. The portrait of Stephen Foster was a gift of the Pittsburgh Chamber of Commerce.

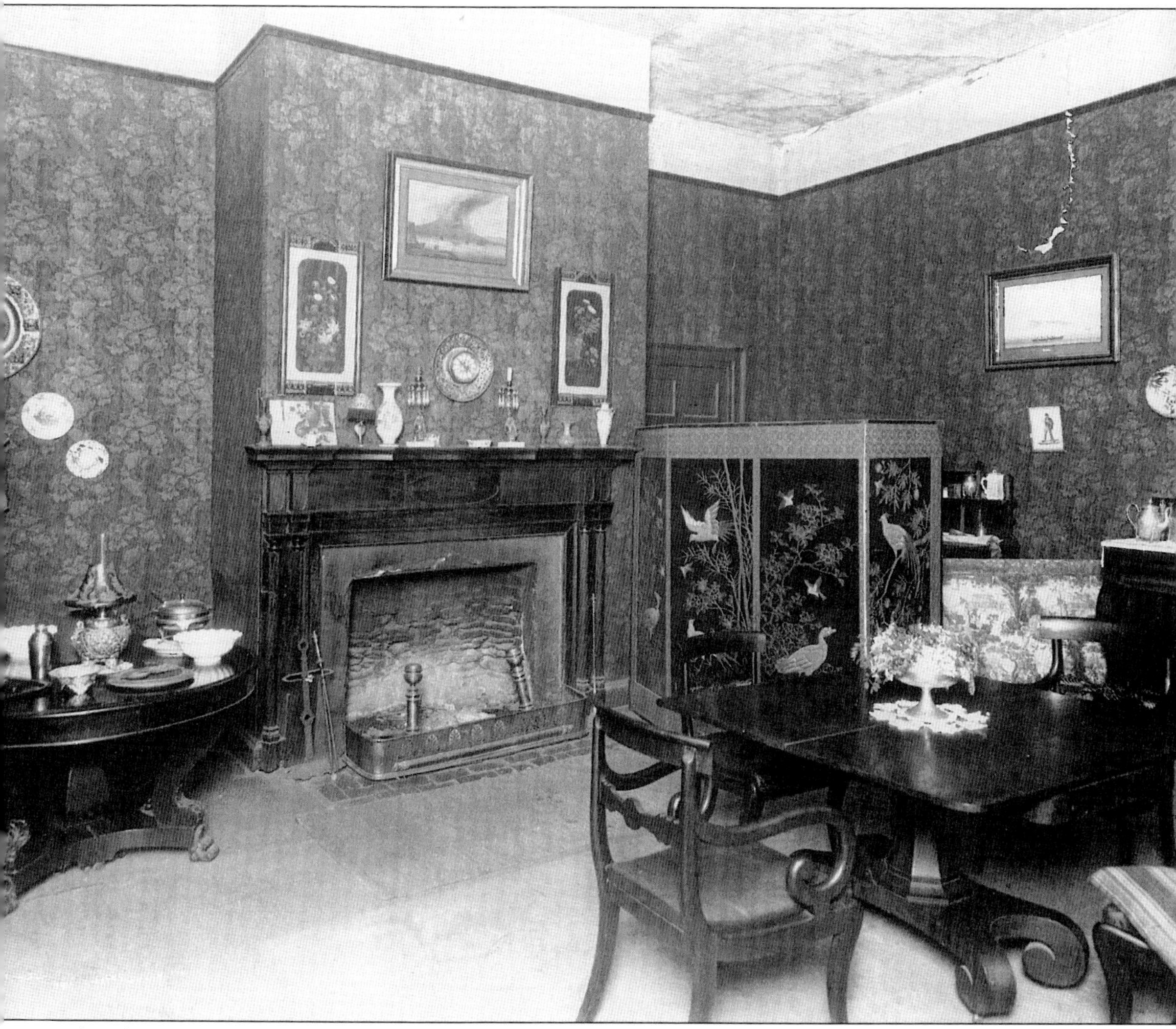

The dining room picture shows the oriental screen that hid the entrance from the outside kitchen. Food was brought into the room and served from behind the screen. This pre-purchase view shows the sideboard, table and chairs, and two watercolor prints that are still displayed. The absence of a grate indicates that the fireplace must have burned wood rather than coal. A kerosene lamp on the round table provided light.

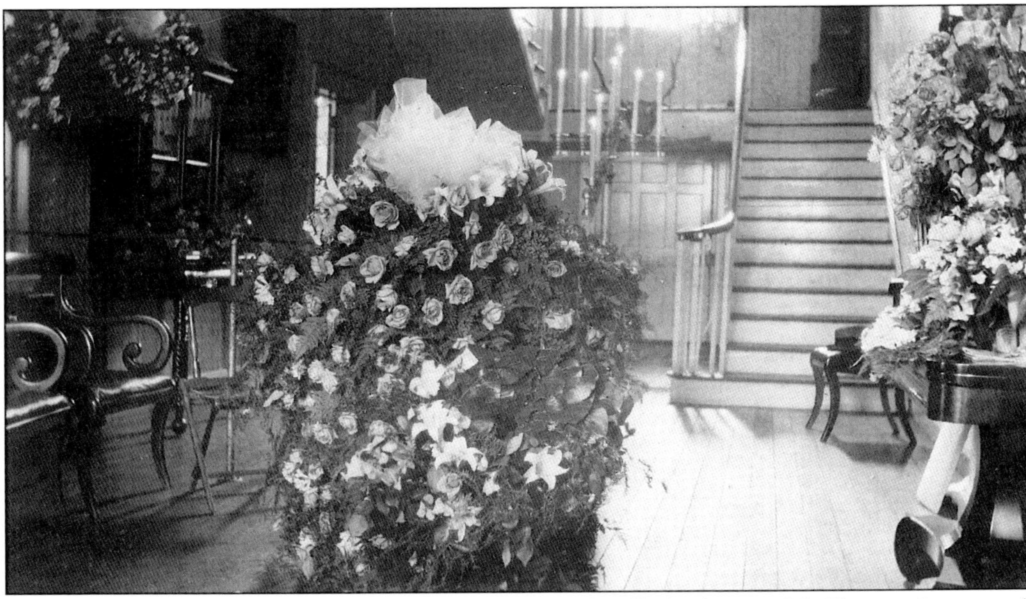

In 1925, Madge Rowan Frost, the last owner of Federal Hill, died at age 70. She was living with the C.R. Barnes family, across the highway from the home. Her coffin was placed in the front hallway of Federal Hill until it was taken to St. Joseph Cathedral for funeral Mass. She is buried in the family graveyard close by the home.

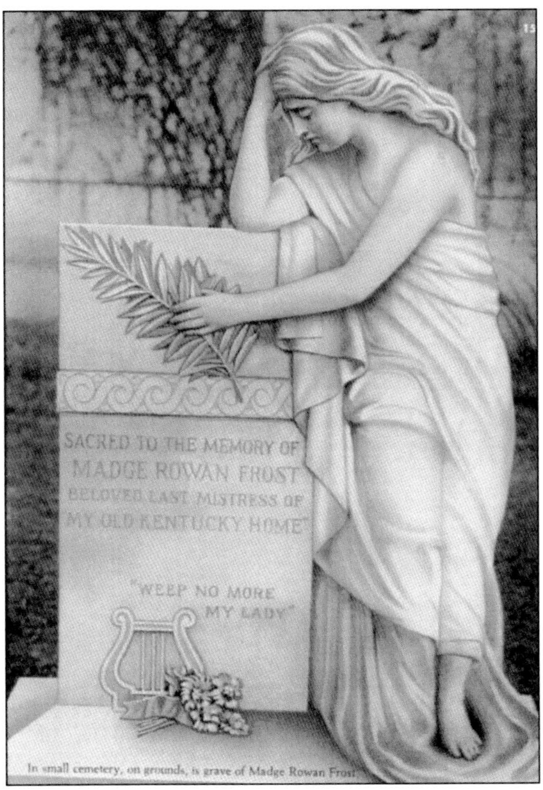

Her monument reflects the theme "Weep No More, My Lady." This graveyard was enclosed by a tall, iron fence when Mrs. Frost was buried. A brick wall was erected by the State about 40 years ago. John Rowan's monument is a tall marble obelisk noting his death in 1843.

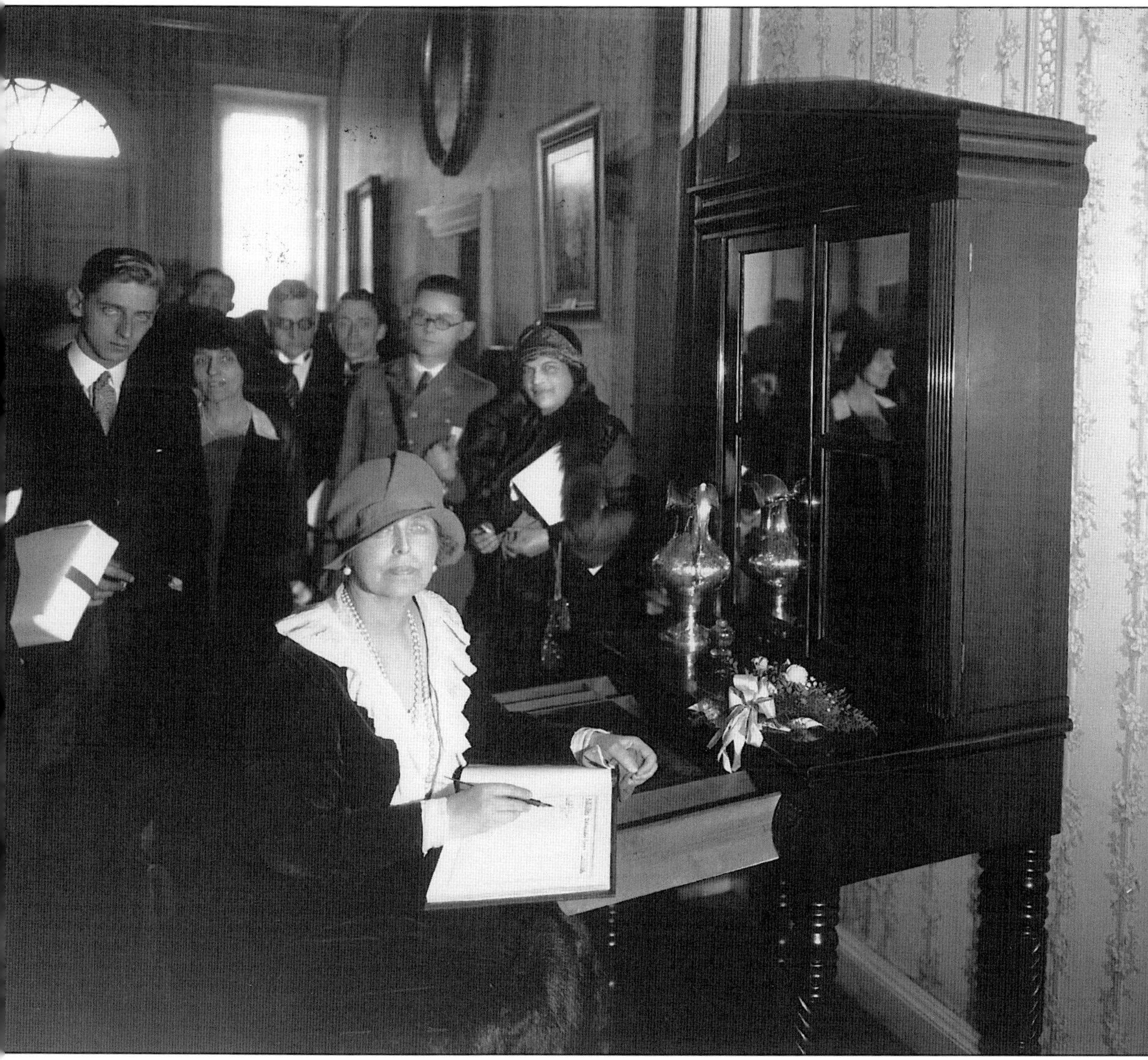

Royalty came to Bardstown on November 18, 1926, when Queen Marie of Rumania and her party arrived in a convoy of touring cars. Congressman Ben Johnson was chairman of the Governor's Committee and escorted Her Highness. The party left Louisville at 11:30 for Bardstown, speeding at an average of 45 miles per hour led by two motorcycle policemen. Crowds of people lined the streets of Bardstown and greeted them as they drove to Federal Hill. Pictured here, signing the register in the hallway of the home, is the Queen and her son, Prince Nicholas. A luncheon was served in the home for 65 guests. The dining room table at My Old Kentucky Home was set with the Johnson family china and decorated with flags of the United States and Rumania. Souvenir menus were given to each guest. Tables were also set up in other rooms to accommodate all of the guests at the party.

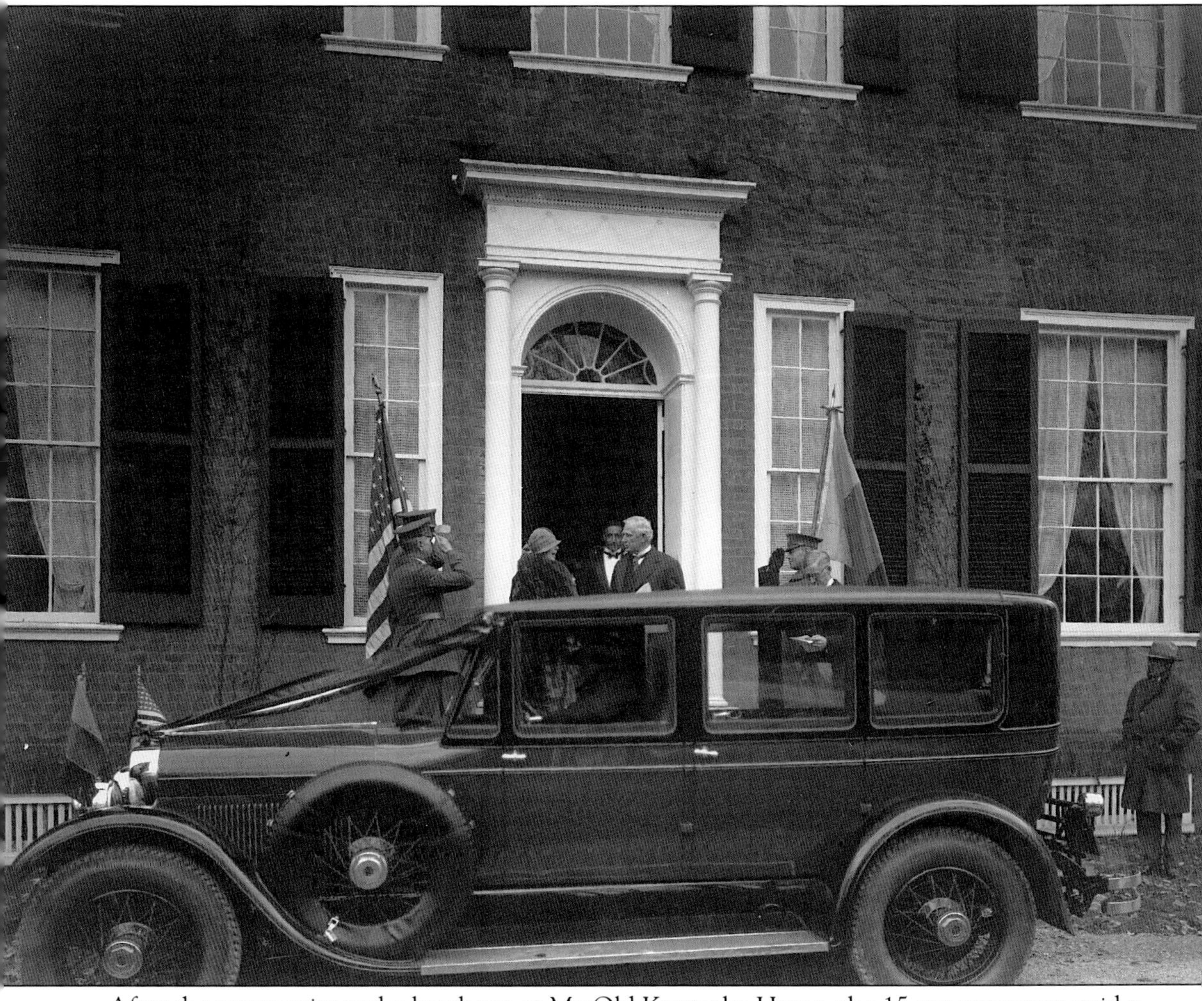

After the ceremonies and a luncheon at My Old Kentucky Home, the 15-car entourage paid a short visit to St. Joseph Cathedral, where the Queen endeared herself to the crowd by singling out young Leo Haydon in his "rolling chair" for comments. She pinned her corsage of yellow roses and lilies of the valley on the youngster. Then the motorcade raced off to Hodgenville and the Lincoln Memorial. Dust flew from the roads as this parade set speed records averaging 60 miles per hour! Uphill and down, speeding cars slid into ditches, overheated, and threw bearings. Both motorcycles were disabled, leaving the Queen's car to proceed with only the national flags flying to denote the importance of this visitor.

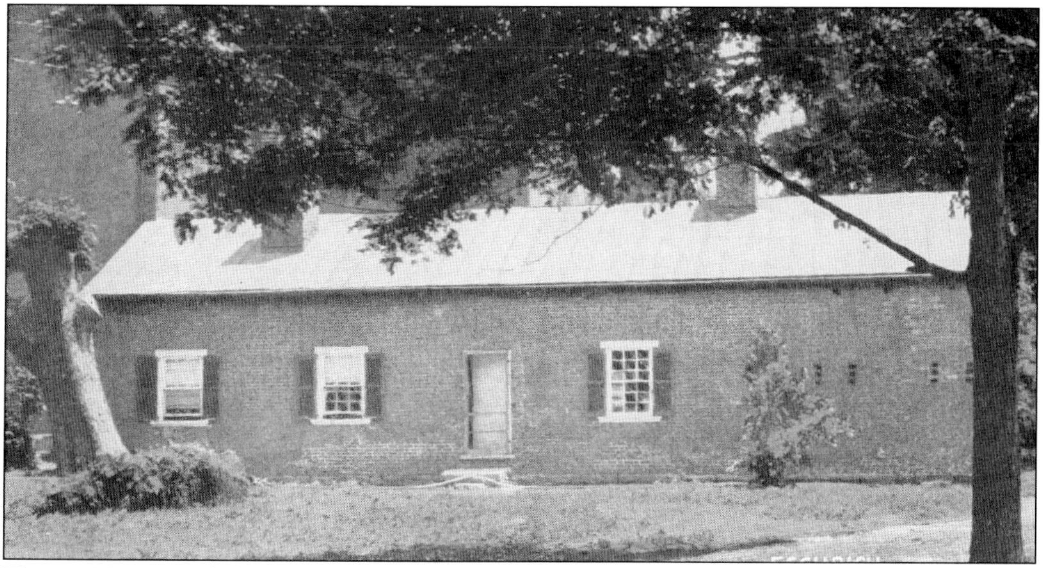

This 1923 postcard shows the back wing of the structure. This is the oldest section. Built in the early 1800s, it was occupied during the construction of the main house. Later, it was used as the kitchen, a smokehouse, and two small bedrooms. The home has been open to the public since 1923, and thousands of visitors have enjoyed the beauty that inspired the song. On September 19, 1932, U.S. Vice-President Charles Curtis visited the park.

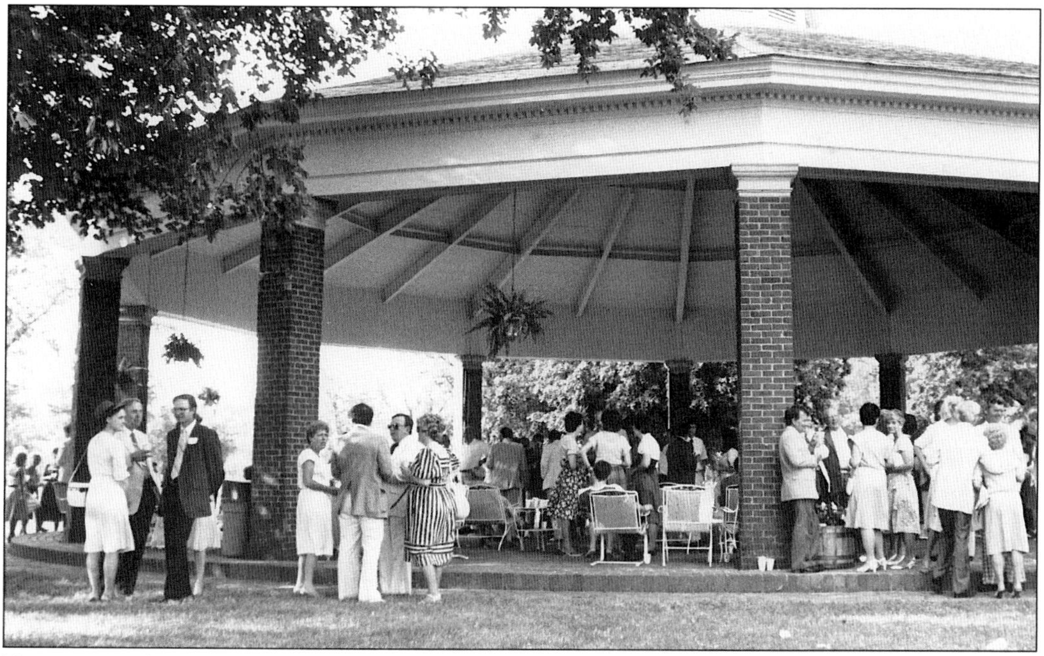

Newspaper clippings indicate that a pavilion was being built at My Old Kentucky Home in May of 1933. It was to be finished by July Fourth at a cost of $5,000. Fourteen years later, an advertisement for bidders to demolish this pavilion drew bids that the state considered too high. The area is still being used today for receptions, weddings, official ceremonies, and entertainment.

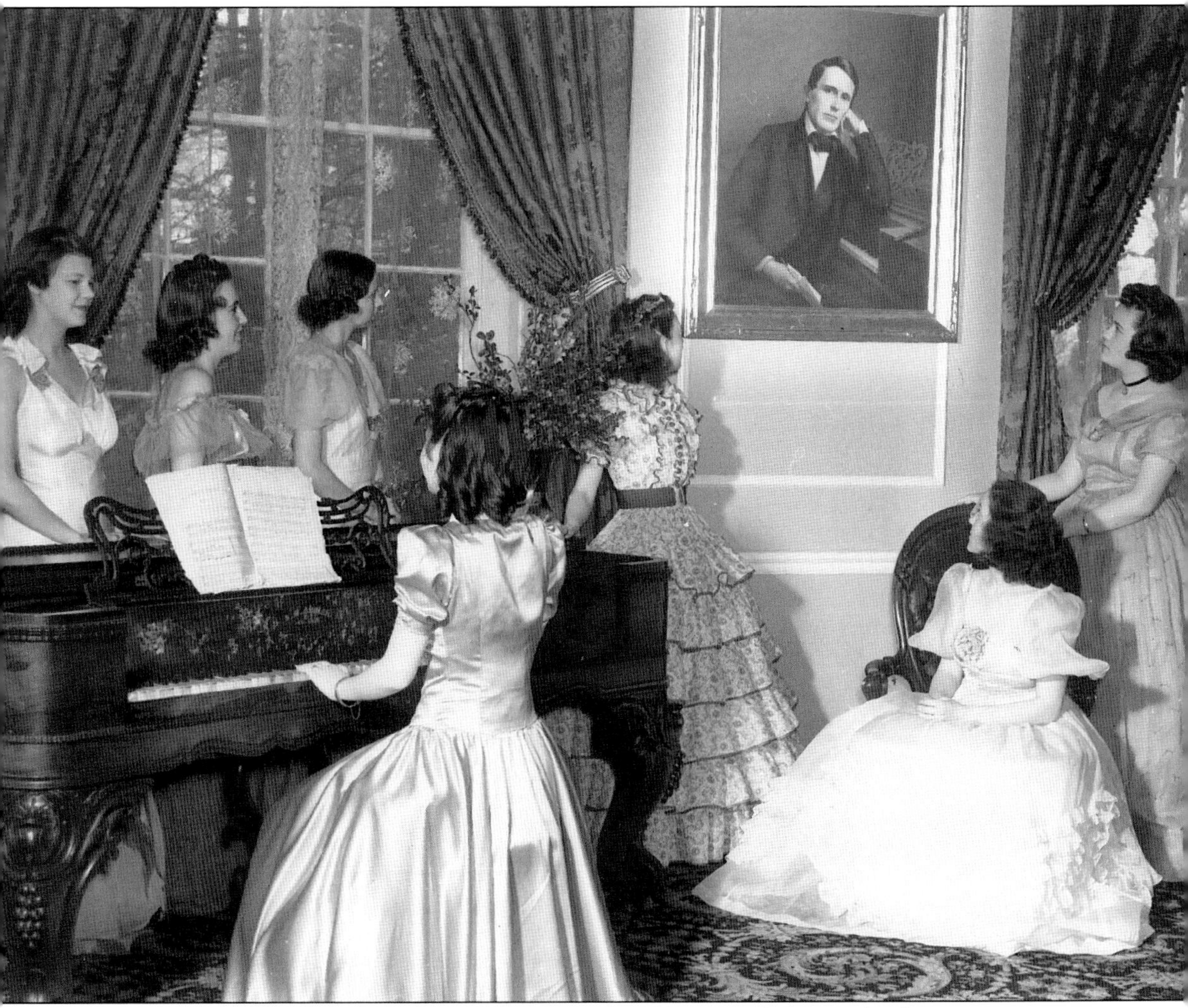

On Friday, May 3, 1940, the Stephen Foster Stamp was issued. It was the first time a composer had been so honored. Guests were entertained by these lovely hostesses in the parlor of the home. They are, from left to right, Carolyn Elston, Dorothy Sympson, Hayse Hamilton, Mrs. Dan Arnold, Kitty Conway (seated), and Mary Spalding Roby. Sally Edelen is at the Ambler piano. The invitation reads as follows:

"HOME COMING DAY
BARDSTOWN, KY
MAY 3, 1940

The city of Bardstown invites you and your friends to be with us at My Old Kentucky Home on May 3rd to participate in a glorious celebration commemorating the first day issue of a postage stamp honoring Stephen Collins Foster, America's favorite composer. The ceremonies will be broadcast over a nationwide network at 11a.m. with Mr. Leopold Stokowski conducting a symphony orchestra and Bing Crosby singing, assisted by other radio and screen artists. True Kentucky hospitality awaits you." It is signed "J.F. Conway, Mayor."

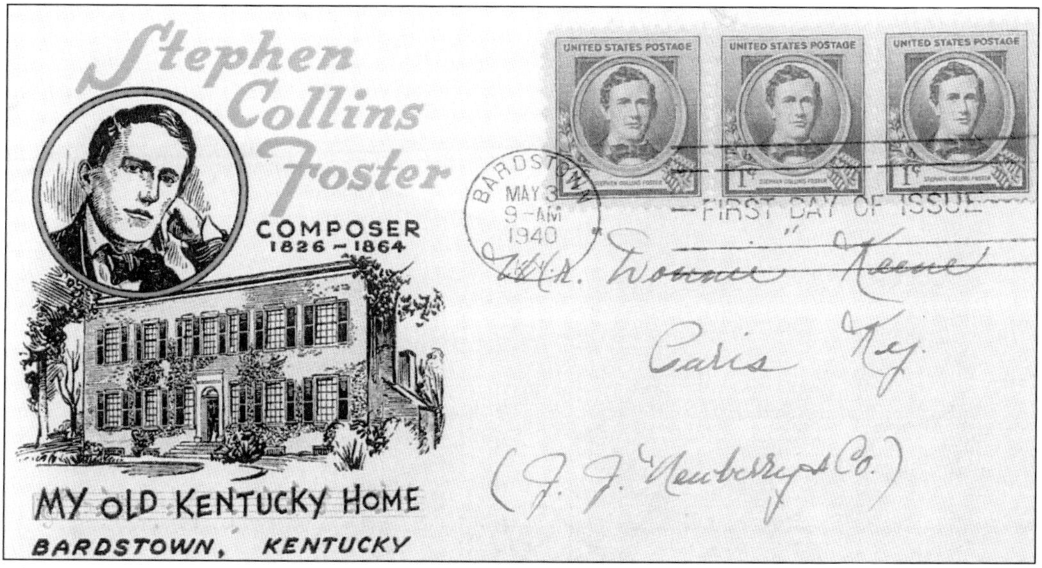

This is a first-day issue of the Stephen Foster Stamp that was stamped and mailed on May 3, 1940. It took three commemorative stamps to pay the 3¢ postage for an envelope.

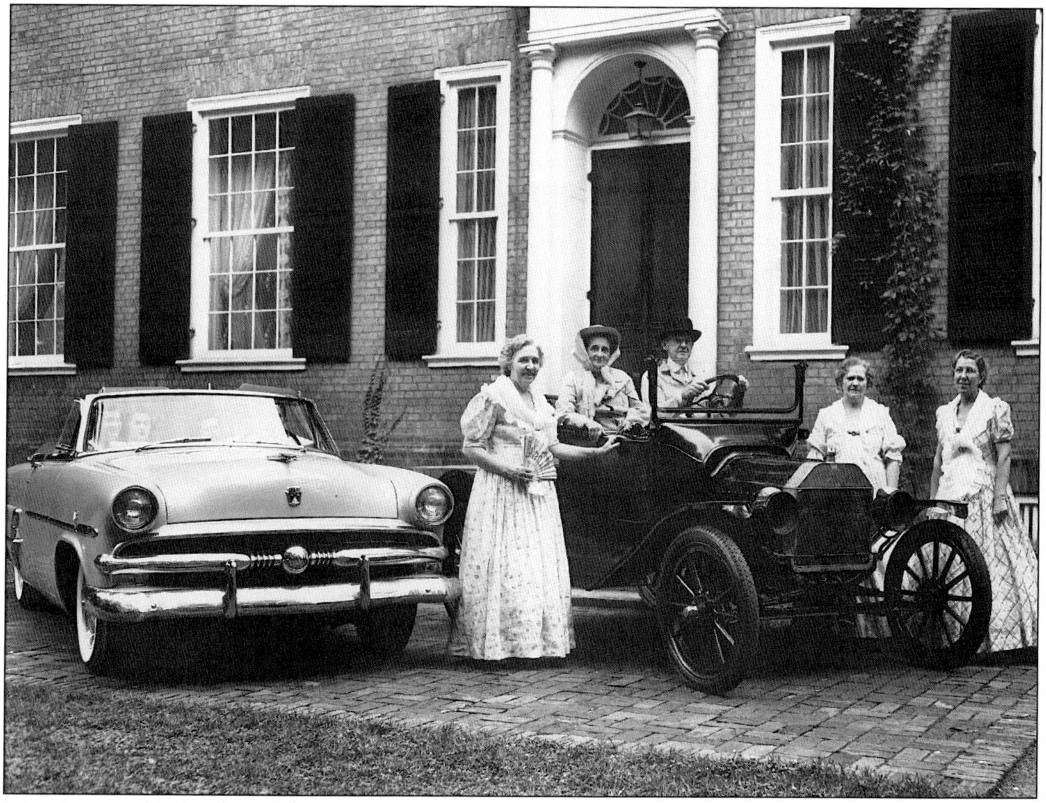

The front of Federal Hill became very popular for advertising pictures. Here are Mr. and Mrs. James F. Conway in a Model-T 1919 Ford. The 1953 Ford is driven by Mr. and Mrs. Pike Conway. The hostesses at the home, from left to right, are Mrs. Ethel Mattingly, Mrs. Jennie Dickerson, and Mrs. Harry Marr.

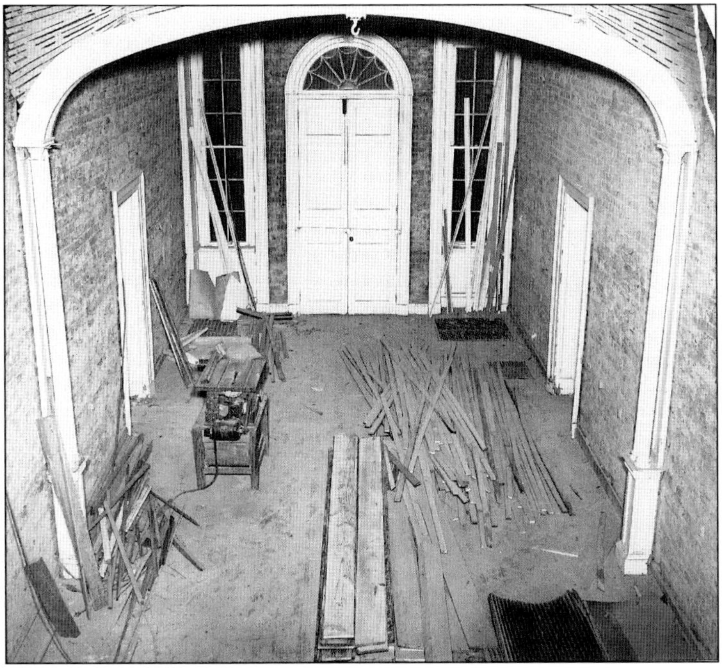

In 1950, Federal Hill underwent extensive renovation. Pictured is a view of the main hallway, looking down from the stair landing. All of the plaster was removed from the brick walls and the lathing was removed from the center arch. It was completely rewired. Eleven more "stars" (attached to reinforcing rods) were added to the original two in order to stabilize the solid brick walls. Below is a picture taken from the same location, showing the finished hallway. It is filled with costumed guides and visitors.

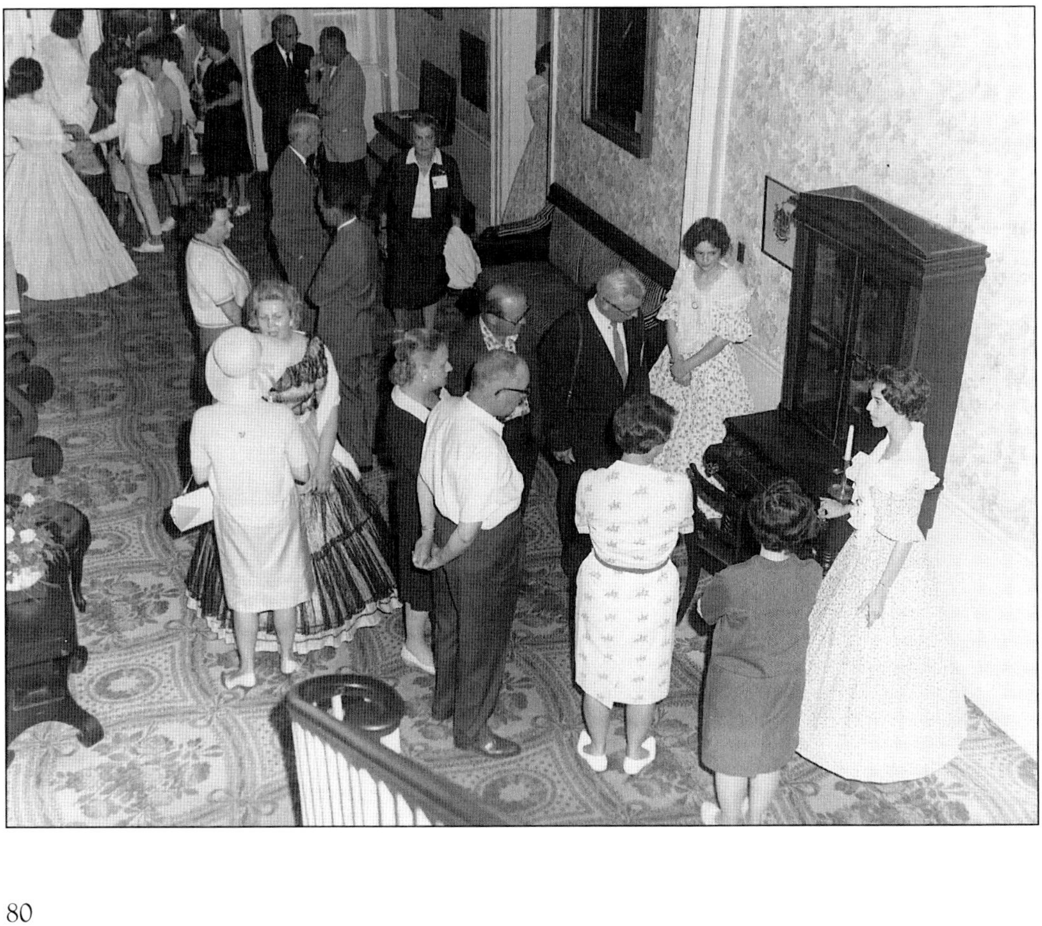

Four

Nelson Distilleries

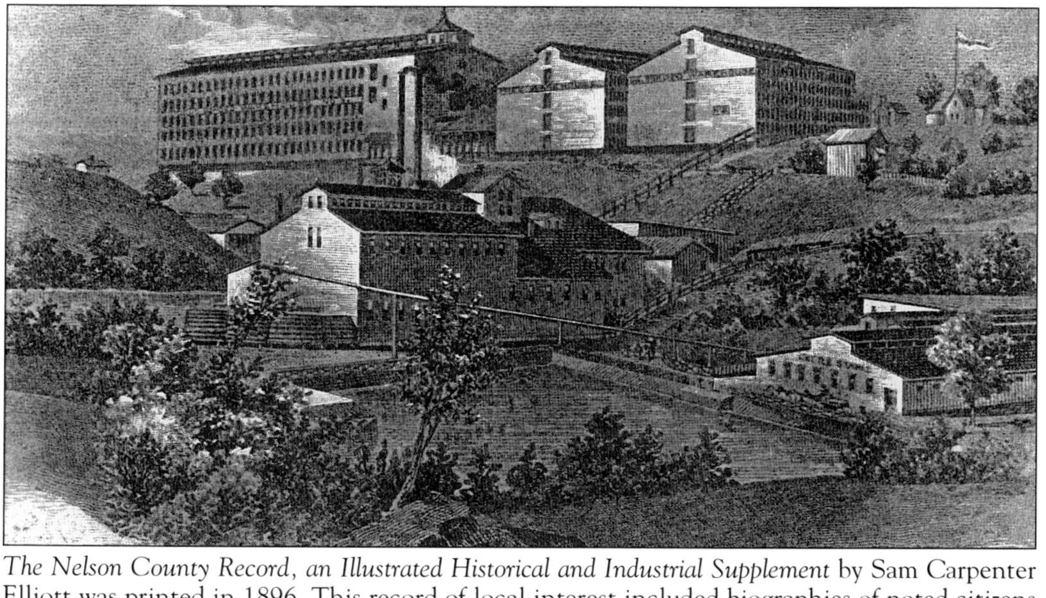

The Nelson County Record, an Illustrated Historical and Industrial Supplement by Sam Carpenter Elliott was printed in 1896. This record of local interest included biographies of noted citizens and accounts of local distilleries. Elliott was a former revenue officer for the federal government who worked at various distilling operations in the area. He wrote in the florid style of the age about the "unblemished character and unquestioned veracity" of the men and the "beauty and accomplishments" of the women. The following condensed accounts are of the operating distilleries of 1896. The sketch above is the Belle of Nelson Distillery Company on the Knoxville branch of the L & N Railroad at New Hope, Kentucky. Belle of Nelson is the brand name. The majority of the distilleries have disappeared. Some brand names continue to be used by other distilleries.

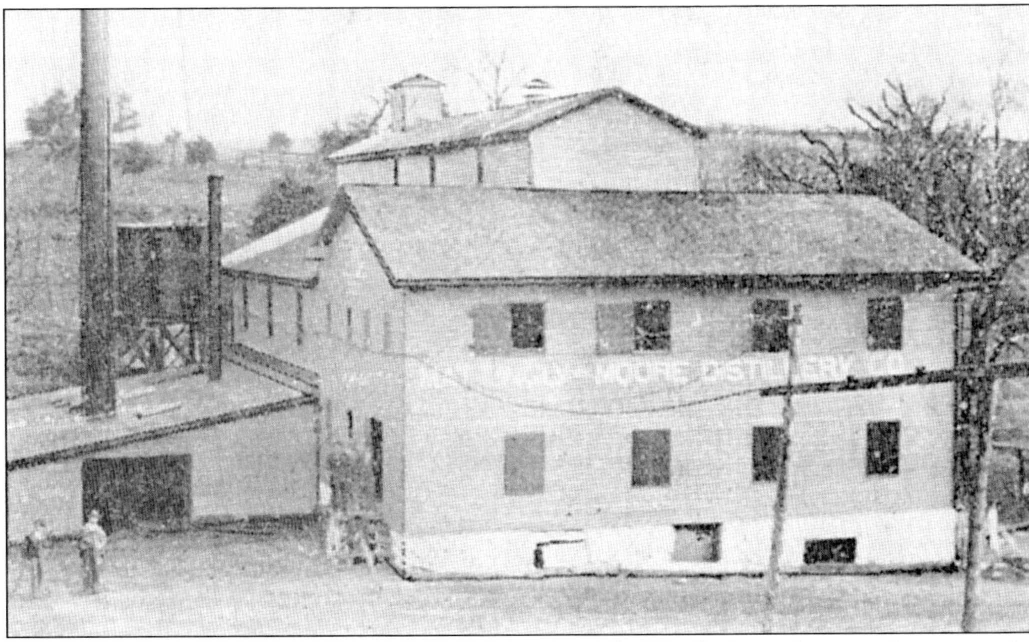

In 1896, the Mattingly and Moore Distillery was one-half mile from the courthouse on the Bardstown-Green River Turnpike. Established in 1876, it was here that the first barrel of Belle of Nelson was made. The never-failing Morton Spring provides the limestone spring water necessary for making good whiskey. Warehouse capacity is 1,800 barrels. Cattle-feeding sheds are built over a running stream to carry off the waste, and slop is piped directly to these sheds from the stillhouse. John Simms and R.H. Edelen are the owners. Simms Edelen is the brand name.

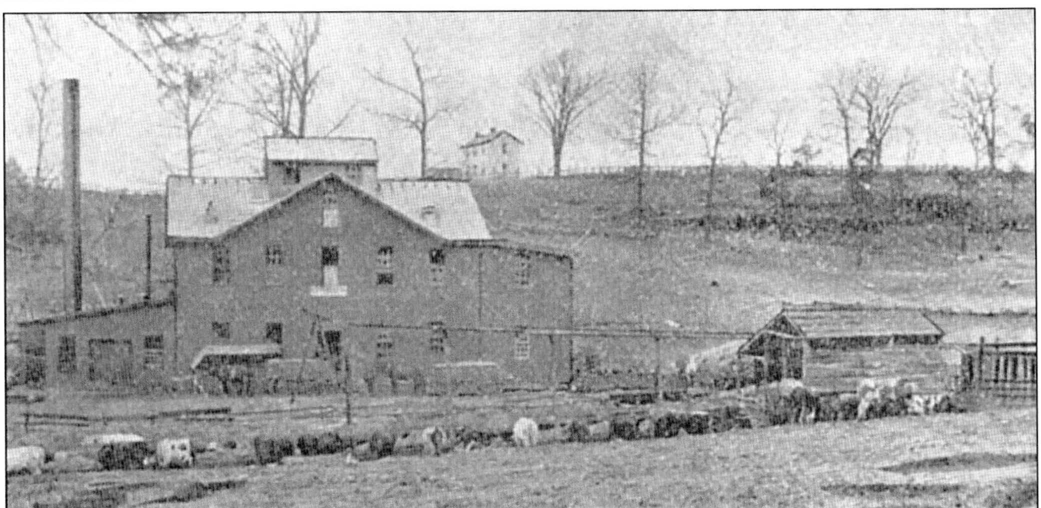

In 1896, the Tom Moore Distillery was on the Bardstown-Green River Turnpike one mile from Bardstown. It was established in 1889 by Thomas S. Moore, a practical distiller with 15 years of experience. He managed the Mattingly and Moore Distillery directly north of this site until 1889. T.C. O'Keefe of Oswego, NY, a full partner in the distillery, was in charge of the distribution. Warehouse capacity is 2,000 barrels. Tom Moore and Woodcock are the brand names.

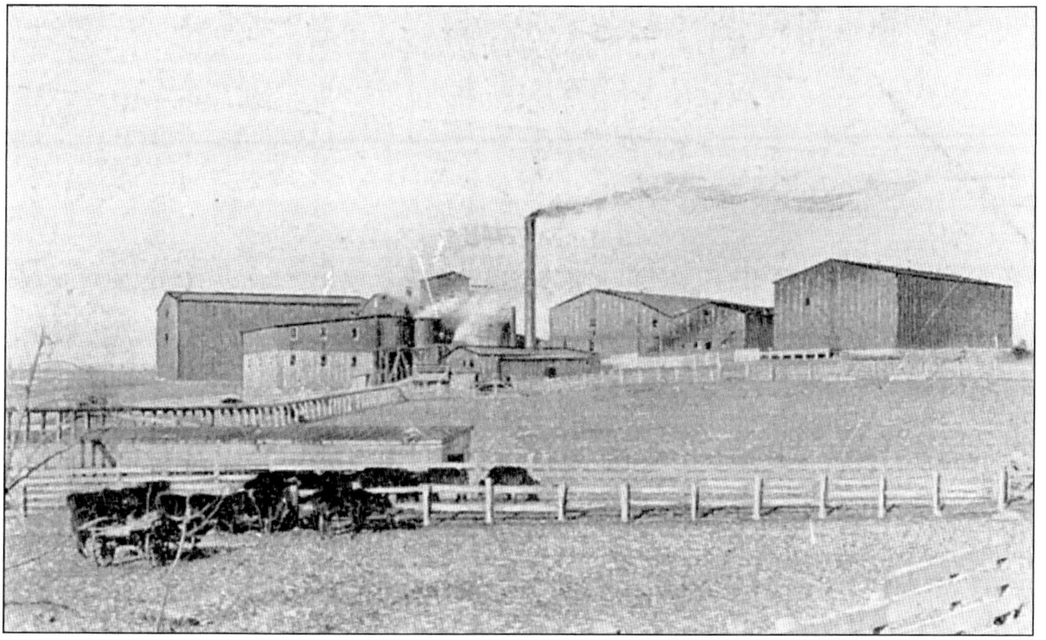

In 1896, the Early Times Distillery was located 4 miles east of Bardstown, on the Springfield branch of the L & N Railroad. The distillery was owned by B.H. Hurt and John H. Beam. Beam believed in the early methods of making whiskey—mashing the grains in small tubs and boiling the beer and whiskey in copper stills over open fires. The employees of the distillery at the time were William E. Brown (general superintendent), Edward D. Beam (general manager), and H.T. Cravens, (distiller). Early Times, A.G. Nall, sour mash whiskies, and Jack Beam sweet mash whiskey are the brand names they manufactured.

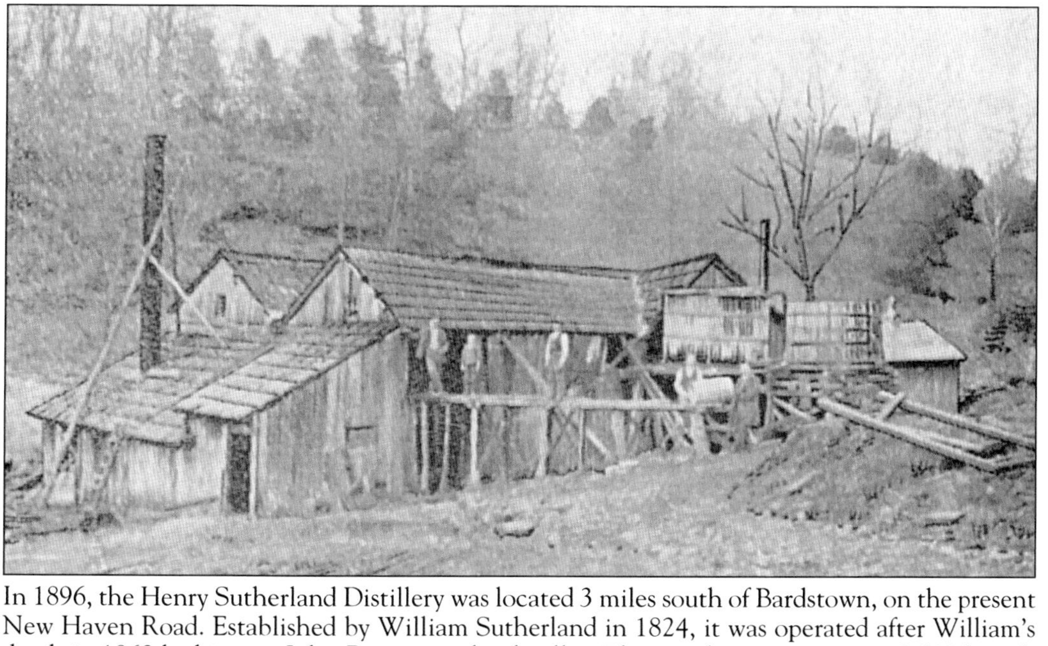

In 1896, the Henry Sutherland Distillery was located 3 miles south of Bardstown, on the present New Haven Road. Established by William Sutherland in 1824, it was operated after William's death in 1862 by his son. John Beam was the distiller. The warehouse capacity is 2,500 barrels and Old Sutherland is the brand name manufactured here.

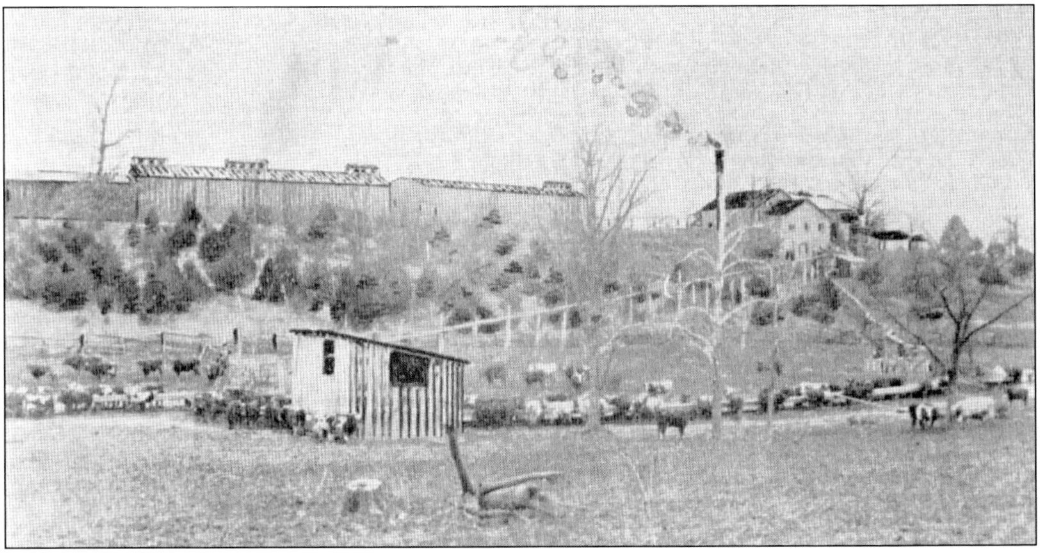

In 1896, the S.P. Lancaster Distillery was located 1.5 miles north of Bardstown, on the Springfield branch of the L & N Railroad. S.P. Lancaster and his brother, J.M. Lancaster, established the present distillery in 1850. Mr. Lancaster, a farmer, produced much of the corn used at this distillery. S.P. Lancaster served as the distiller as well as the superintendent. Warehouse capacity is 15,000 barrels and S.P. Lancaster is the only brand made.

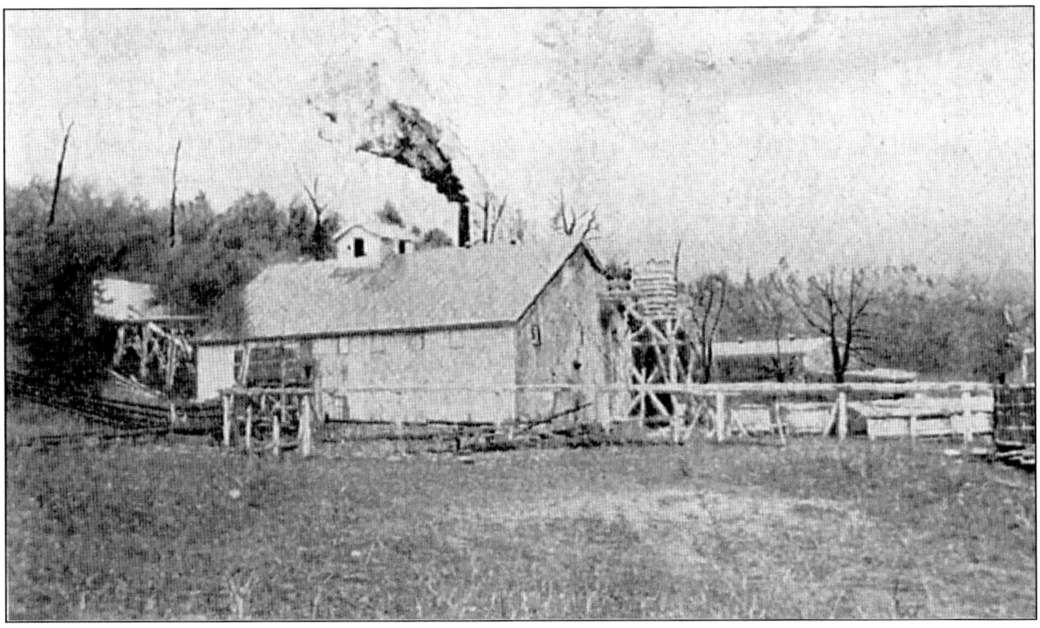

In 1896, the F.G. Walker Distillery was located on College Creek, on the western edge of Bardstown. Established by Walker in 1881, it is now operated by his partner, Charles C. Brown. Morgan Edelen is the distiller and F.V. Bell is the beer runner. The warehouses are dry with a capacity of 8,000 barrels. Frank Stivers is the barrel maker and William E. Abell is the general manager. F.G. Walker and Queen of Nelson are the name brands.

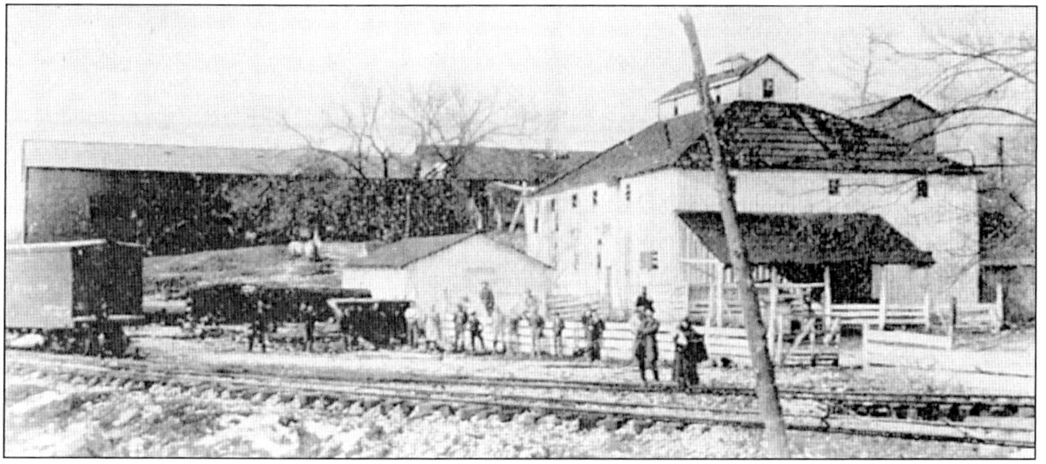

In 1896, Murphy, Barber, and Company was located in Clermont, Kentucky (in Bullitt County). The fountainhead of the springs which supply the water for whisky-making, however, is located in Nelson County. In 1881, Squire Murphy, A.M. Barber, and Calvin Brown established this distillery. Mr. Murphy died in 1893, and Mr. Brown retired soon after, leaving Mr. Barber in charge. John Kurtz is the distiller and Charles Drillette is the general manager. The warehouse capacity is 10,000 barrels. Murphy, Barber, & Company and Clermont Rye are the brands.

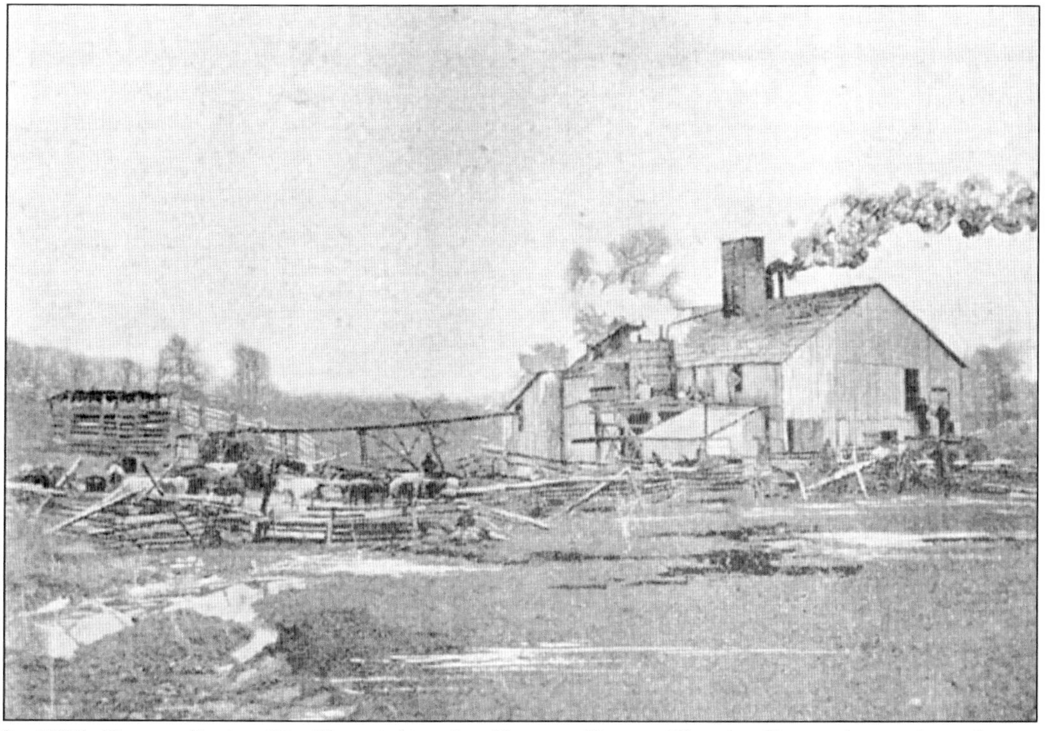

In 1896, Gwynn Spring Distillery is listed as Hunters Depot. The distillery is located northwest of Bardstown, off the maintained roads and deep in the woods. Visitors must have guides to locate it. It was established in the 1870s by Jefferson D. McGee and a Mr. Walker. The operation was destroyed by fire and was rebuilt in 1880. John B. Stoner has been a partner with McGee in this distillery since 1895. Dee Beam is the distiller.

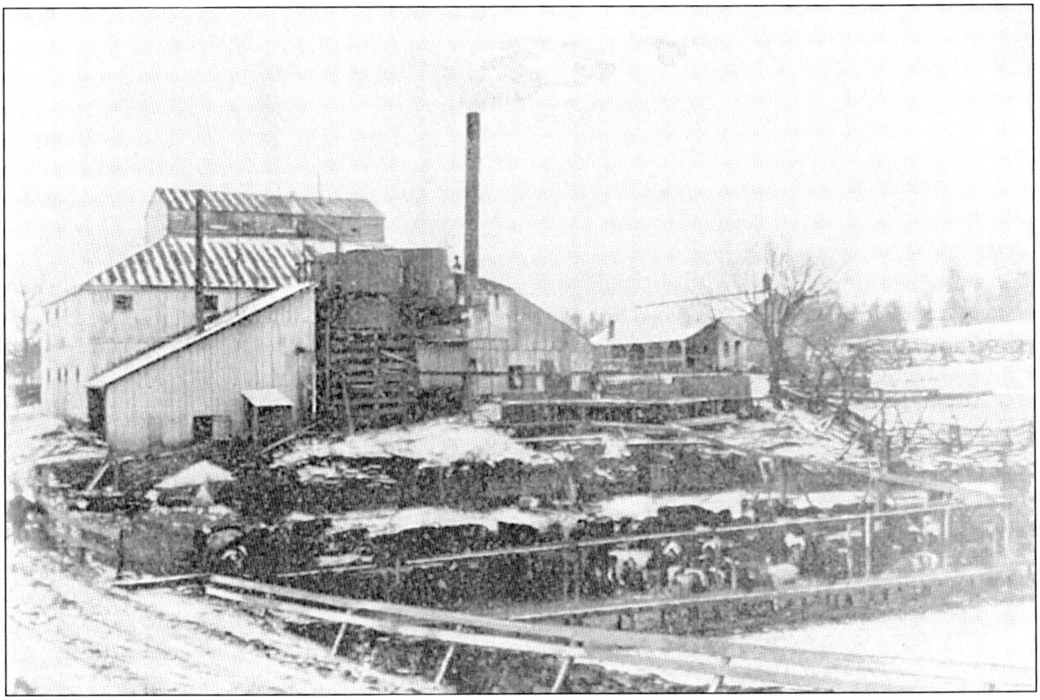

In 1896, the Taylor W. Samuels Distillery was located one-half mile east of Deatsville on the Springfield branch of the L & N Railroad. It was erected by T.W. Samuels in 1844 and has been continuously operated by him. Stephen Hall is the distiller. The warehouse capacity is 14,000 barrels. T.W. Samuels is the brand.

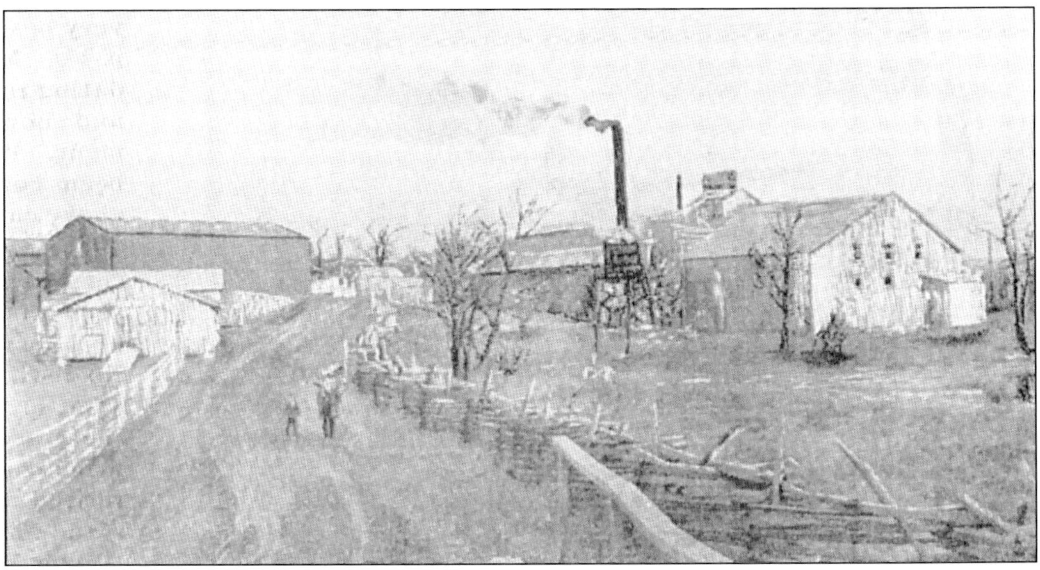

In 1896, the W.B. Samuels and Company Distillery was located at Samuels on the Bardstown branch of the L & N Railroad. It was established in 1869 by Samuels and is now operated in partnership with George R. Burkes. Robert Masters is the distiller. The warehouse capacity is 11,000 barrels. It is located along the railroad "so that a carload of whiskey can be loaded by two men within 40 minutes time." W.B. Samuels Bourbon and Eureka Rye are the brands.

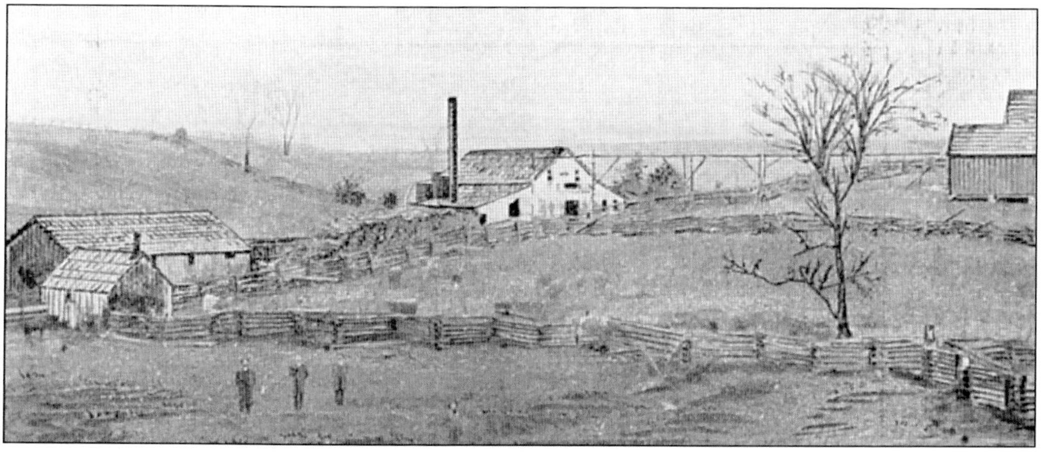

In 1896, Boone and Brothers Distillery was located 2 miles east of Bardstown, on the Loretto Turnpike. Wattie Boone and Stephen Ritchie began making whiskey in this area in 1780. The Boone family descended from Wattie and continued the tradition of whiskey-making for the last 116 years. Warehouse capacity is 2,000 barrels. Charles Boone purchases the grain and sells the finished product, Nicholas R. Boone is the superintendent, and Frank N. Boone is the distiller. Boone Brothers and Old Maid are the brand names.

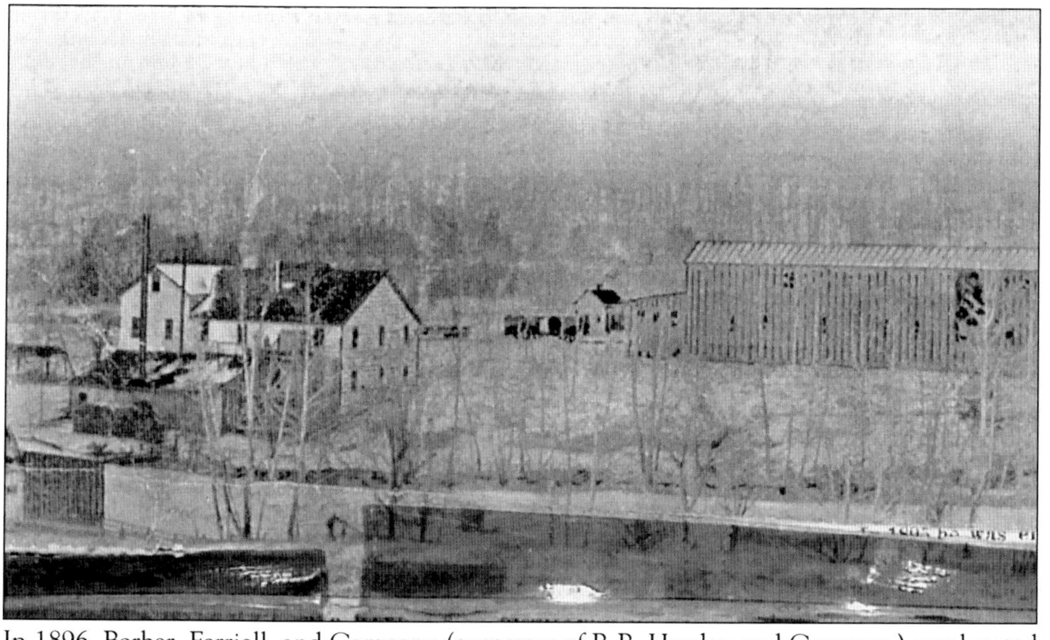

In 1896, Barber, Ferriell, and Company (successor of R.B. Hayden and Company) was located in Hobbs, Kentucky, on the western edge of Nelson County. R.B. Hayden's grandfather began distilling in 1796, and his father followed in 1819. Hayden continued the family tradition in 1840. In 1882, Hayden and F.L. Ferriell built the present distillery. After Mr. Hayden's death in 1885, P.S. Barber purchased Hayden's estate's interest in the operation. Warehouse capacity is 7,000 barrels. R.B. Hayden & Company, Pure Rye Whisky, and Old Gran-Dad, Nelson County Kentucky Whiskey are the brands.

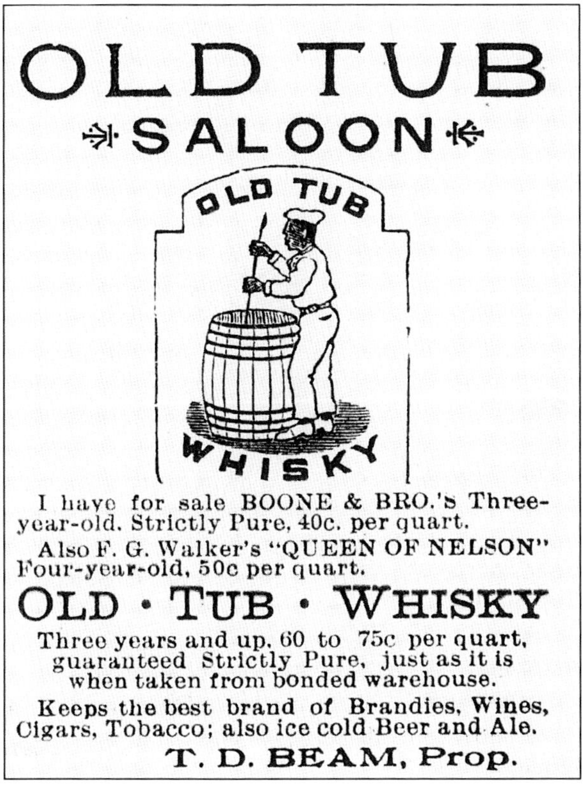

In 1896, the Beam and Hart Distillery was located about 2 miles north of Bardstown on the Springfield branch of the L & N Railroad. David M. Beam began the distillery in 1853. He retired in 1892, and transferred the distillery business to his son, James B. Beam, and son-in law, Albert Hart. The warehouse capacity is 10,000 barrels. James B. Beam is the distiller, and Hart buys the grains and supervises the storage and shipping. Old Tub is the only brand.

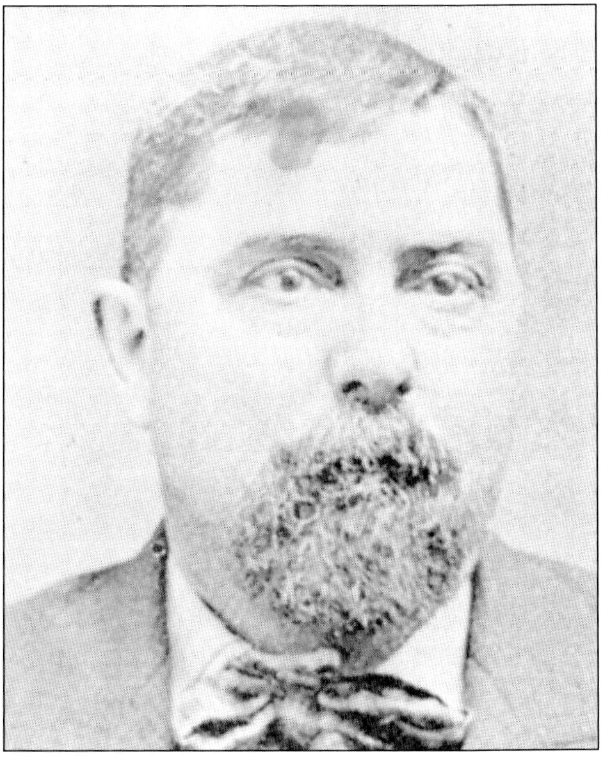

In 1896, Ford Brothers Distillers were located one mile north of New Haven on the Bardstown-Green River Turnpike. R. Monroe Ford (pictured) was president and general manager. His brothers, Thomas R. and Curtis J., served as silent members. The mashing capacity is 50 bushels a day. Richard Bowling worked for E.L. Miles and Company of New Hope in 1880. "He is a believer in signs as displayed by the moon. When he is making whisky in the dark of the moon he always exceeds 4 gallons per bushel, while in the light of the moon he can only produce about 4 gallons per bushel." Green Price is the assistant distiller and superintendent of the mash floor. Pride of Nelson is the only brand.

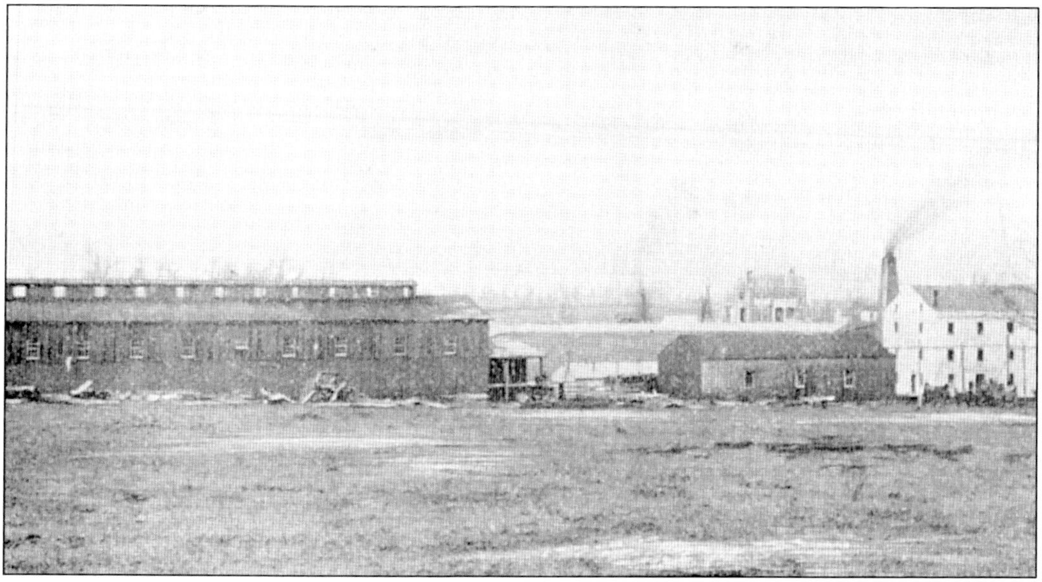

In 1896, the McKenna Distillery, located in Fairfield, Kentucky, was making "old-fashioned, handmade whiskey." Henry McKenna began the operation in 1855 with a flour mill. He made less than one barrel of whisky per day. In 1883, he built a new brick distillery and increased production to three barrels a day. He died in 1893, leaving his sons to continue the business. Warehouse capacity is 8,000 barrels. Employees of the distillery are Daniel McKenna (general manager), James S. McKenna (assistant manager), Stafford McKenna (traveling man), and Patrick Sweeney (distiller since 1860). H. McKenna, Old Line, Handmade Sour Mash Whiskey is the brand.

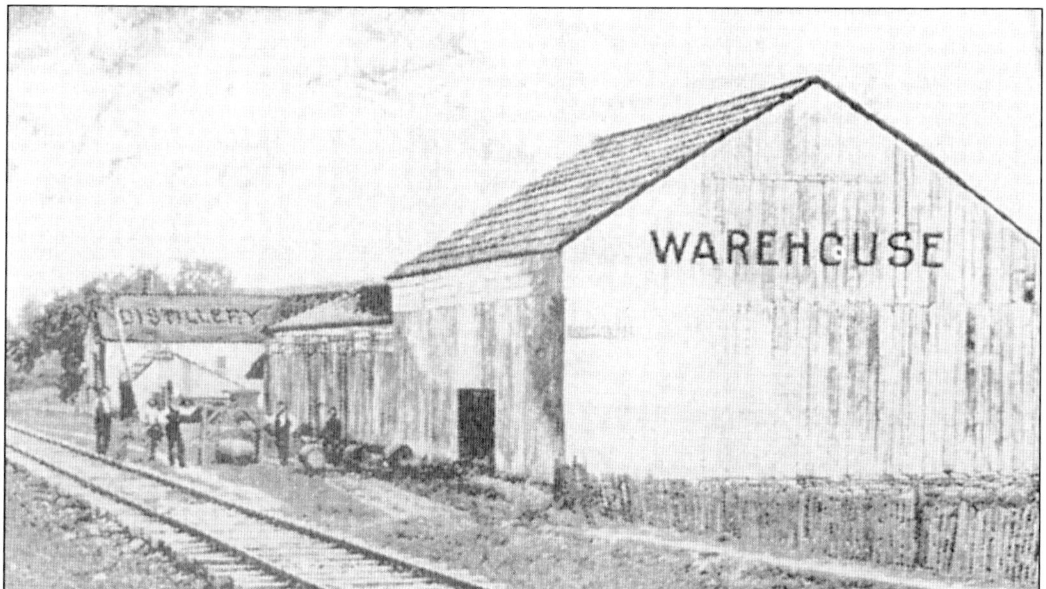

In 1896, Sugar Valley Distillery was located in the suburbs of Bloomfield, northeast of Bardstown. Bodine and Samuel McClaskey purchased it from David Brooks in 1889. It has a warehouse capacity of 2,500 barrels.

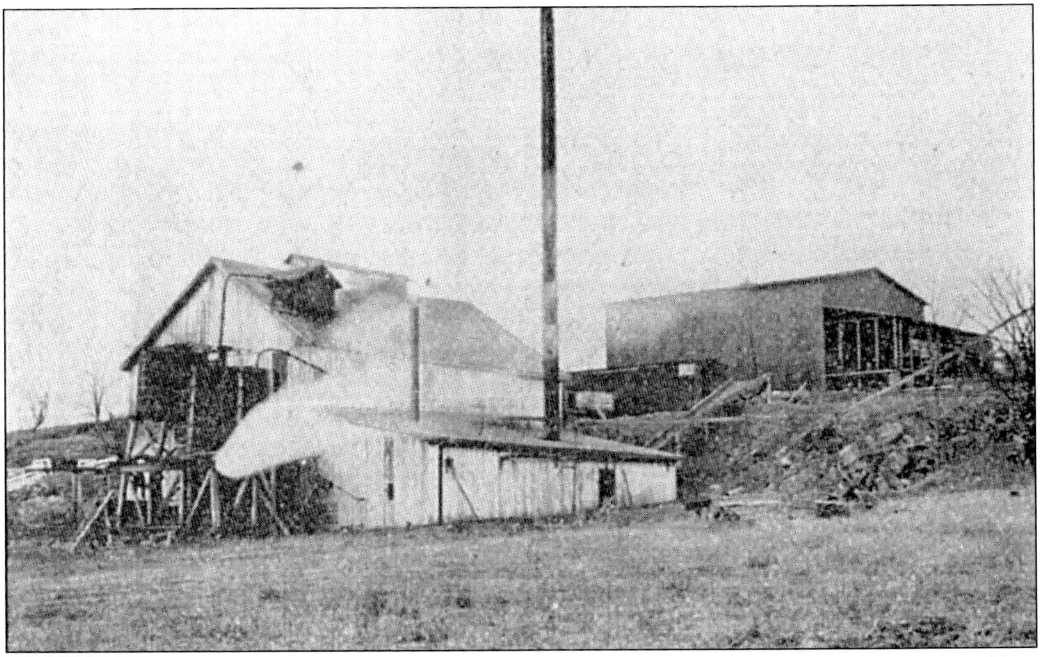

In 1896, the Willow Springs Distillery was located a few hundred yards from Coon Hollow Station. Owned by P. and M.J. Cummins, it was operated by Martin J. Cummins. Willow Springs sour mash and Minway Club sweet mash are the brands.

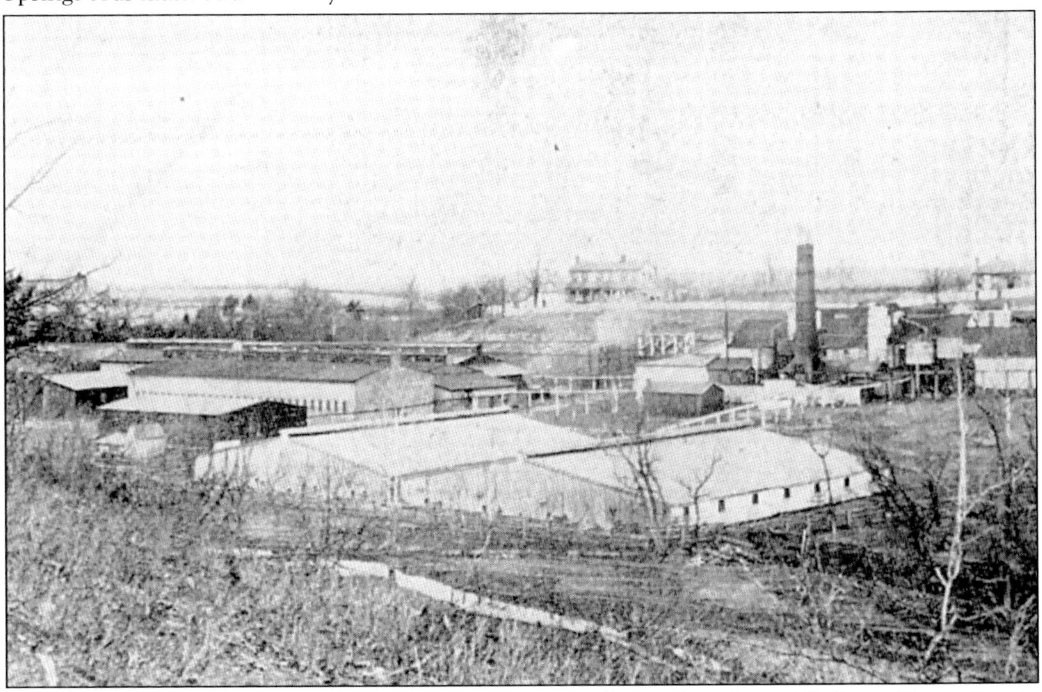

In 1896, the Nelson County Distillery Company was located at Coon Hollow, Kentucky, in the southern part of Nelson County on the Knoxville branch of L & N Railroad. The company operates two distilleries: Coon Hollow and Big Spring. They have six new warehouses. Coon Hollow is a sour mash and Big Spring is a fire copper bourbon.

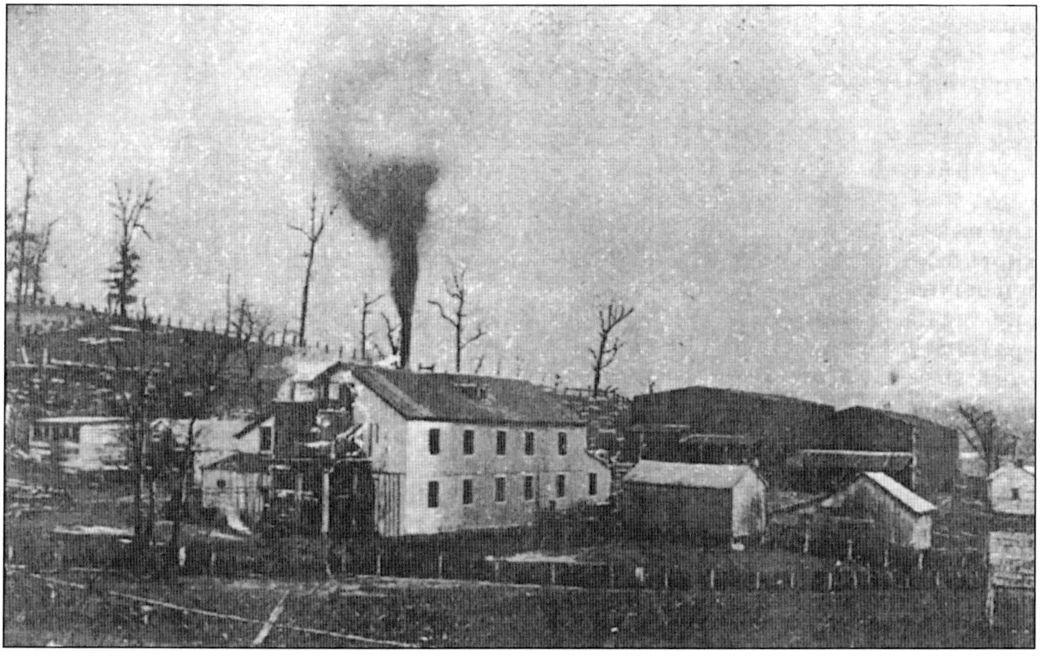

In 1896, Cold Spring (at Gethsemane Station on the Knoxville branch of the L & N Railroad, in the southern part of Nelson County) was operated by J. Bernard Dant and Crittenden Clark, distiller. The barrels were made locally, and Dant selected the timber to be used in the process. Nelson County Club pure rye and Cold Spring sour mash whisky are the brands.

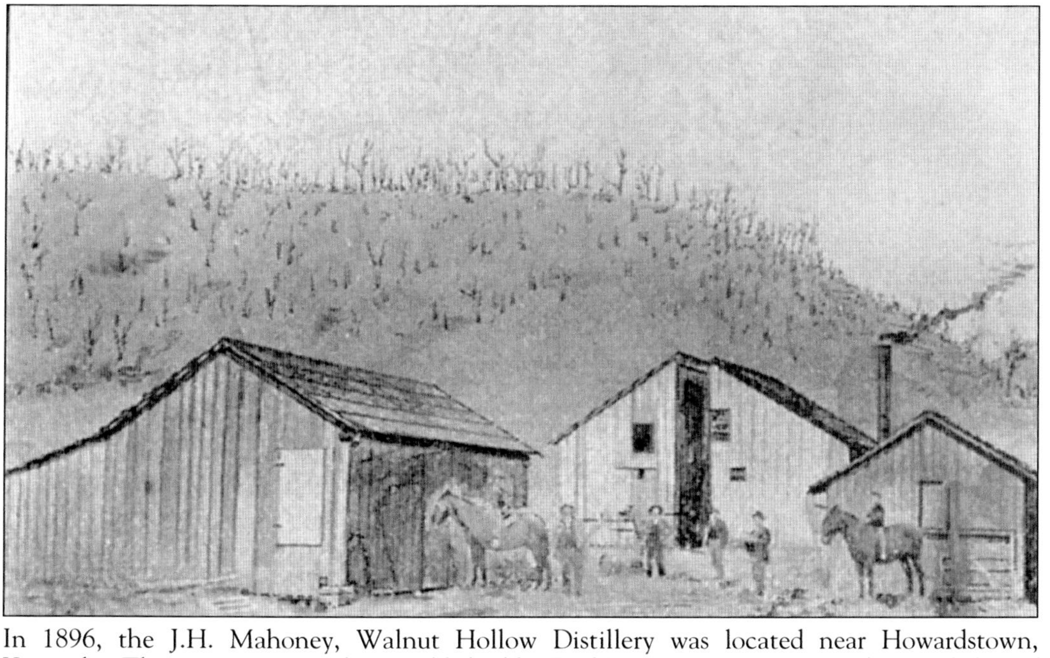

In 1896, the J.H. Mahoney, Walnut Hollow Distillery was located near Howardstown, Kentucky. This operation was first established by Fred Bray in 1831. James Mahoney, father of the present owner, operated it until 1888, when he entered into a partnership with Miles A. Howard. In 1895, James H. Mahoney bought Mr. Howard's interest and is now the sole owner. Uncle Richard Bowling is the distiller, and Walnut Hollow is the brand.

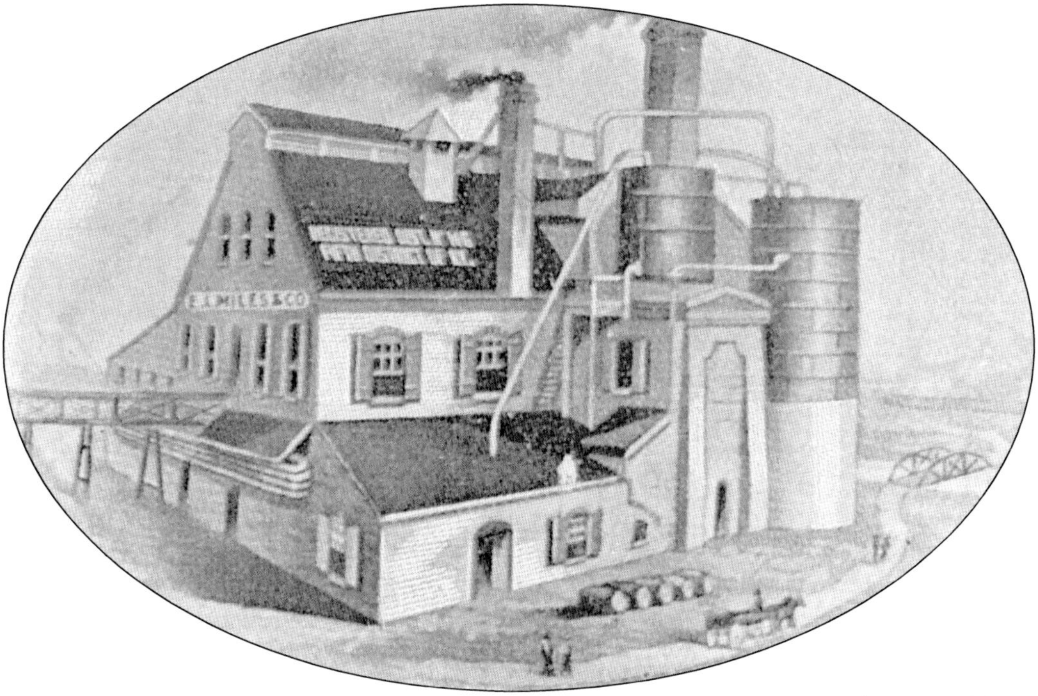

In 1896, the E.L. Miles Distillery and the New Hope Distillery were located in New Hope, Kentucky, on the Knoxville branch of the L & N Railroad. The whisky-making operation, established in 1796 by Henry Miles, has been in operation continuously, except for three years during the Civil War. Edward L. Miles built the distillery in 1867. The mashing capacity is 800 bushels of grain per day. Thomas H. Sherley is the distiller. The New Hope Distillery, established in 1875, is operated by Mr. Miles and Mr. Sherley.

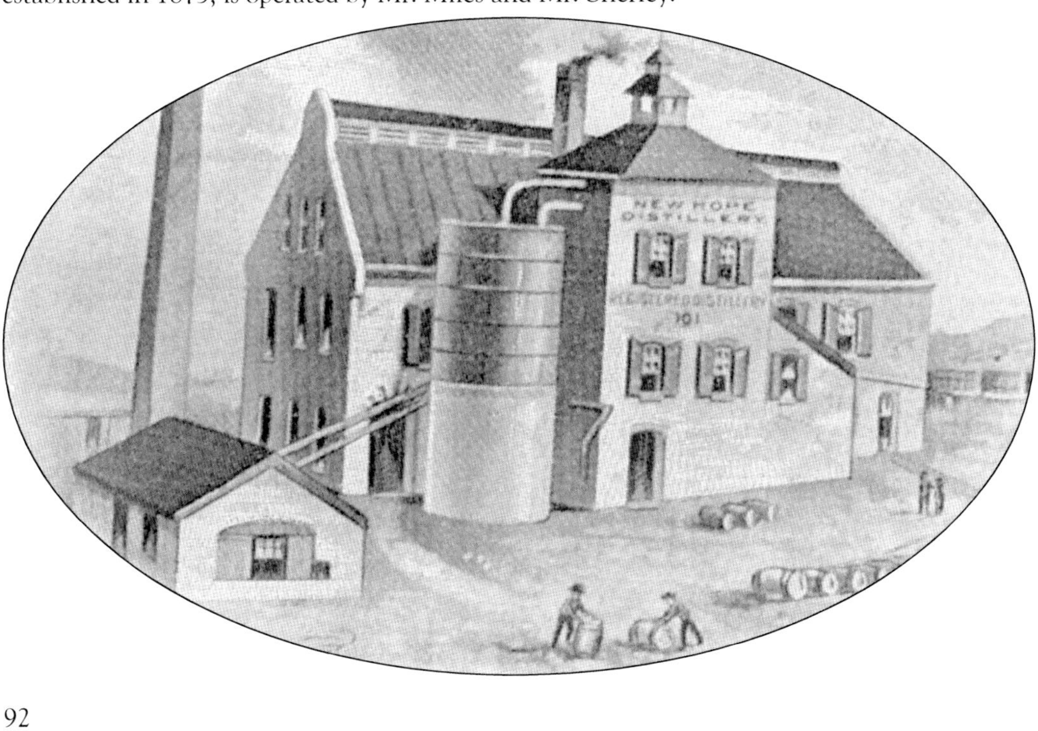

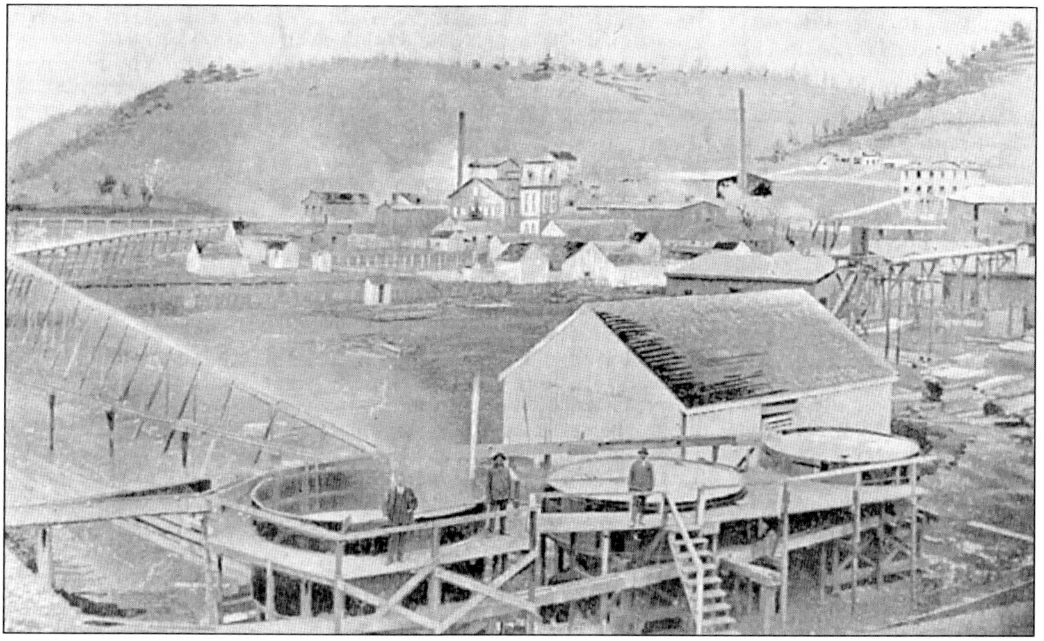

In 1896, the J.M. Atherton Distilleries were located across the Rolling Fork River in LaRue County. Mr. Atherton began manufacturing whisky in 1867 on the present site of the Mayfield House (pictured below). The other large distillery was the Atherton (pictured above). Old Johnnie Boone, whose father (Wattie) was probably the oldest distiller in Kentucky, made whiskey here for years. It was at this location that Thomas Lincoln worked for Boone's Distillery. Taylor Whitehead is the present distiller. Peter Lee Atherton, son of the owner, is in charge of the distillery plant. Warehouse capacity is 150,000 barrels. Atherton, Mayfield, Clifton, Windsor, Howard, Carter, Kenwod, Brownfield, and Baker are the popular brands.

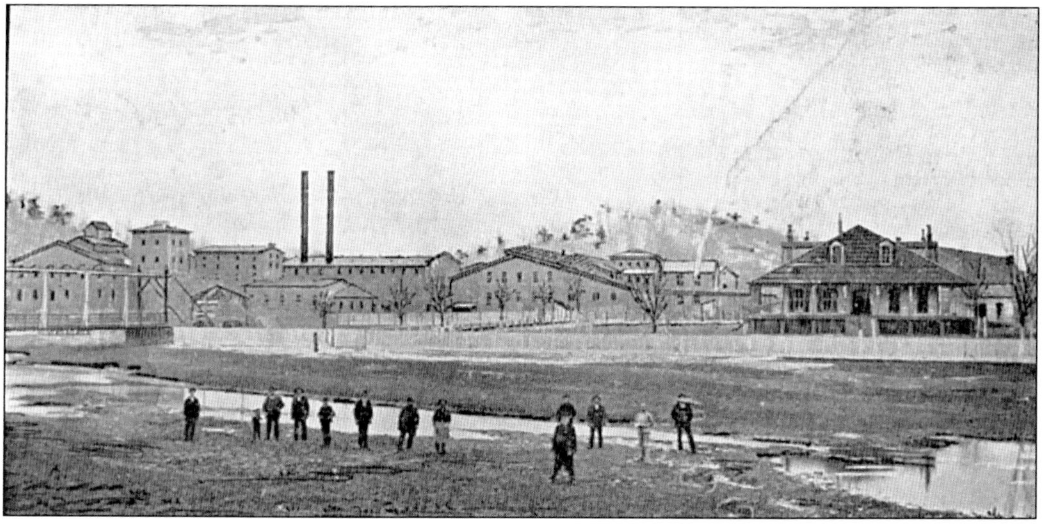

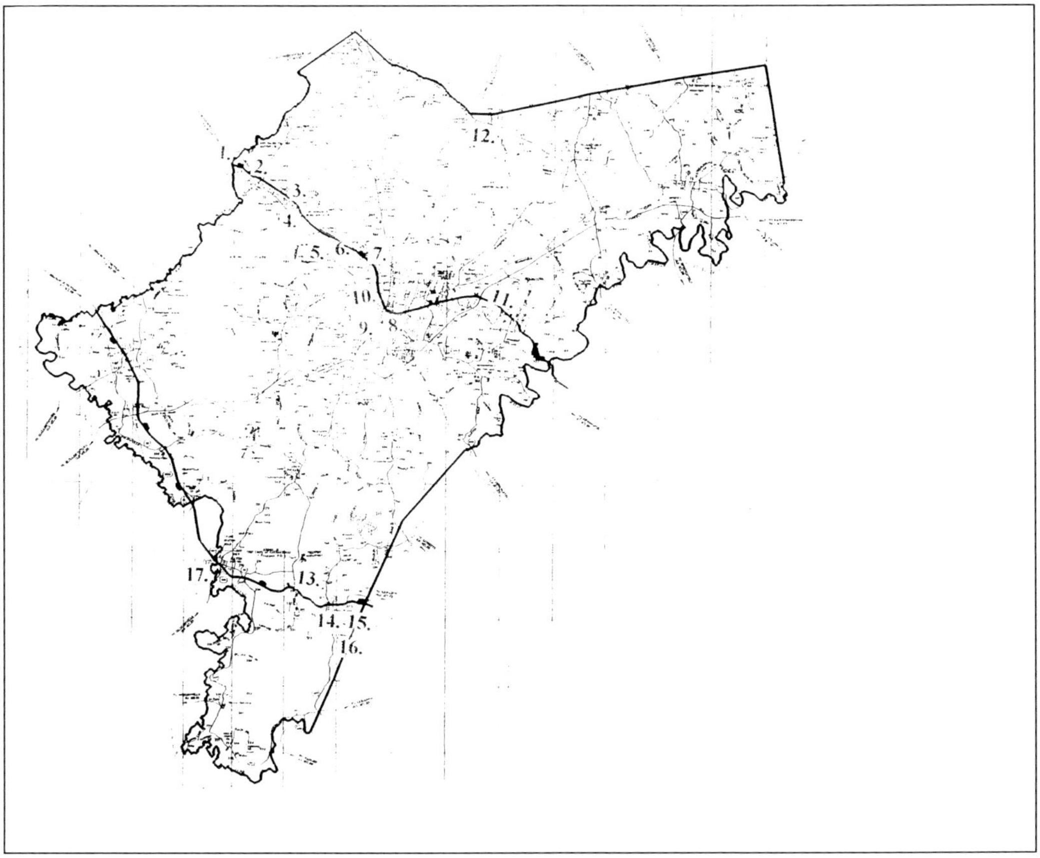

Pictured is a map of Nelson County, showing the location of the distilleries located along or near the railroad.

1. Murphy, Barber, and Company, Clermont
2. Barber, Ferriell, and Company, Hobbs
3. T.W. Samuels
4. W.B. Samuels and Company
5. Gwynn Spring
6. McGee and Beam
7. Beam and Hart
8. The Mattingly and Moore Distillery Company
9. Tom Moore
10. F.G. Walker
11. The Early Times Distillery Company
12. The McKenna Distillery
13. J.B. Dant
14. The New Hope Distillery
15. The Belle of Nelson Distillery Company
16. The Coon Hollow and Big Spring Distillery
17. The J.M. Atherton Company Distilleries

Five

Bourbon and Water at Heaven Hill Distillery

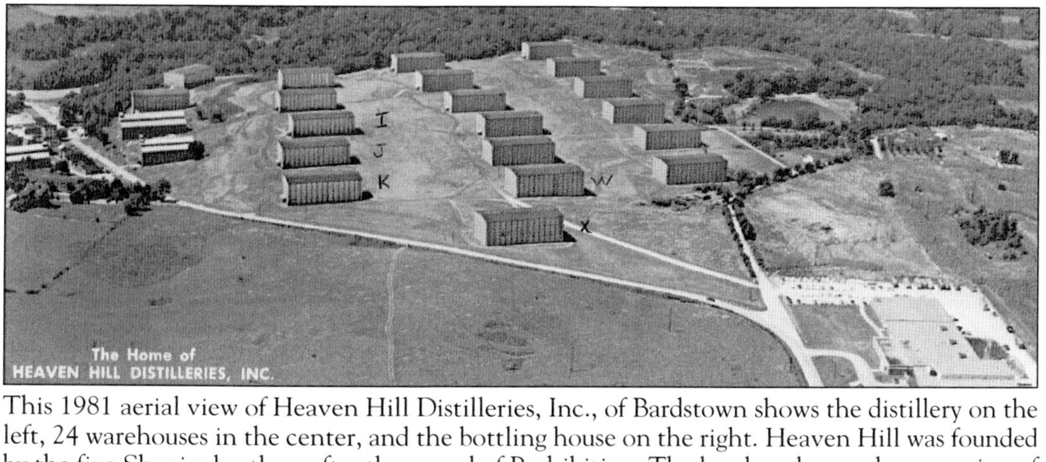

This 1981 aerial view of Heaven Hill Distilleries, Inc., of Bardstown shows the distillery on the left, 24 warehouses in the center, and the bottling house on the right. Heaven Hill was founded by the five Shapira brothers after the repeal of Prohibition. The brothers began the operation of the largest family-owned distillery in the U.S. Because they built their company on Heavenhill plantation and used water from the Heavenhill Spring, it was logical to name the distillery after the family. Elijah Craig, Heaven Hill, and Evan Williams are the best known brands of bourbon whiskey made by Heaven Hill Distillery.

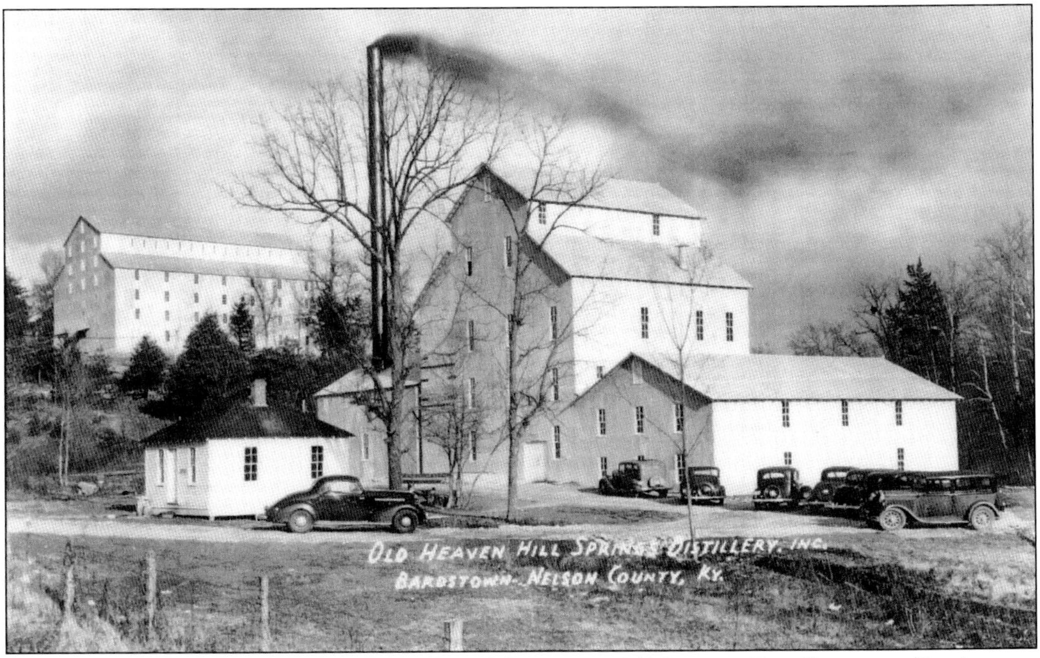

This advertisement reads as follows: "The Old Heaven Hill Springs Distillery near Bardstown, organized in 1935 with Gary Shapira, president; Ed Shapira, General Manager, is operating a complete new plant. Joe Beam, whose grandfather is credited with being Kentucky's first distiller, is the master distiller and helped Joe Brant, the architect, plan the buildings. H.D. Shain, distillery superintendent, was in charge of construction." During World War II, the distillery joined others in producing alcohol for the war effort.

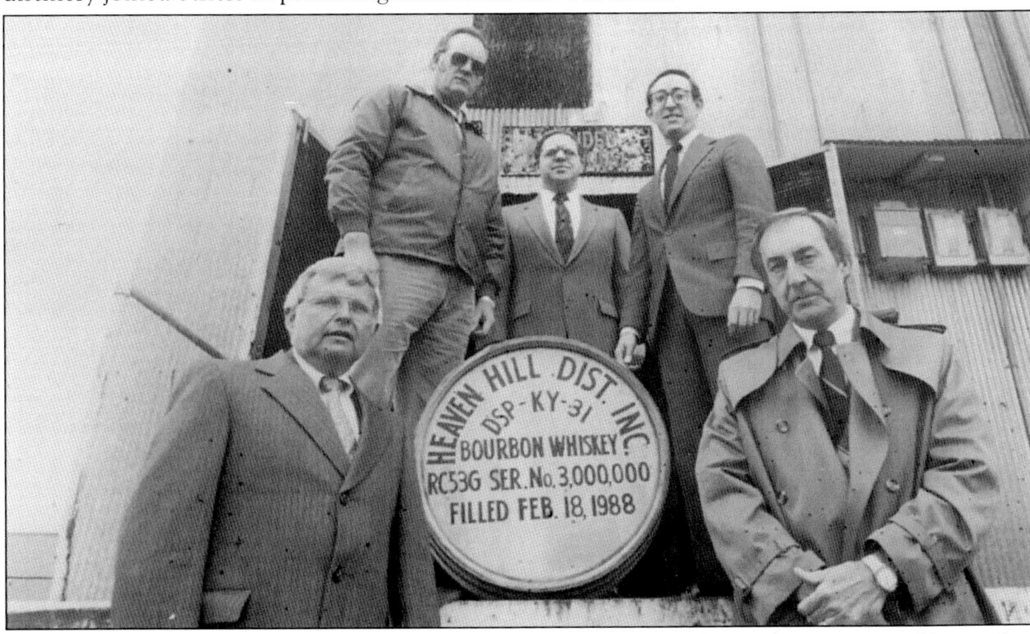

Posing with the 3,000,000th barrel in 1988 are, from left to right, Robert Murray, Kenny Ice, Harry Shapira, Max Shapira, and Parker Beam. These gentlemen are still involved in production at the distillery in 1998, the year the 4,000,000th barrel will be filled.

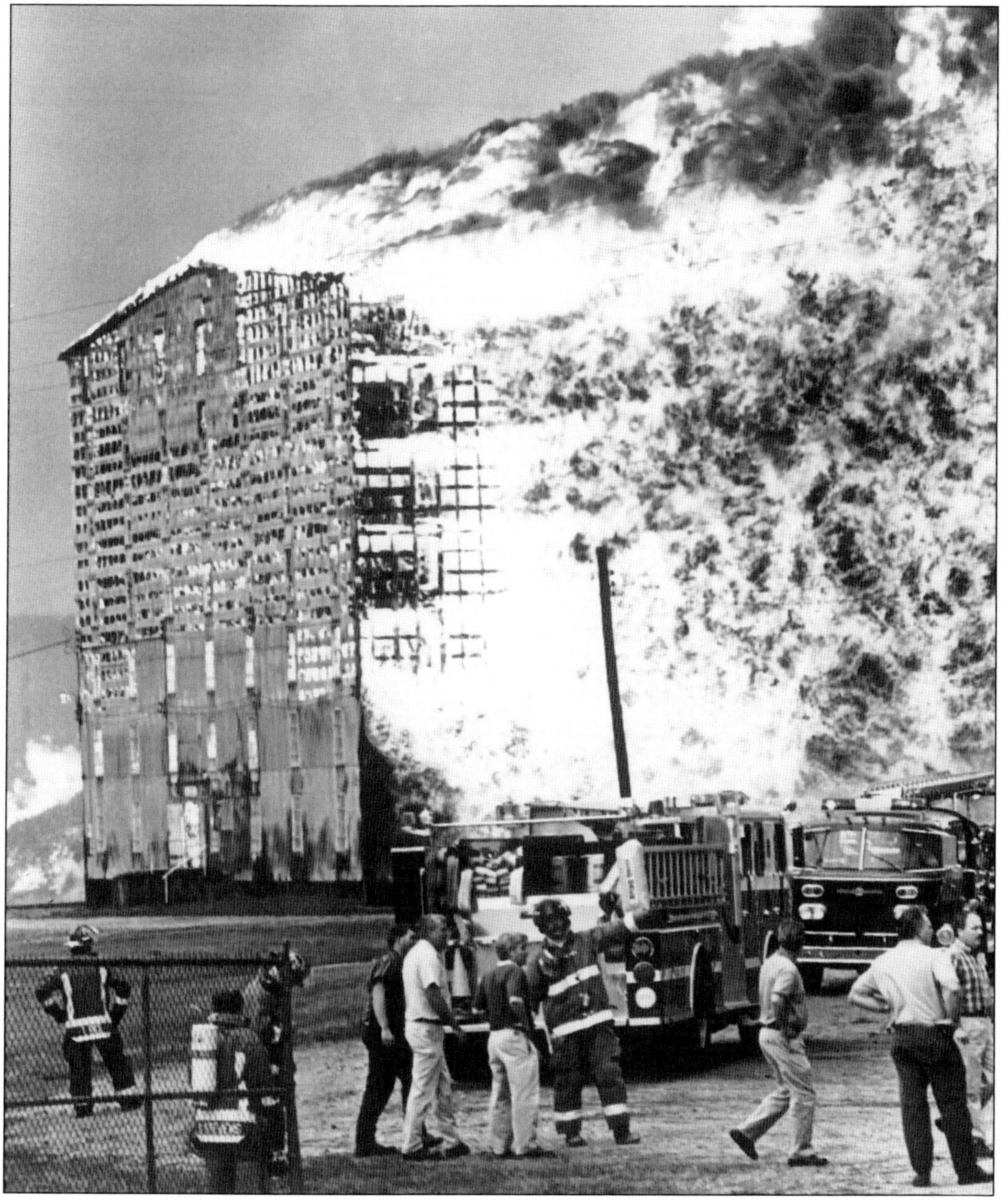

On November 7, 1996, a wind-driven single warehouse fire became a disaster for Heaven Hill Distilleries. At 2:03 p.m. the alarm was sounded and the Bardstown Volunteer Fire Department immediately responded. The first building, Warehouse I (left), is a pile of burning debris—it was engulfed in flames. The heat and flames were blown horizontally to the next building, Warehouse J. Set in rows with more than 250 feet between them, this site had 24 warehouses. The call for assistance went out immediately, and more than 18 companies responded. Whisky warehouses are wooden buildings full of wooden barrels filled with alcohol. If the wood is burning, water can be used to fight the fire, but once the whisky starts to burn, water just spreads the flames. The flames reached a height of 330 feet. The large timbers are outlined by flames in this photo, taken less than an hour after the alarm was sounded.

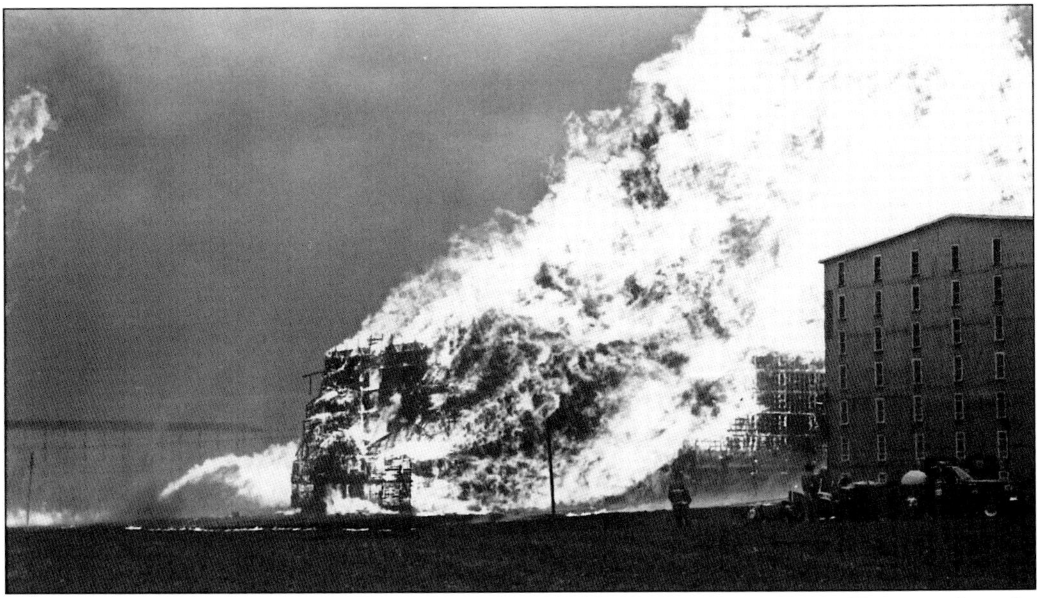

Three buildings are burning. The warehouse on the right is starting to ignite. Two aerial trucks with elevated water ways were ordered to concentrate on two warehouses (W and X), which are in peril. An estimated 1 million gallons of water was directed toward these metal-clad buildings to cool the surface and prevent them from burning. The flames are from the first building. When it collapsed, a surge of burning liquid ran over the hill, toward the distillery.

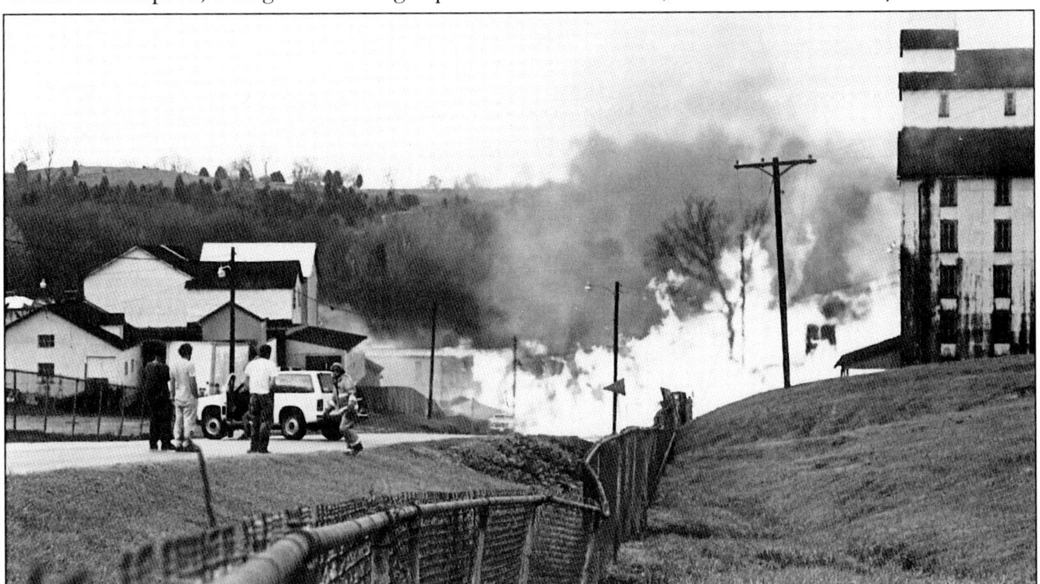

Burning whisky ran downhill toward two other warehouses and the distillery. This view shows the river of flames as it consumed buildings, 34 vehicles, the highway, and the distillery buildings. The buildings on the left also burned. Nineteen million dollars worth of whiskey, seven warehouses, and the distillery were destroyed in less than 8 hours. It was investigated and analyzed by agents from ATF. The cause was filed as "undetermined." The extreme heat consumed all evidence. It was considered to be "the hottest fire to have occurred in the United States."

Six

Talbott Tavern

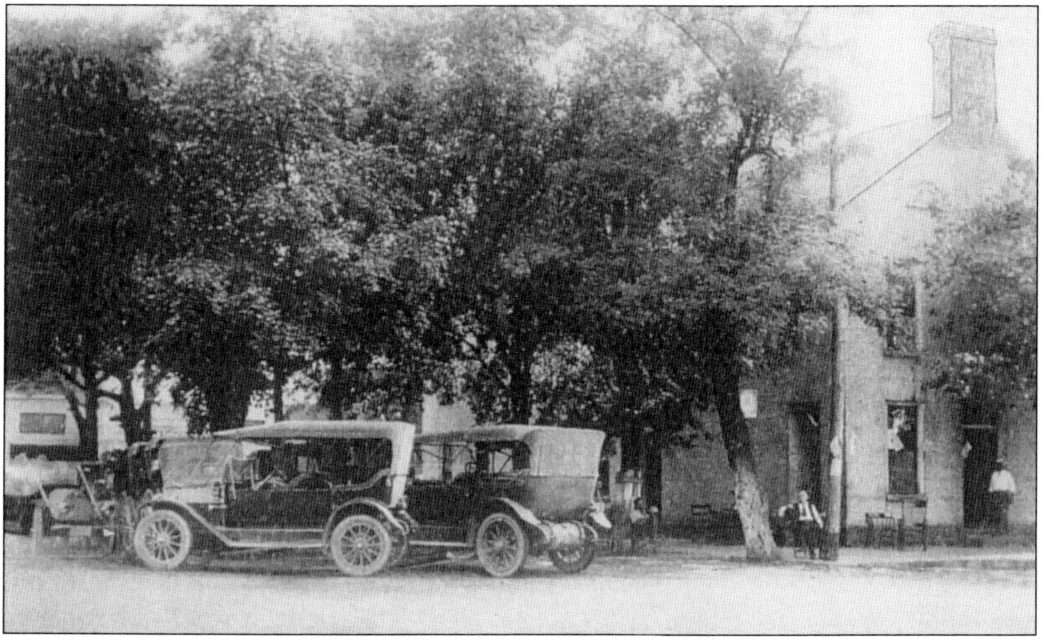

This postcard's caption reads as follows: "The Talbott Hotel, Bardstown, Kentucky. A good hotel where special attention is given to automobilists." This building wasn't called Talbott Hotel until after the death of the owner, George Talbott, in 1912. Merchant W. R. Hynes, the first owner, resided there in 1812. He rented the tavern house and contents to Thomas R. Elder in 1830. An 1831 advertisement for the "Celebrated Comedy, *The Rivals*, to be presented by the Bardstown Thespian Corps in the ballroom at Elder's Hotel" shows the use of the building.

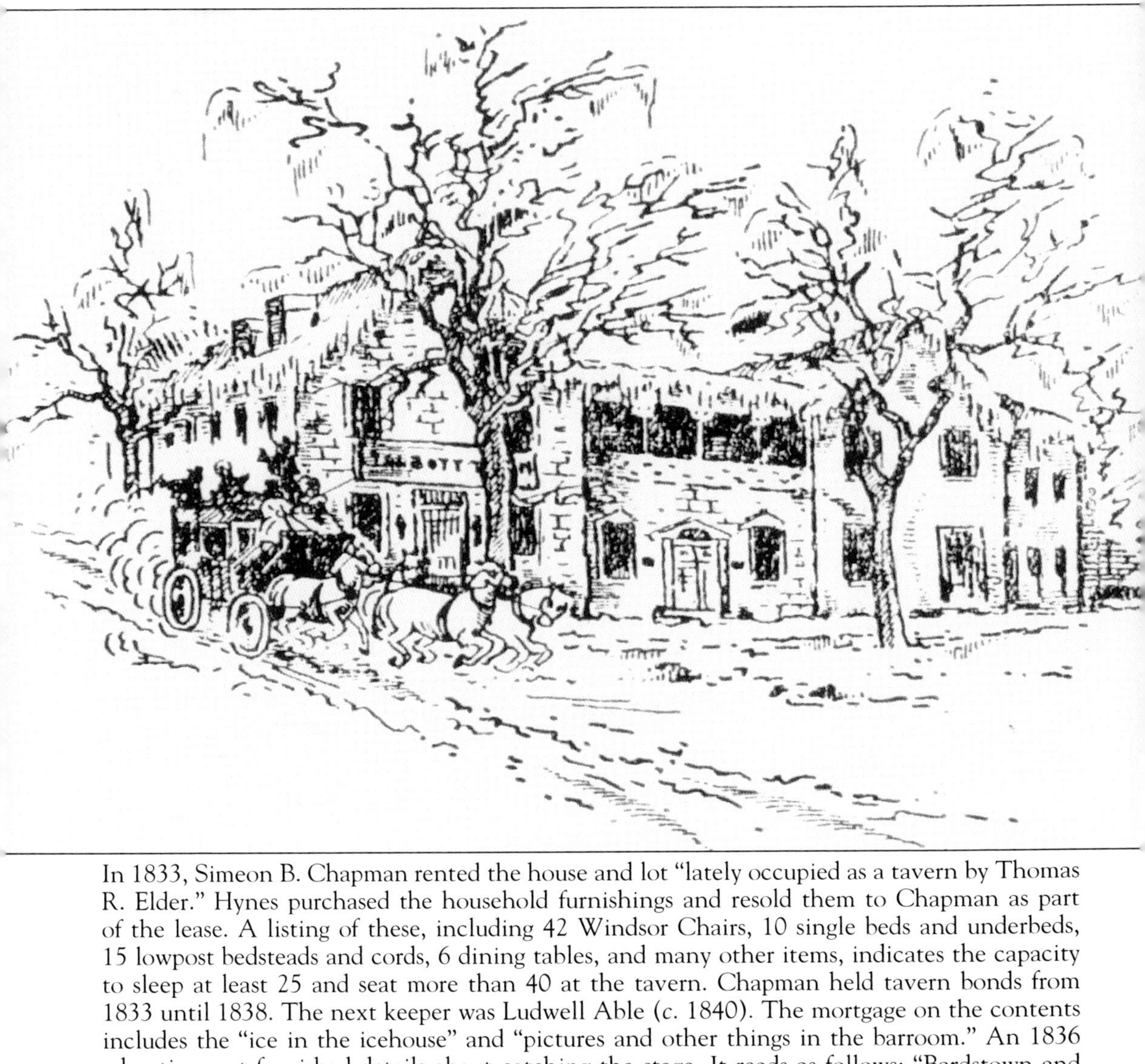

In 1833, Simeon B. Chapman rented the house and lot "lately occupied as a tavern by Thomas R. Elder." Hynes purchased the household furnishings and resold them to Chapman as part of the lease. A listing of these, including 42 Windsor Chairs, 10 single beds and underbeds, 15 lowpost bedsteads and cords, 6 dining tables, and many other items, indicates the capacity to sleep at least 25 and seat more than 40 at the tavern. Chapman held tavern bonds from 1833 until 1838. The next keeper was Ludwell Able (c. 1840). The mortgage on the contents includes the "ice in the icehouse" and "pictures and other things in the barroom." An 1836 advertisement furnished details about catching the stage. It reads as follows: "Bardstown and Louisville Accommodations Stage. George Penny's Stage will leave Bardstown on Mondays, Wednesdays, and Fridays—and Louisville on Tuesdays, Thursdays and Saturdays, continuing throughout the season. He has good drivers, good teams, good stages. The time of leaving will be regulated to suit passengers. The passenger at Bardstown will enter at Chapman's Hotel."

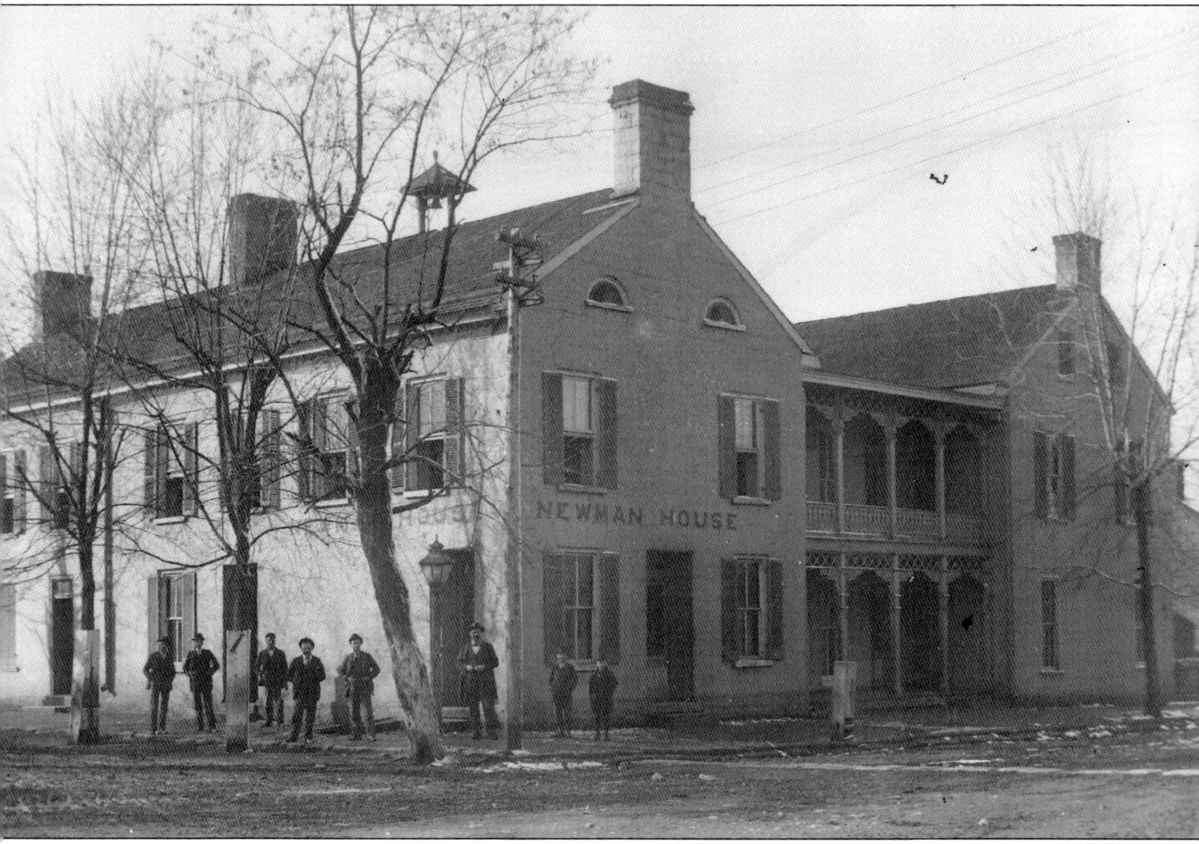

Hynes heirs sold the "Hynes House" to Michael Donohoo in 1845. In 1865, he sold it to Rev. George W. Robertson, who renamed it "Shady Bower." Thomas Newman sold the Newman House to a partnership of Isaac Hughes, Geo. M., and Ben Talbott in 1885. A former owner, Bob Briggs, held the lien on the furniture and contents. By 1893, only George Talbott was still involved in the operation of the Newman House. Mr. Talbott was appointed postmaster in 1896 and hired Jack Daugherty to manage the hotel. At this time, the rates were $2 per day. While the Talbott family resided there, 12 children were born to George and Annie Spaldling Talbott. George was a teetotaler and didn't have a saloon there. His father was killed by an intoxicated saloon patron. After George's death in 1912, the name became Talbott Hotel. Mrs. Talbott operated it until she sold the property to T.D. Beam in 1916. Mr. Beam sold the stable that later became the Service garage. He operated the Talbott Hotel until 1926, when he sold it to C.P. Moore.

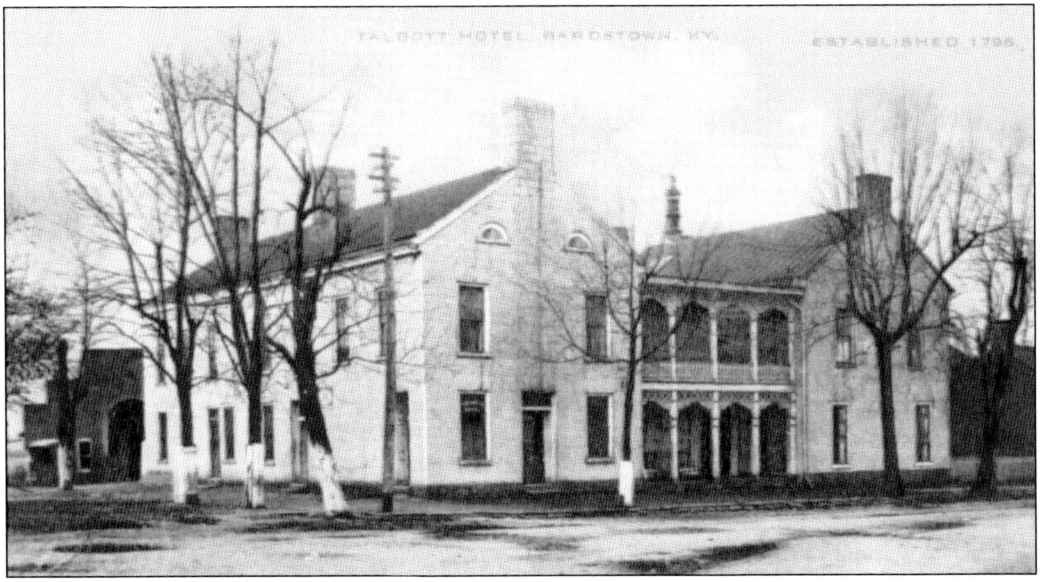

This brick livery stable (back left) was built *c.* 1885 on lot 89. Hughes, Talbott, and Company operated the stable. Hacks, buggies, and horses could be hired, and guests' horses could be stabled while they stayed overnight at the Newman House. According to the memories of Ben Johnson, cock-fighting occurred in the livery stable behind the tavern when Jim Caldwell and Beverly Grigsby Sr. operated it. When it became too cold, they took the cocks into the lobby. Games of draw poker also took place in the stable.

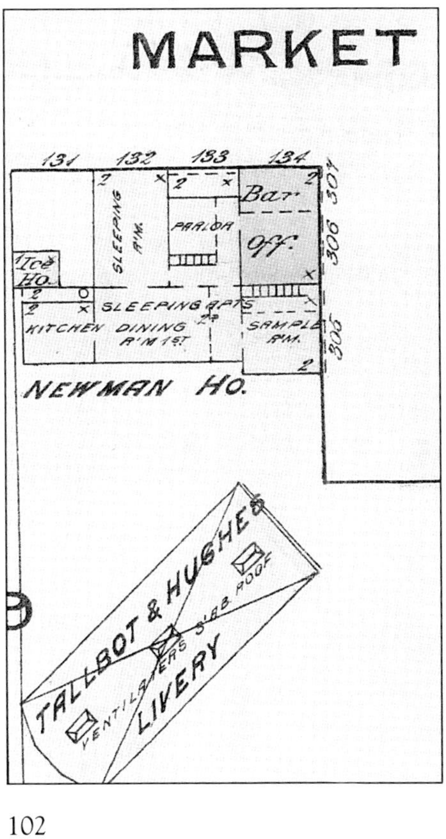

This excerpt from an 1886 map shows how the different sections of the hotel were used. The main entrance was on the east with customers coming into the office-bar section. The second floor housed sleeping rooms.

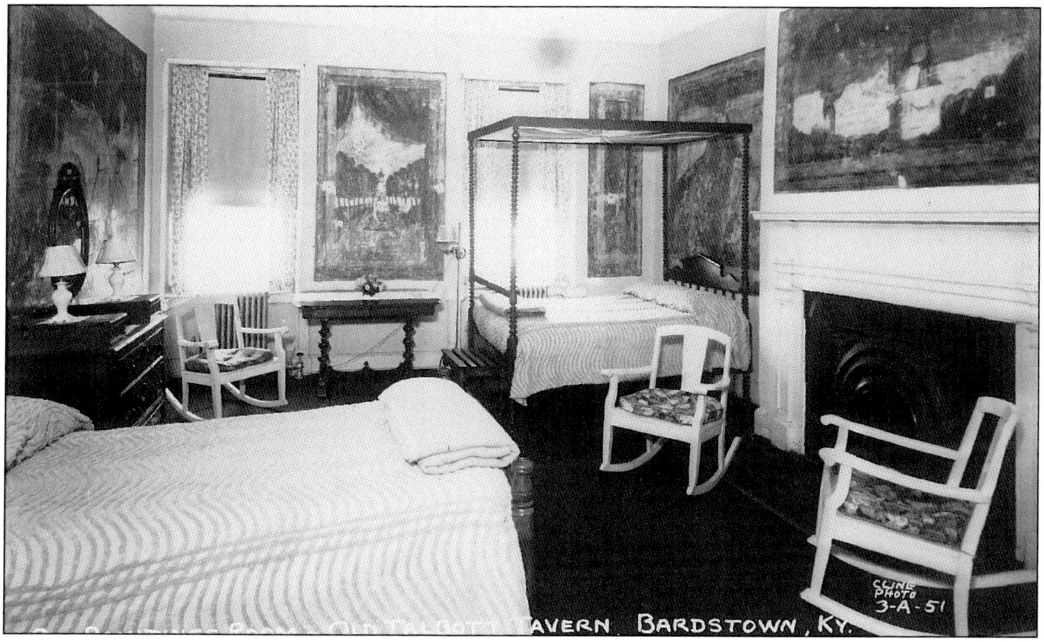

In 1928, paperhangers removing three thicknesses of paper discovered a "weird picture" sketched on the plaster in an upstairs room in the 1815 brick addition. Mrs. Talbott remembered them from 30 years before, when repapering was done. She remembered a penciled date of "1842" and a signature "Jefferson, October 22, 1830." These murals stimulated much conjecture over the years. Mistaken credit is given to the brothers of Louis Phillipe for the art. Phillipe's brother was an artist, but according to his dairy in 1797, the French party stayed at Captain Bean's Tavern (lot 54) on Arch Street.

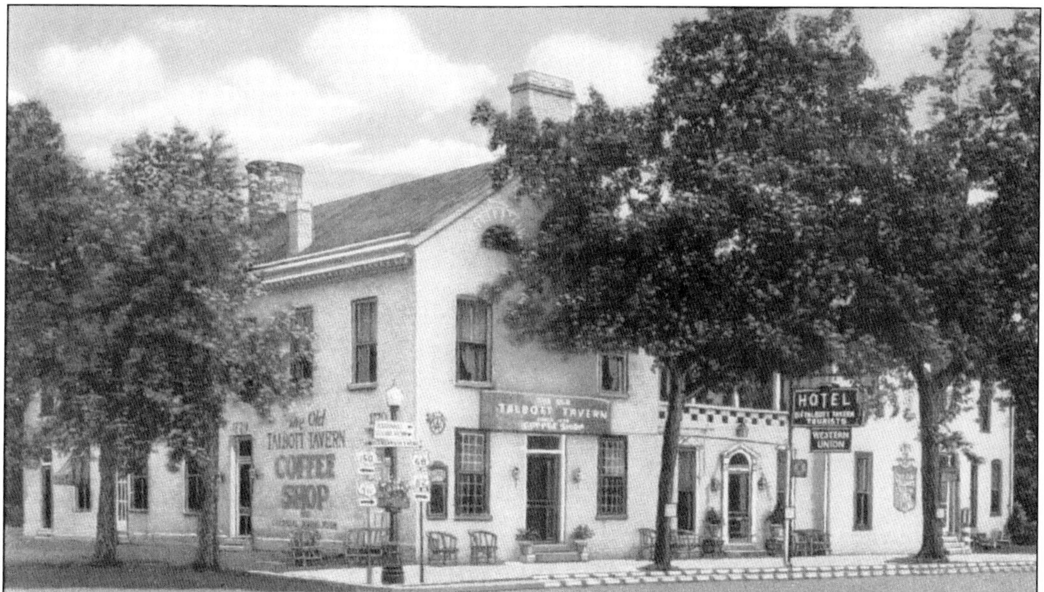

This 1930s view shows the main door to the coffee shop and the lobby entrance in the middle. The chairs on the sidewalk were frequented by those Bardstown elders who liked to discuss the "When, Who, and Why of the past." This was known as the "Dog Walk."

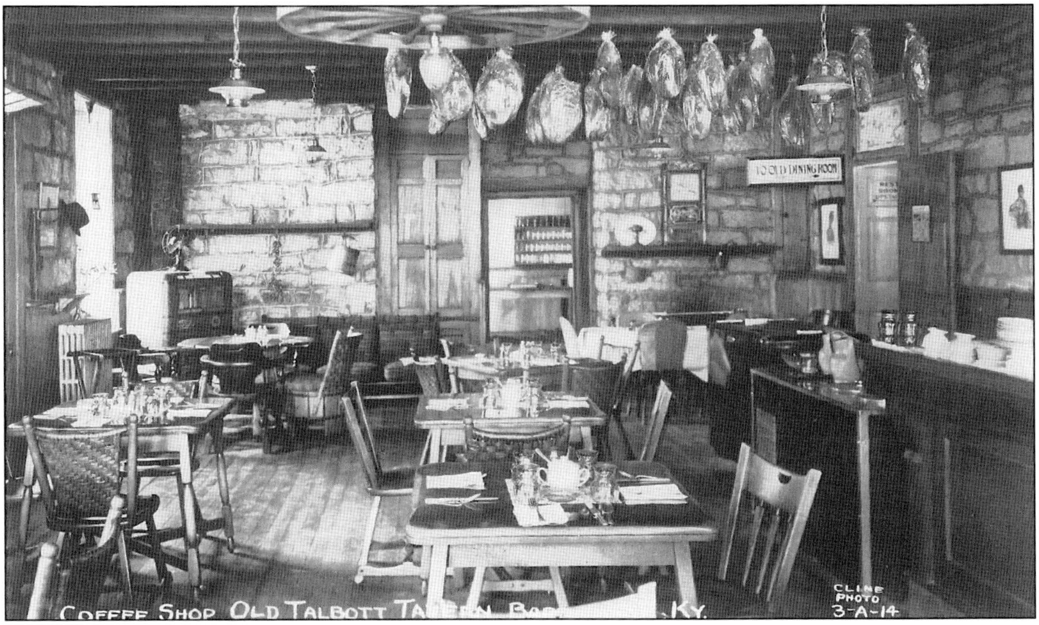

These 1940s postcard views of the coffee shop reveal the stone walls of the original building, which measured 24 feet by 40 feet. The double fireplaces at one end were separated into two rooms. One had an outside entrance off the square (left) and the other had an entrance at the end (which is now the kitchen). Hams hang from the rafters in this view. The business advertised that they cured their own hams and their red-eye gravy was sought by all. The bar on the right was used for food service from 1885. The front section of the room shows military visitors from Fort Knox.

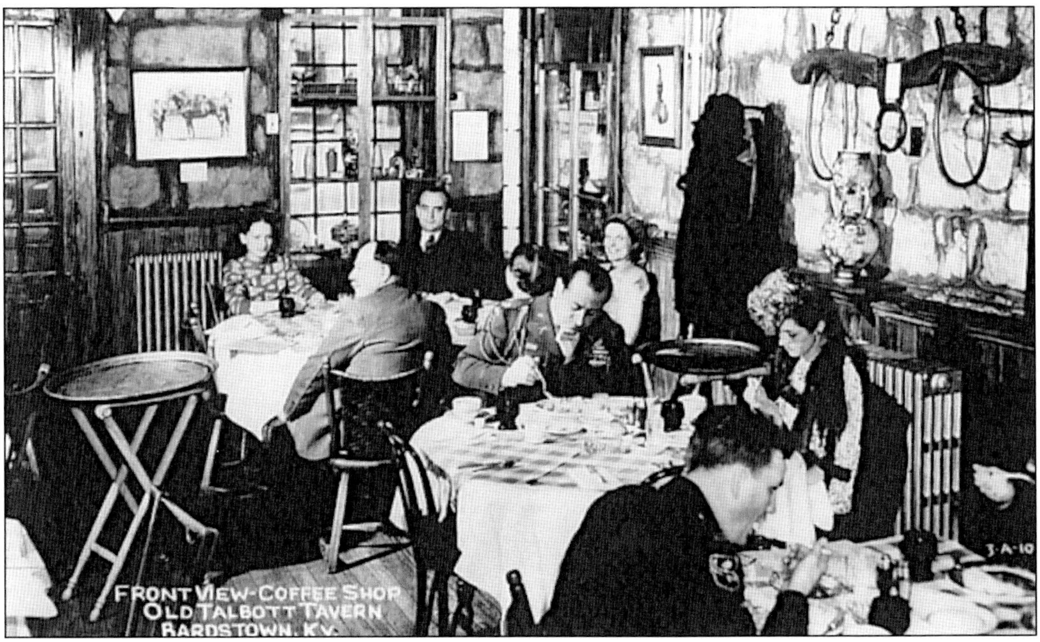

"Bussie" is the dog greeter at the front door of Talbott Tavern in this 1940s postcard. This finely carved doorway was moved from the 1820s brick addition to the old stone section. The stone wall was brought out flush with the two wings under the porch sometime after 1920. Hardy Kieffer, hotel manager, had a stone mason carve the date 1779 in the front step of the building in the 1930s. Earlier claims gave the date as c. 1797.

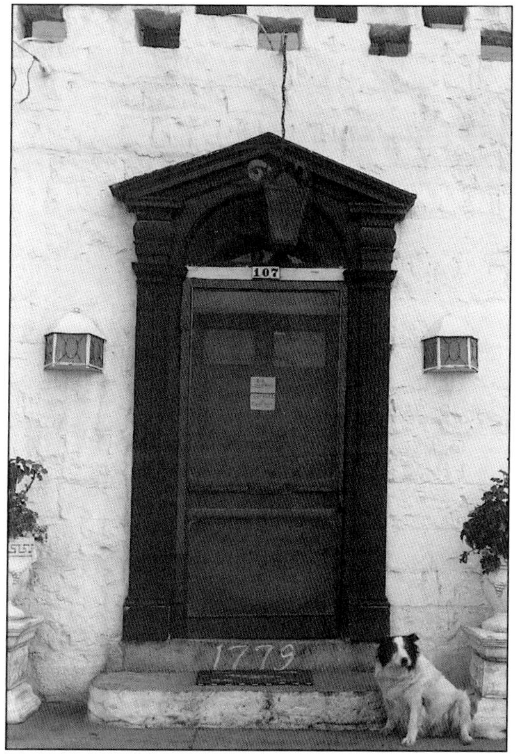

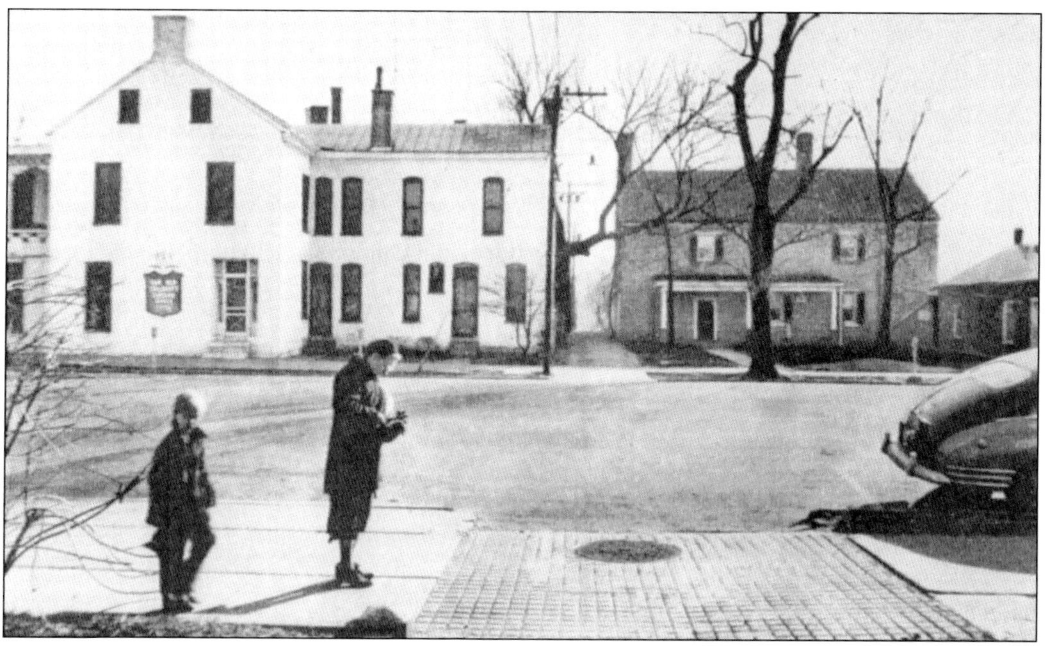

In this 1954 view, the west wing of Talbott Tavern is shown. Built after 1910, it had apartment-style rooms that were used by long-term guests. The lower floor had two separate doors for offices or shops. This wing was torn away to provide a site for the Old Talbott Drug Store in 1964. The stone building (right) is the county jail. It was built in 1819 and used until 1987.

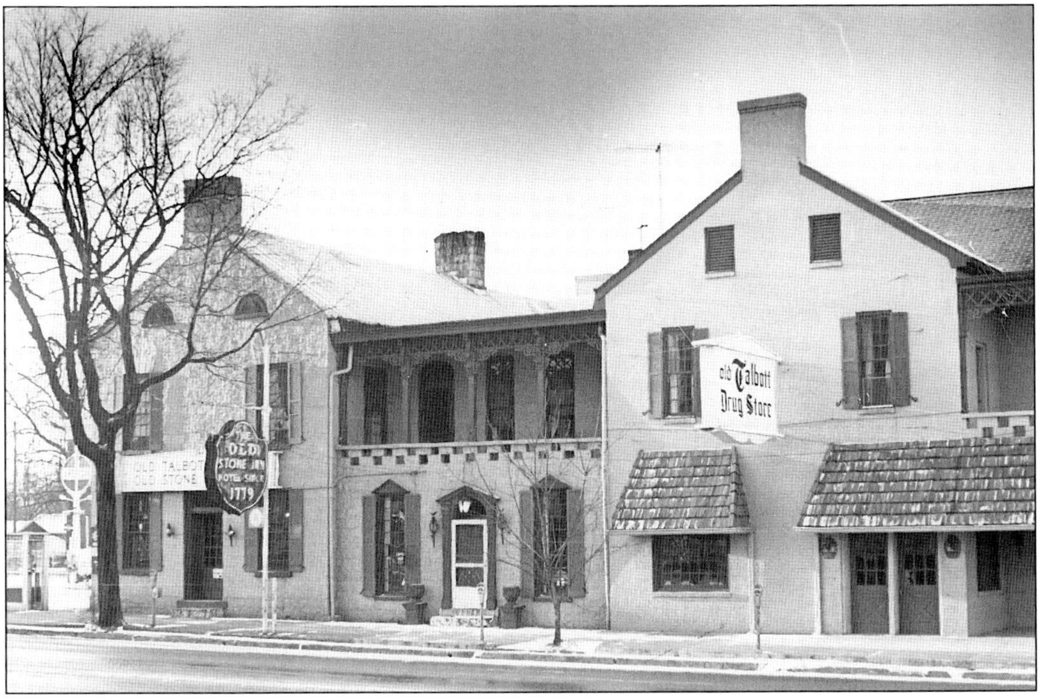

This is how the building looked after new owner, J.E. Willmes, completed the drugstore addition. He installed a new kitchen, new chandeliers, and had a mural painted behind the bar to replace a mirror. Notice the name "Old Stone Inn."

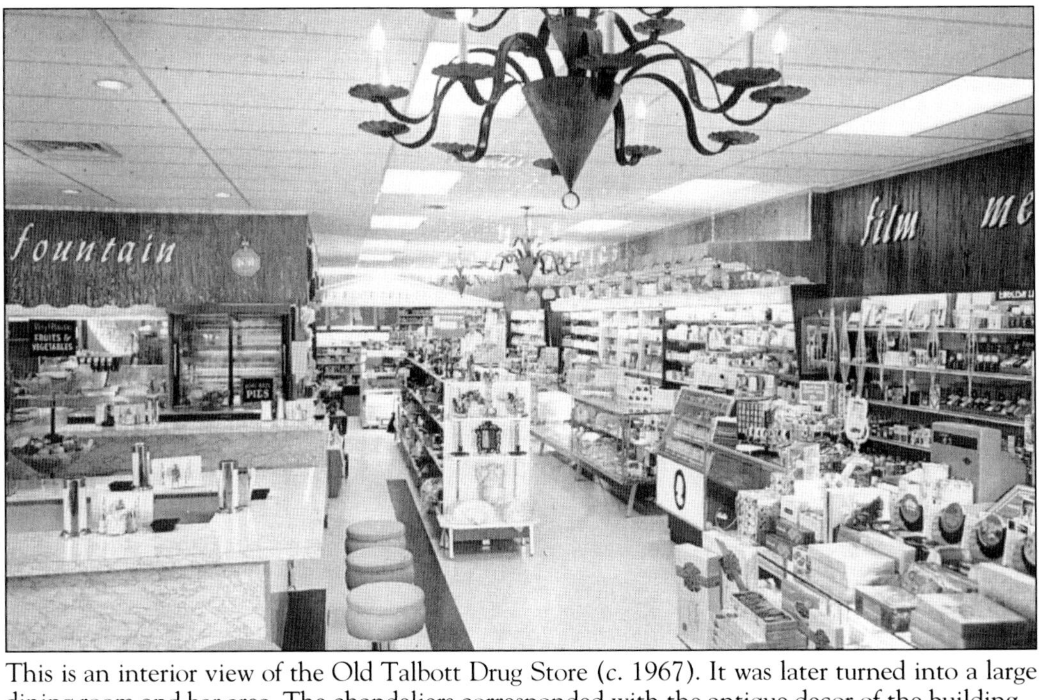

This is an interior view of the Old Talbott Drug Store (c. 1967). It was later turned into a large dining room and bar area. The chandeliers corresponded with the antique decor of the building.

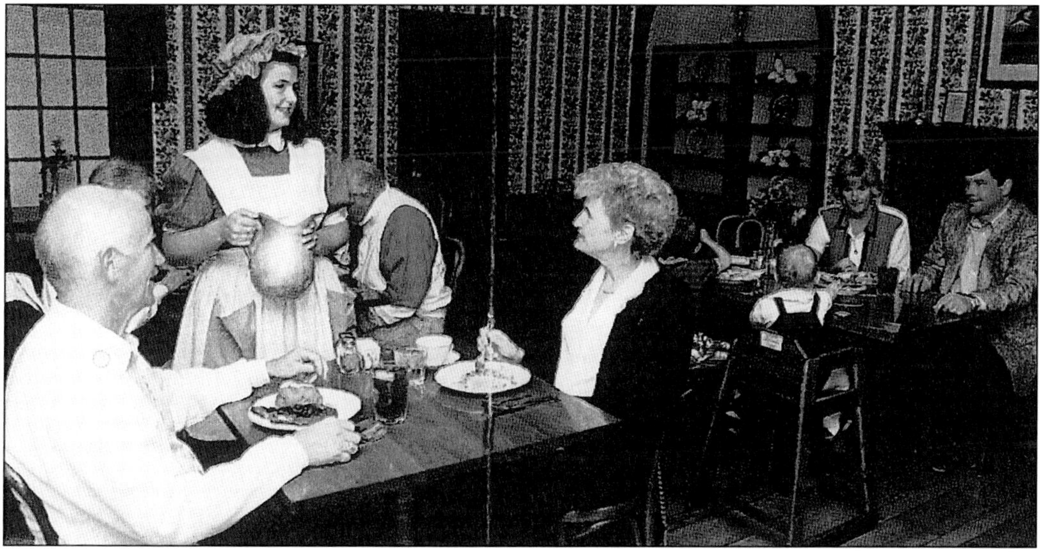

This is a 1990s view of the colonial dining room, located in the 1820 brick wing. The 1886 map indicates that this room was used for dining at the time. The kitchen was located directly west but today it is in the room shown on the map as the sample room. Recessed cupboards flank the fireplace.

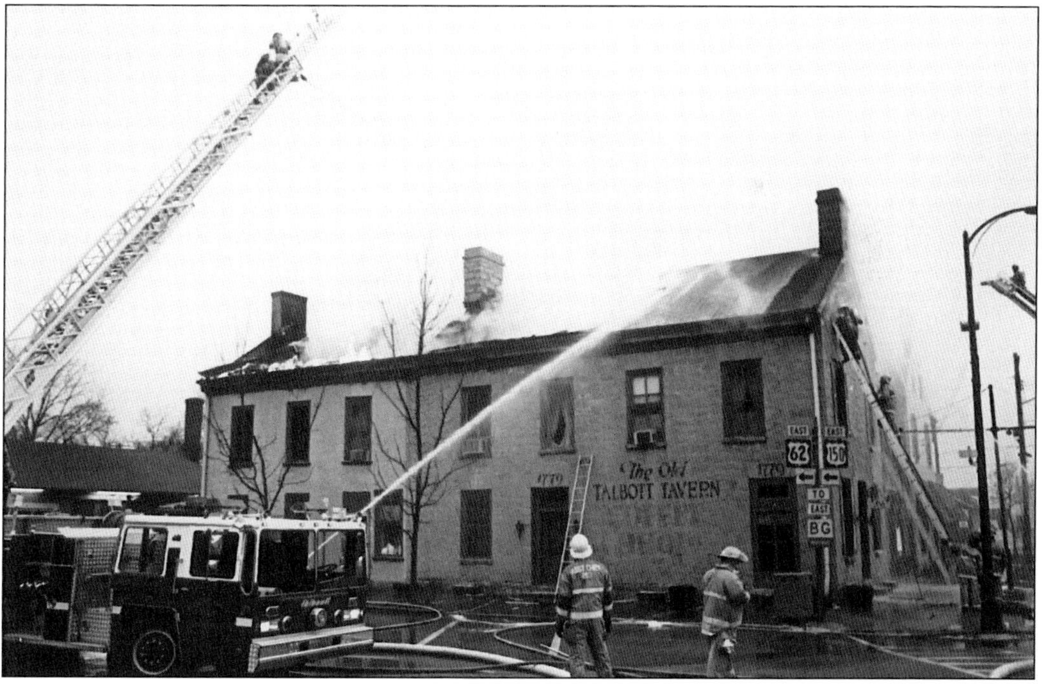

On March 7, 1998, an electrical fire began under the interior stairway and completely destroyed the roof and ceilings of the second floor. Firefighters were able to save the stone and brick walls but there was considerable water damage. This photo, taken about two hours after the alarm, shows the water streams directed to the roof of the oldest stone section. It was completely burned. Various additions over the years with different roof tie-ins complicated fighting the fire. Bardstown volunteer firefighters stayed at the site until the smoldering debris was controlled.

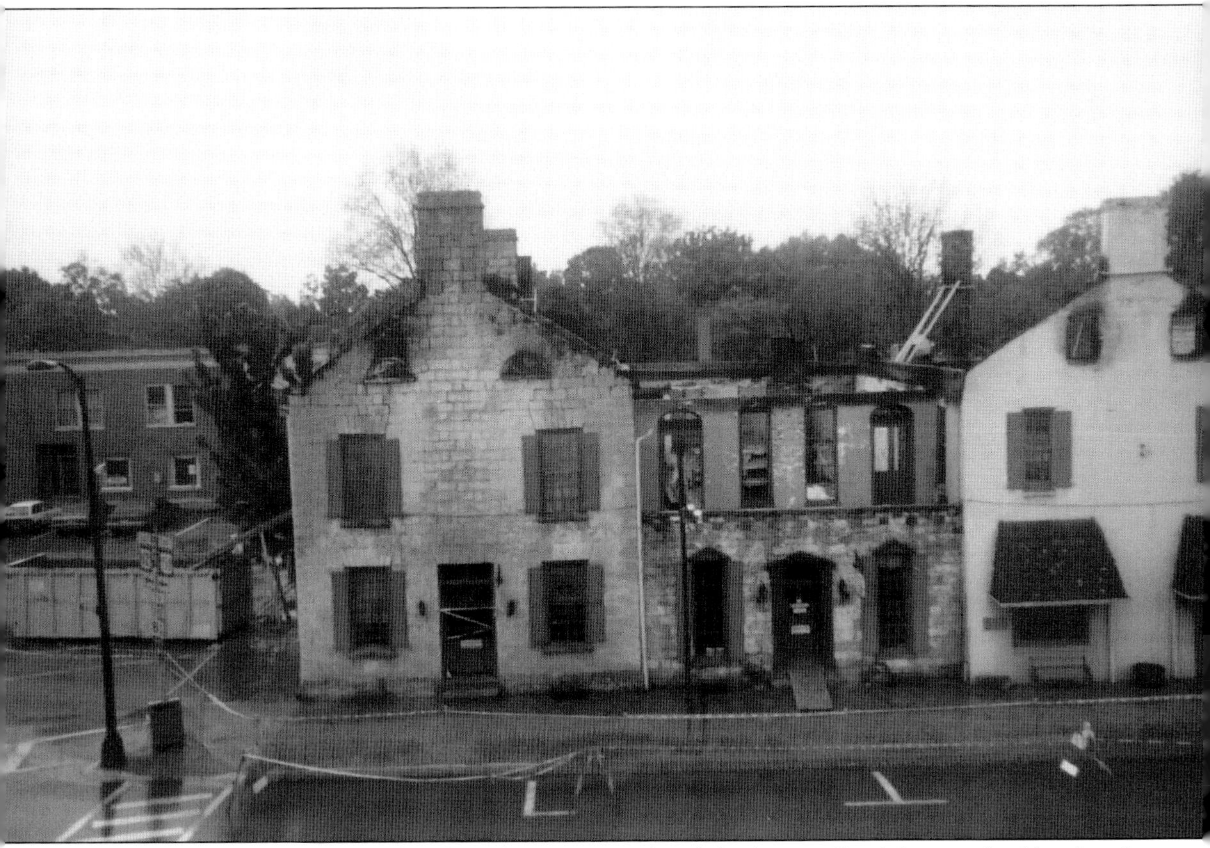

The charred timbers and debris have been removed and the bare walls of the scorched landmark are exposed. Many emotional memories were shared among the mourners of this landmark's tragedy. A visit to Talbott Tavern was a step back into Bardstown's past. At its location on the court square for 200 years, its walls have witnessed the passing of the soldiers of 10 wars. As the site of wedding receptions, anniversary dinners, and birthday parties, it houses memories for all ages. The building is presently being reroofed and repaired.

Seven

1917 Louisville Train Wreck

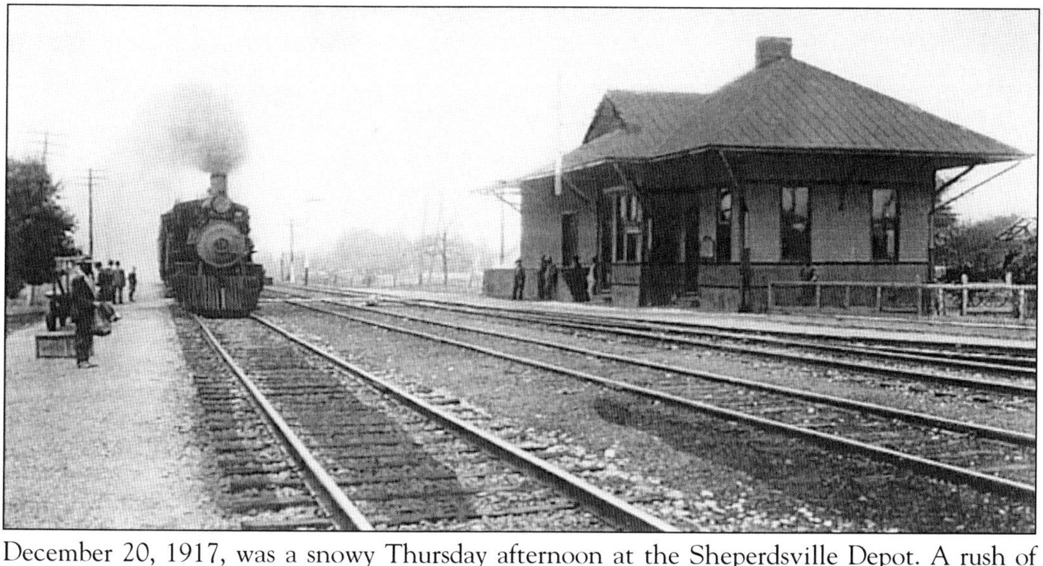

December 20, 1917, was a snowy Thursday afternoon at the Sheperdsville Depot. A rush of warmly clad shoppers, gentlemen, ladies, children, servants of all ages, many of them family groups, hurry to board the train for Bardstown and other points east. Mrs. Joseph Hurst had taken her infant son Raoul into Louisville to consult a specialist about his health. She was accompanied by her nurse, Annie Reed. Ben Talbott, a deputy U.S. Internal Revenue collector, was attending tax school with Mr. James Thompson, also of the IRS. They hurried to catch the Bardstown accommodation. As the time drew near to departure, Mr. and Mrs. John Phillips and their daughter Ella left another daughter, Mae Phillips, at the hospital. Redford Cherry, county attorney, and his wife and son met at the station. Little Redford Jr. had been excited about his trip to see Santa Claus. Many of these passengers were carrying the Christmas gifts they had made the trip to Louisville that morning to obtain.

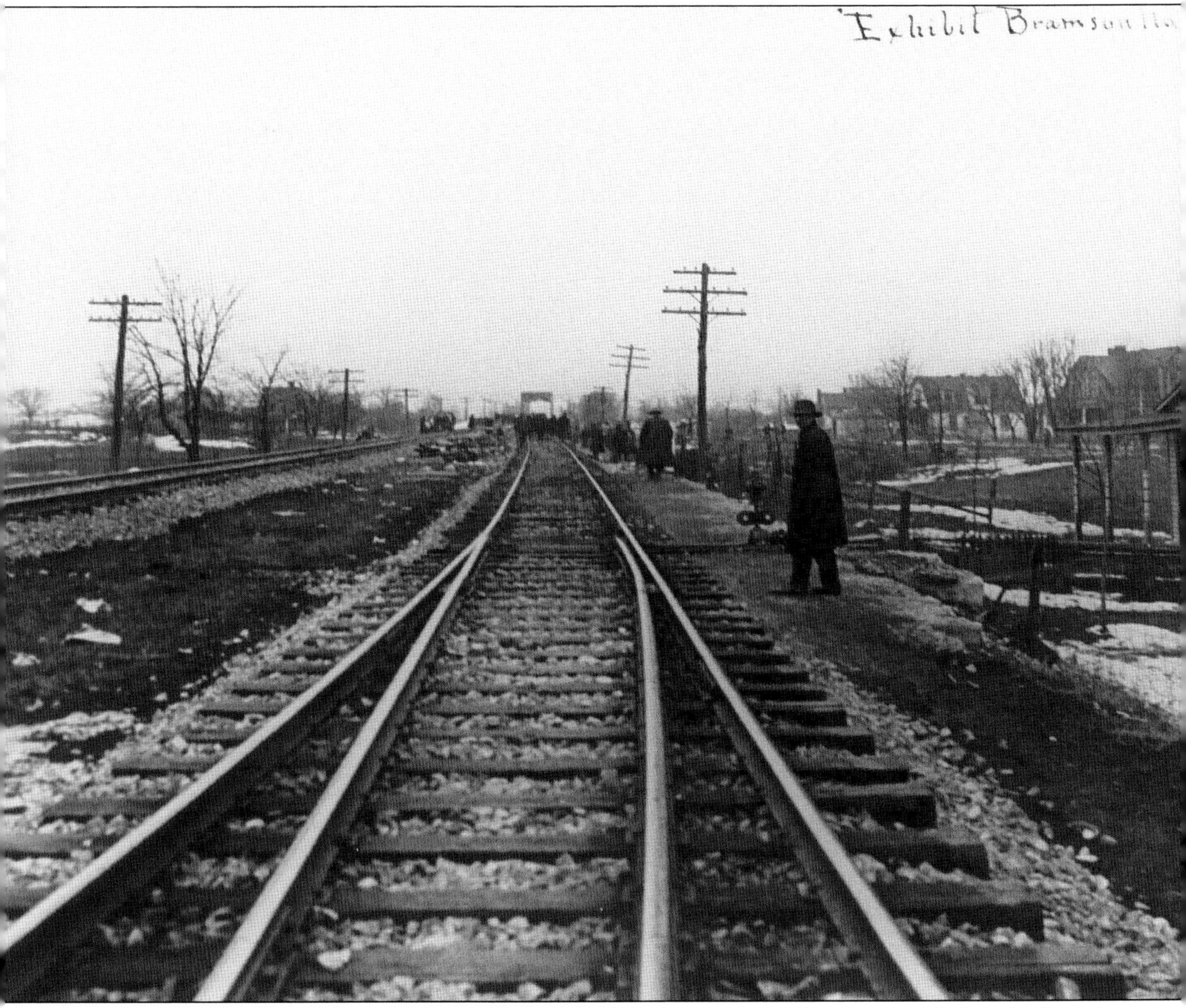

The train, loaded with more than 100 people, left the station a few minutes behind schedule. Due at Shepherdsville at 5:19 p.m., it arrived about six minutes late. The telegraph operator, aware that the Cincinnati and New Orleans Flyer Number 7 was running three hours late and due to arrive, asked the dispatcher what arrangements to make. The answer was to arrange a passing at this station. He gave orders to the Accommodation to take the siding. The four cars and engine pulled up about 200 feet past the siding, prepared to back off the main track. The signal was set against the fast train, but the roar of the approaching train was clearly heard. The telegraph operator grabbed a red lantern and ran out to signal frantically. The 20 passengers who had just left the cars watched in horror as they realized that they were to witness the terrible fate of their traveling companions. The faster train made up of the heavy engine, several baggage cars, and passenger coaches, all of steel construction, plowed into the wooden passenger cars of the Accommodation. The two rear passenger cars were splintered into fragments and shattered bodies. The impact threw people out into the snowdrifts, the cars were pushed over the sides of the tracks, and 150 feet after the impact, the mass of wreckage was halted.

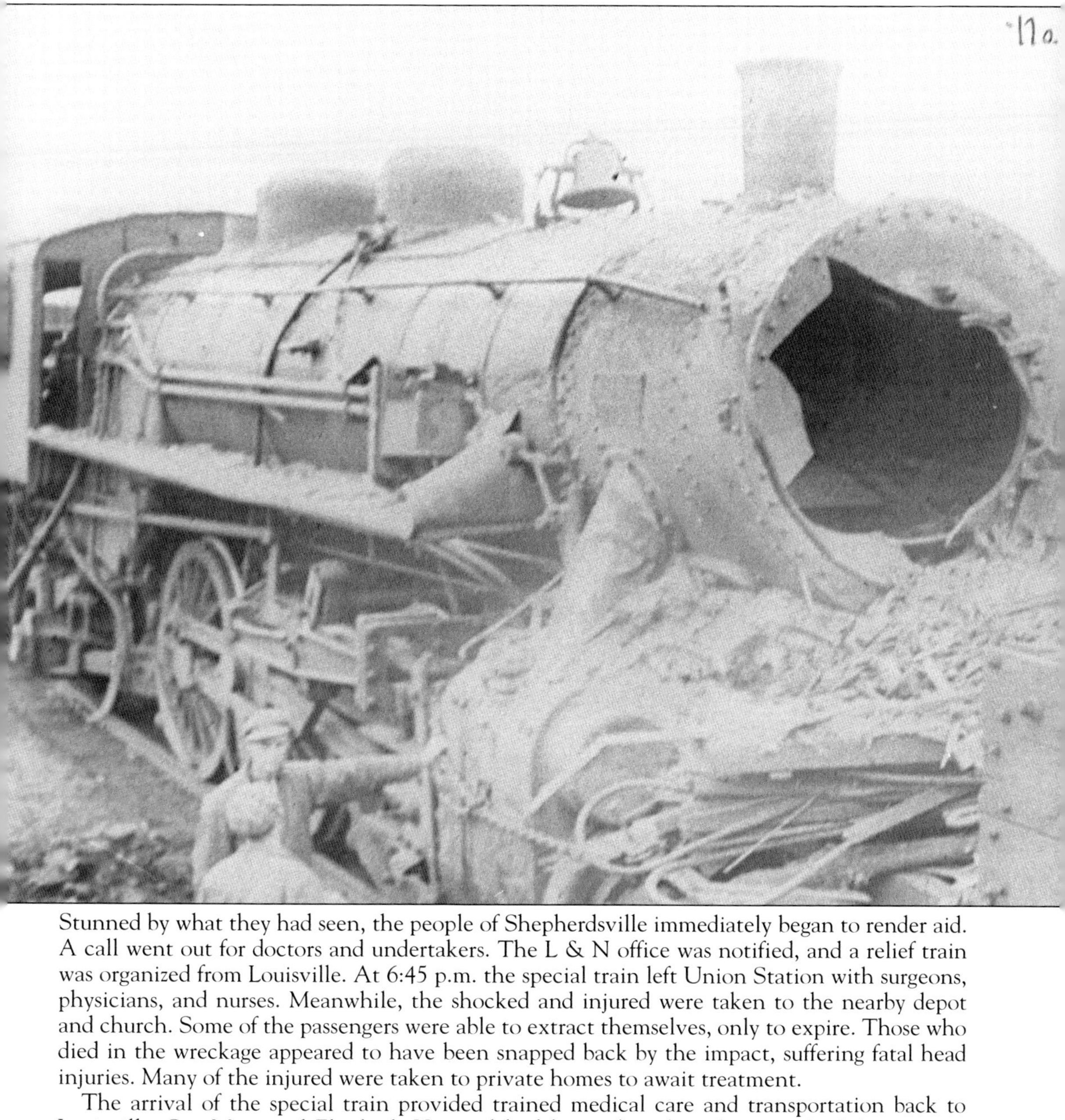

Stunned by what they had seen, the people of Shepherdsville immediately began to render aid. A call went out for doctors and undertakers. The L & N office was notified, and a relief train was organized from Louisville. At 6:45 p.m. the special train left Union Station with surgeons, physicians, and nurses. Meanwhile, the shocked and injured were taken to the nearby depot and church. Some of the passengers were able to extract themselves, only to expire. Those who died in the wreckage appeared to have been snapped back by the impact, suffering fatal head injuries. Many of the injured were taken to private homes to await treatment.

The arrival of the special train provided trained medical care and transportation back to Louisville. Sts. Mary and Elizabeth Hospital had been alerted to the arrival of the victims. The Louisville Police Department arranged policemen and vehicles to help transport patients from the depot to the hospital. The Army Ambulance Corps from Camp Taylor sent 100 men, doctors and interns, and 30 ambulances to the station to assist.

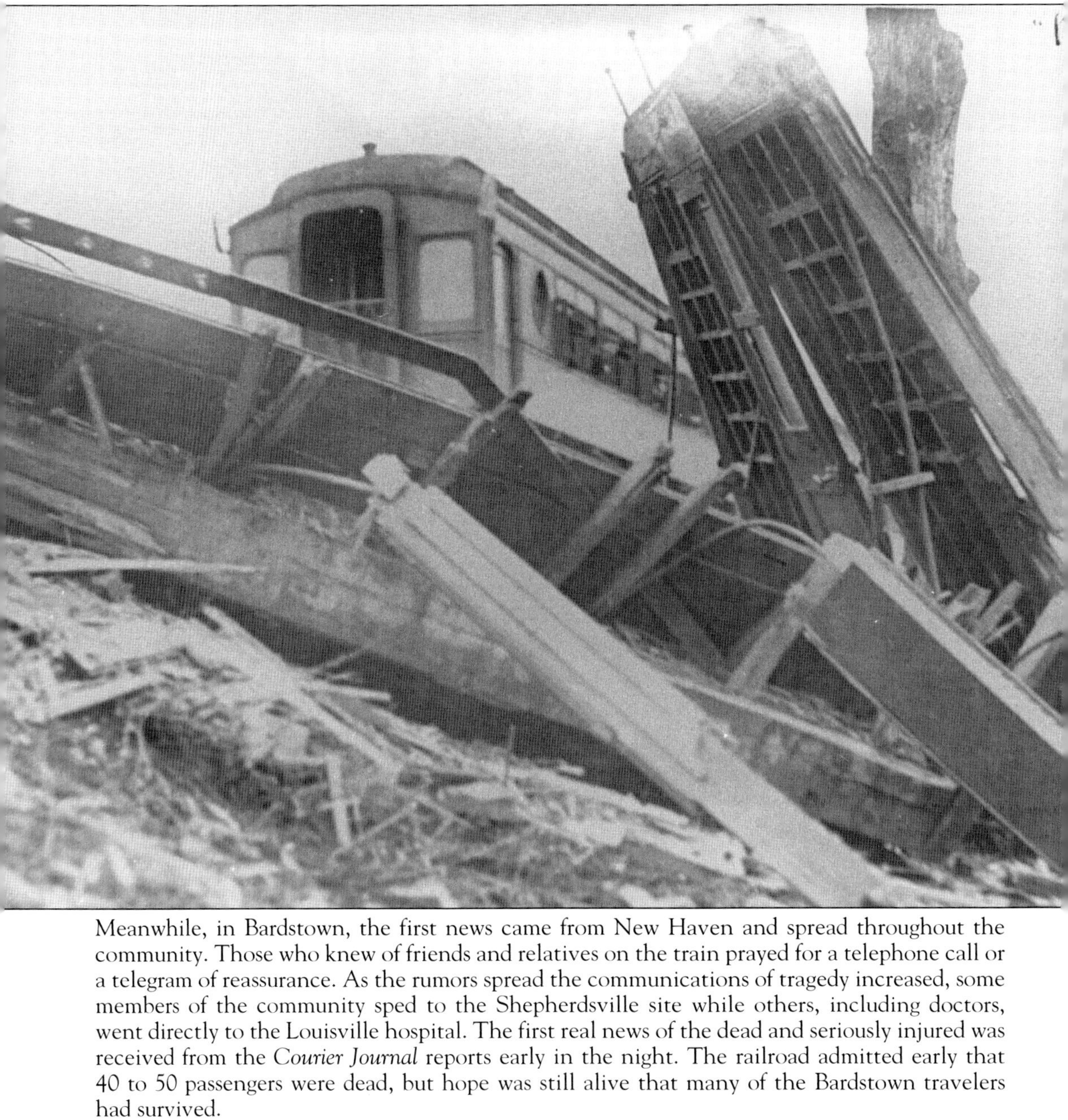

Meanwhile, in Bardstown, the first news came from New Haven and spread throughout the community. Those who knew of friends and relatives on the train prayed for a telephone call or a telegram of reassurance. As the rumors spread the communications of tragedy increased, some members of the community sped to the Shepherdsville site while others, including doctors, went directly to the Louisville hospital. The first real news of the dead and seriously injured was received from the *Courier Journal* reports early in the night. The railroad admitted early that 40 to 50 passengers were dead, but hope was still alive that many of the Bardstown travelers had survived.

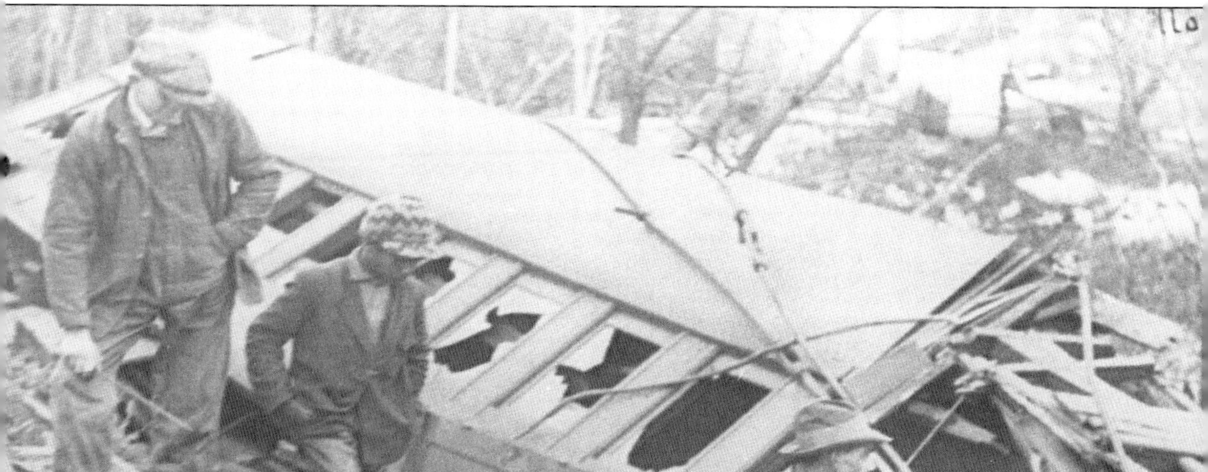

The Sisters of Charity at Sts. Mary and Elizabeth Hospital were praying at the altar of the hospital as they awaited the relief train. When they heard the whistle announcing its immediate arrival, they arose to render what comfort they could to the injured and sorrowing. Joseph Muir obtained the news of his brother's death in the wreck at the hospital. His sister-in-law died as she was brought into the building. His nephew also died in the accident. The relatives of Mrs. Tom Moore, accompanied by Dr. Grigsby, were met with the sad tidings of her death. On and on the sorrows multiplied. As the first papers were distributed, the impact of this, the worst wreck in the history of the L & N Railroad, became known through out the country. Forty-seven people were killed at the time, and many others were seriously injured. Ten more died from their injuries. Telegrams from California, Florida, Texas, and many other states began to arrive at the office in Bardstown.

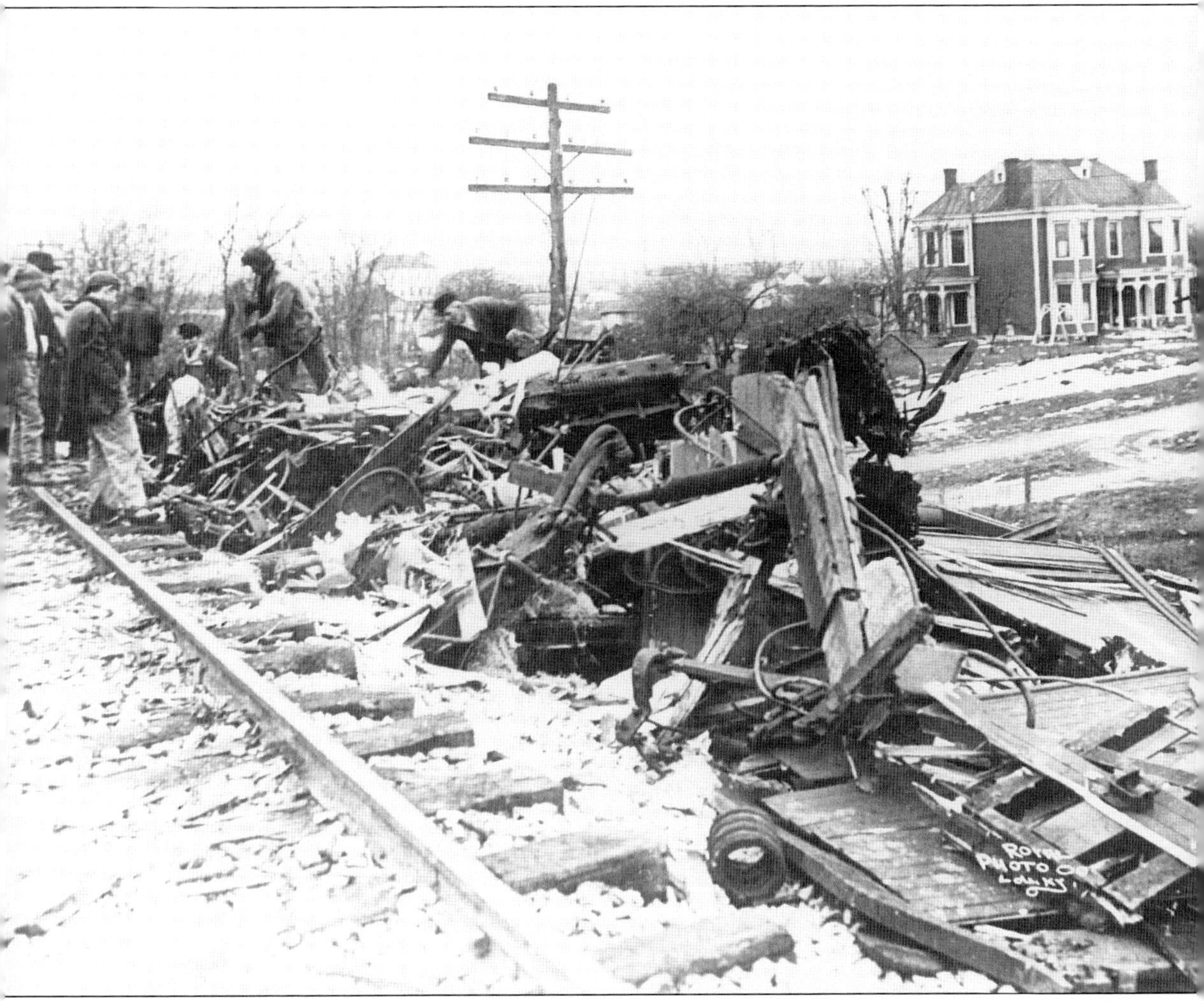

On December 21, 1917, a special train left the Tenth Street Station at 3 p.m. Carrying the bodies of 23 victims of the railroad wreck, it finished the journey these poor souls began 24 hours before. Eighteen bodies were taken to Bardstown, where they were received by a town in mourning. Undertaker George Mann would buried them—nine in one day. People had been waiting an hour or more for the bodies that were carried in a baggage car. The coffins were strewn with flowers. As the coffins were carried up the street, mourners could be seen walking alongside saying the rosary. Three of the bodies were taken to Springfield, and two were delivered to Samuel's Station. Twelve other bodies remained at Shepherdsville until they were sent home to Bullitt and Jefferson County.

The city of Bardstown was still numb with grief. Almost all businesses were closed. The city council and mayor issued an unnecessary appeal to forego the usual festivities of the Christmas season. Bells toll and flags droop at half-mast. Bardstown continues to mourn this tragic loss.

A total of 57 people were killed in the Shepherdsville train wreck. It is considered by many to be the most traumatic event in Bardstown and Nelson County's history.

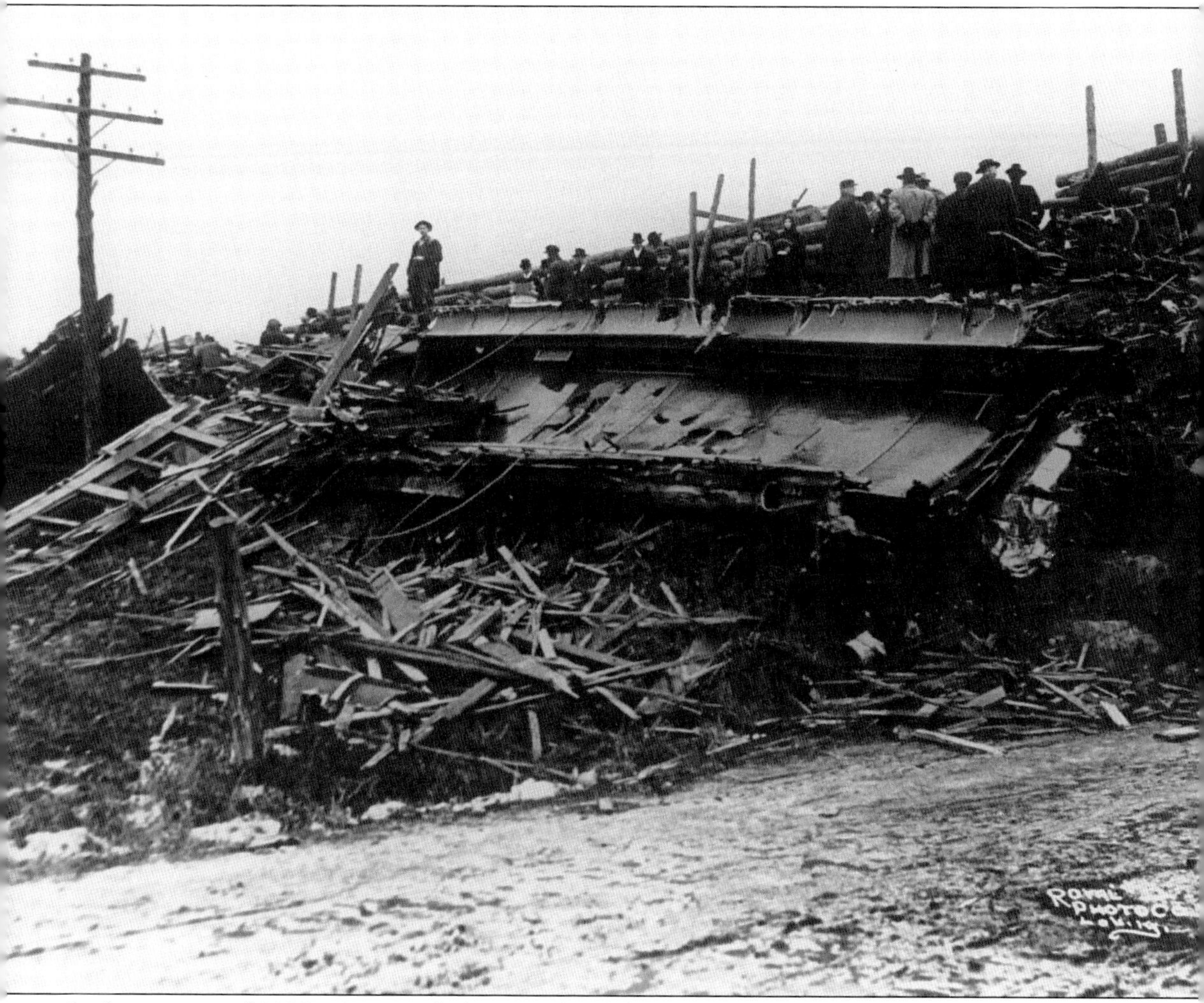

In the summer of 1992, 12 original photographs of this train wreck were discovered in evidence folders in the 1918 Nelson Circuit Court records. They were used in the lawsuits instigated by the injured and heirs of the deceased. Of the multitude of law suits that grew out of the wreck, only one went to trial, and the L & N Railroad settled with the injured and the heirs of the deceased. The fault was determined to be divided between the engineer of the fast train and the flagman and conductor of the wrecked train.

Two Louisville photographers, J.L. Bramson and A.S. Piers, took these photographs, some of which were published in the newspapers at the time. These views are of the wreckage-strewn track and splintered remains of the wooden passenger cars. They illustrate, better than the written accounts, the force of the crash and the miracle of those who survived. This wreck brought public pressure on the railroads to use metal for their passenger cars.

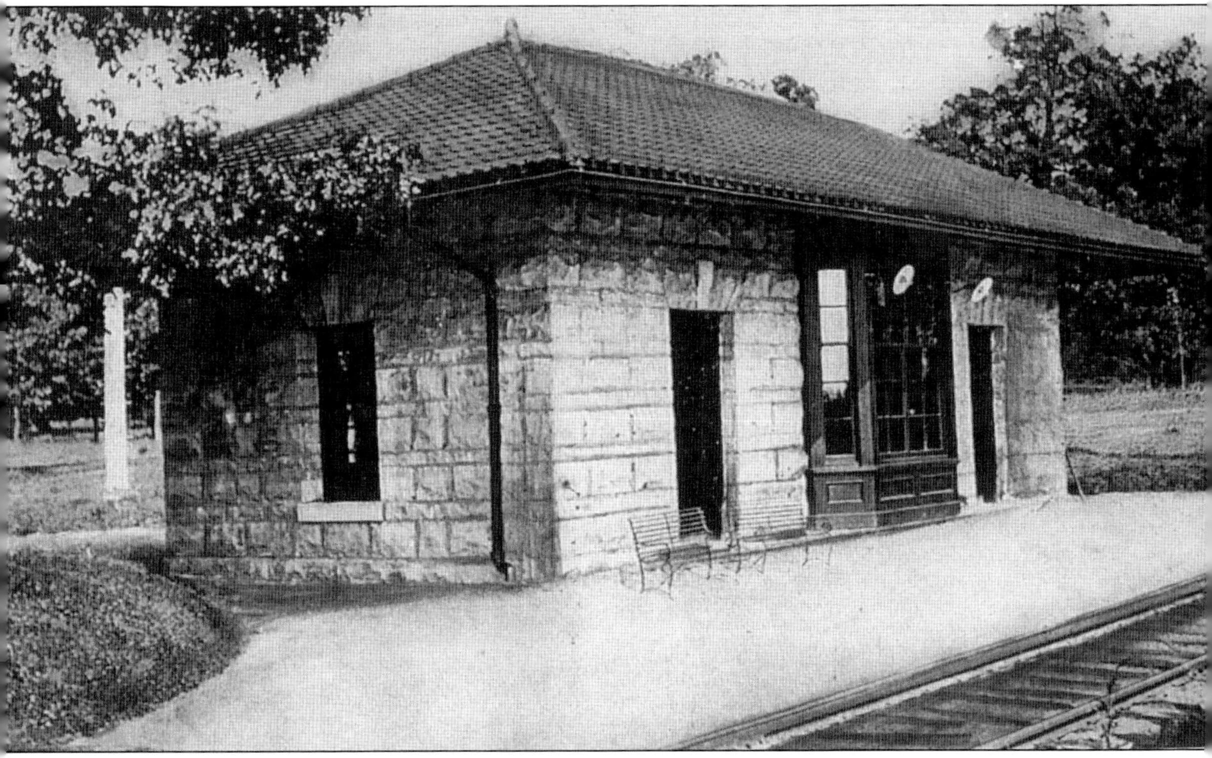

The extension of railway service to Bardstown in 1857 was supported by Nazareth with a "subscription to the stock of the Bardstown and Louisville Railroad Company not to exceed $15,000." The B&L Railroad Company was purchased by the Louisville and Nashville Railroad before its completion to Bardstown in 1860. Daily passenger train service allowed the Sisters of Charity and the students at Nazareth College to travel from Louisville and to ride into Bardstown 2 miles away. The passenger train service stopped in 1953. The original invoices of the construction of this depot, shows that the design and construction in 1907 cost Nazareth $4367.71. D.X. Murphy and Brothers, Louisville, were the architects. Requests to the L & N for help in the funding only resulted in $400 being expended. This is the second station. The first station, constructed in 1860, was connected with the convent by an avenue.

Eight

St. Joseph College and Preparatory School

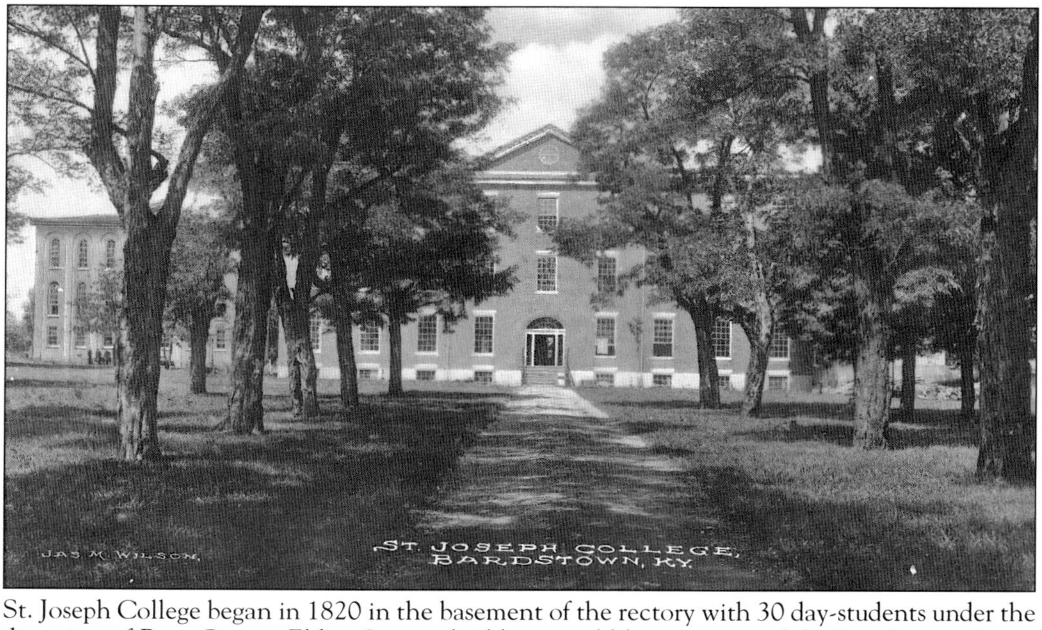

St. Joseph College began in 1820 in the basement of the rectory with 30 day-students under the direction of Rev. George Elder. Soon a building would be constructed for boarding students. Incorporated in 1823, it was described as able to accommodate 200 boarders. Local clergy were the instructors. The minutes indicate that "all students in the seminary either teach or are taught there." To keep good will no effort was made to convert, but all boarders attended high mass and vespers and listened to the sermons at the cathedral.

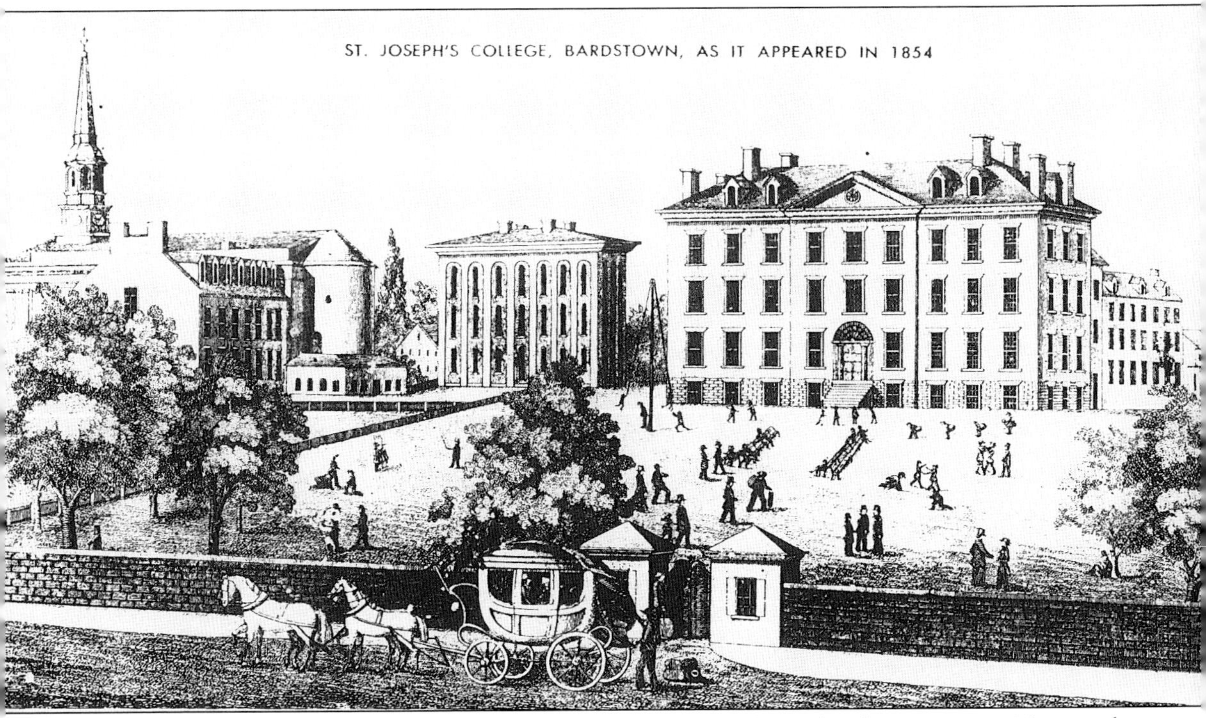

This 1854 engraving shows a view of the campus. The school term was 10 months (September to July). The students ranged from age 10 to 18. In 1824, Father Martial brought 40 students from Louisiana and Mississippi to increase enrollment. In September 1825, there were 90 boarders and 100 externs. The president of the college, Fr. George A. Elder, was considered lax in discipline and was replaced by Fr. Ignatius Reynolds in 1828. An 1828 letter reveals the belief that "Martial's Creoles have corrupted the college." The Southern students' habits of drinking, smoking, and provoking rebellious behavior continued to haunt the school. More students meant more expenses. Father Hazeltine traveled south to meet parents, dispel bad rumors, and collect debts. A devious agent withheld parents' money in New Orleans but a personal visit in 1827 obtained $18,000 owed to the college. In 1848, the Society of Jesus took over the college and brought all its talents to bear. They paid off the debts, increased enrollment, and enhanced the school's reputation.

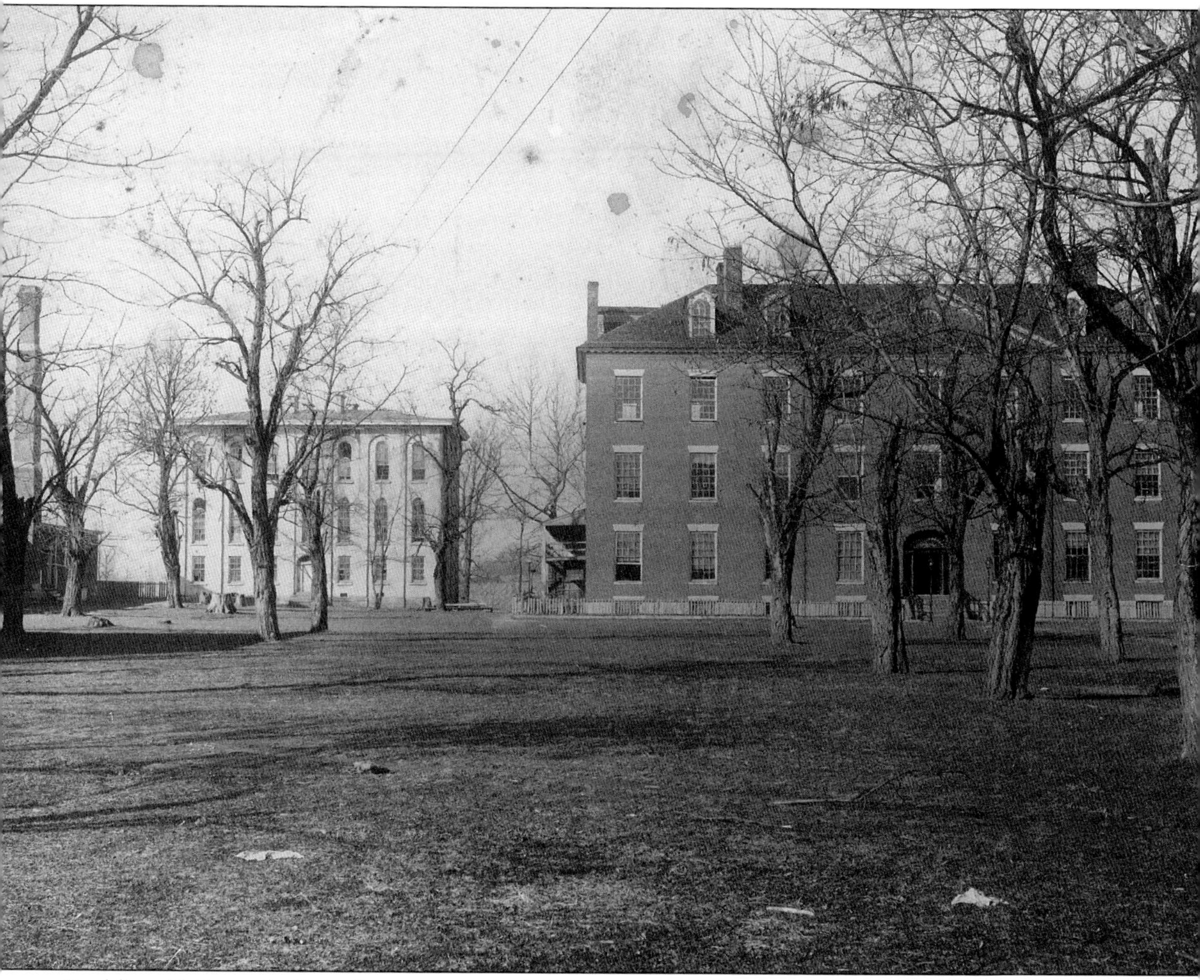

Spalding Hall was built in three stages. In 1820, a two-story brick structure running east to west was built; in 1824, the "chapel wing" was added; and in 1825, the large five-story connecting front completed the construction. It was finished within one year at a cost of $10,000. A disastrous fire on January 25, 1837, began under the eaves and destroyed the interior of the front section of Spalding Hall. By December 1837, the college was repaired but painting was put off until the spring. Fr. Martin J. Spalding became president after the 1837 death of Fr. Elder. In October 1838, he mourned because only one-eighth of the students were Catholic. In 1846, to tighten discipline, he required that all students without parents or guardians in Bardstown stay at the college. This photo shows the porch on the 1820 wing, which was removed in 1911. Flaget Hall, the three-story classroom building, can be seen on the left. The building was erected in 1852 by the Jesuits, who named it in honor of the first bishop of Bardstown, Benedict Joseph Flaget.

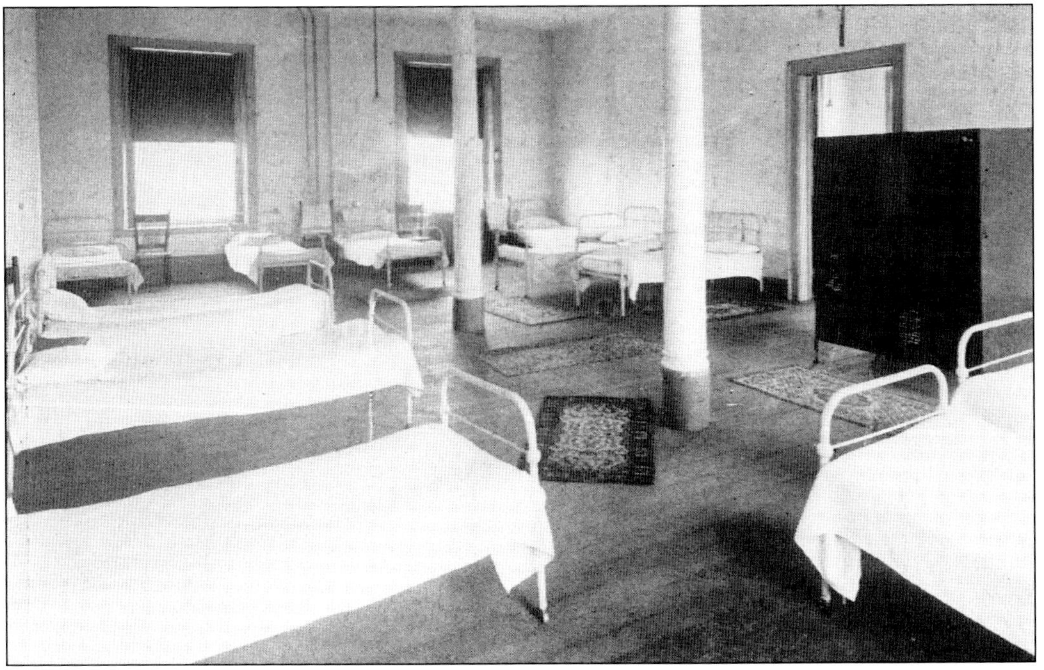

This is a 1926 view of the third-floor dormitory in the main section of Spalding Hall. Pictured is one-quarter of the space on this floor. During the Civil War, the Union army leased the college from October 1861 until May 1862 for use as a hospital. Their training camp, located south of Bardstown, had soldiers from Michigan, Illinois, Wisconsin, Minnesota, Ohio, Indiana, and Pennsylvania, all of whom brought their own germs. The college had beds, bedding, and cooking facilities to provide medical care for these sick soldiers. After the Union soldiers left, the Confederates brought their injured and ill here.

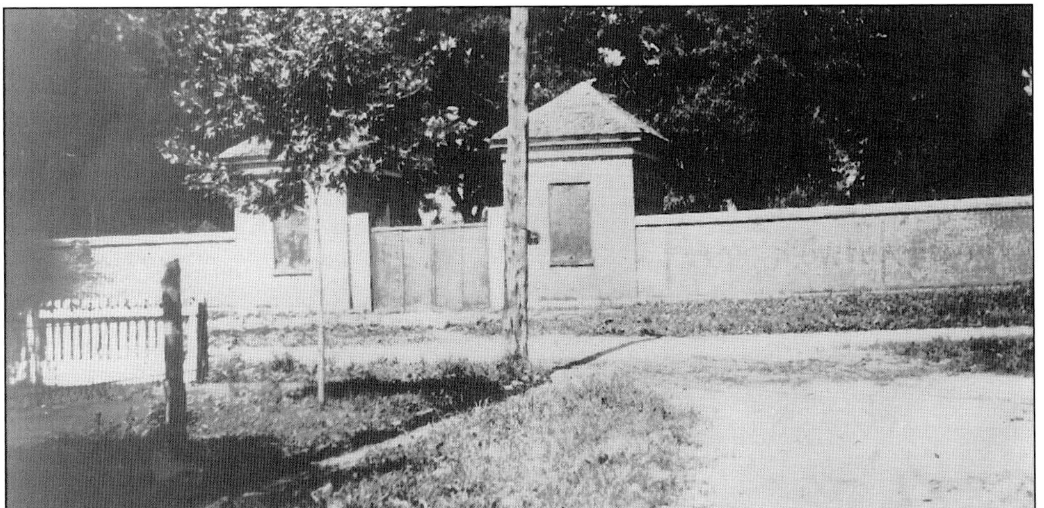

During the 1854–1855 school year, a wall was constructed across the front with gatehouses at the entrance. One was for the porter's lodge and the other was a tailor shop. The students' clothing was provided or altered. This allowed visits to the tailor without leaving the grounds. The gatehouses and front wall seen here were removed in 1925.

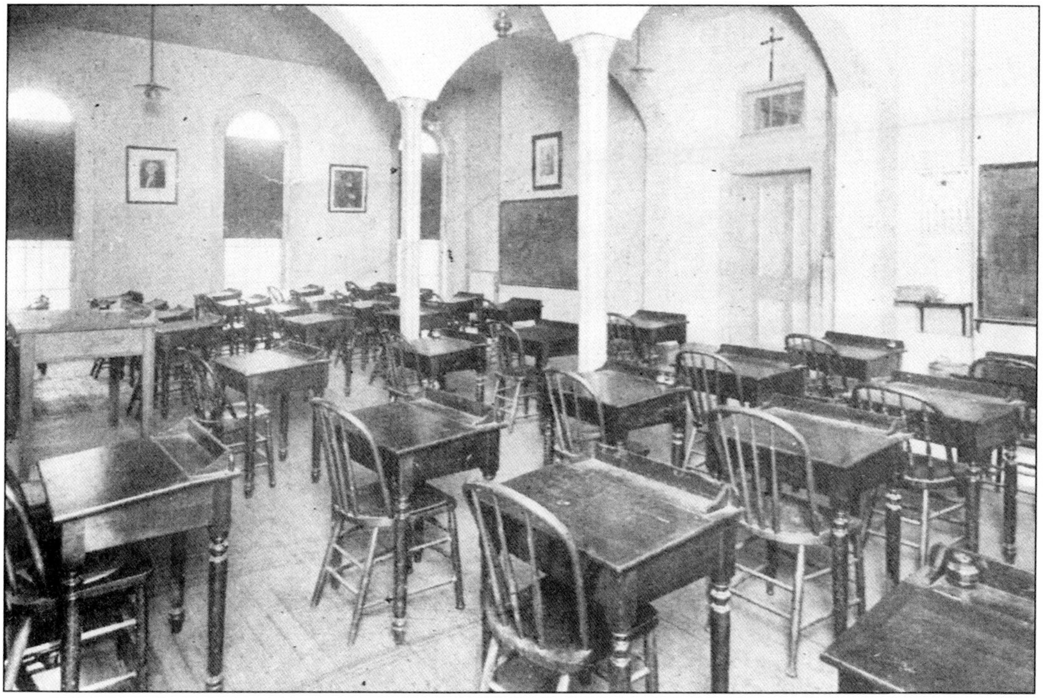

This 1926 picture is a view of the second-floor classroom in Flaget Hall. This Italianate-style building was constructed in 1852 by the Jesuits at a cost of $7,000. It housed a natural science museum and classrooms. The cast-iron columns support the weight of the brick wall above. Two large rooms are located on the second floor, and four classrooms are located on the first and third floors.

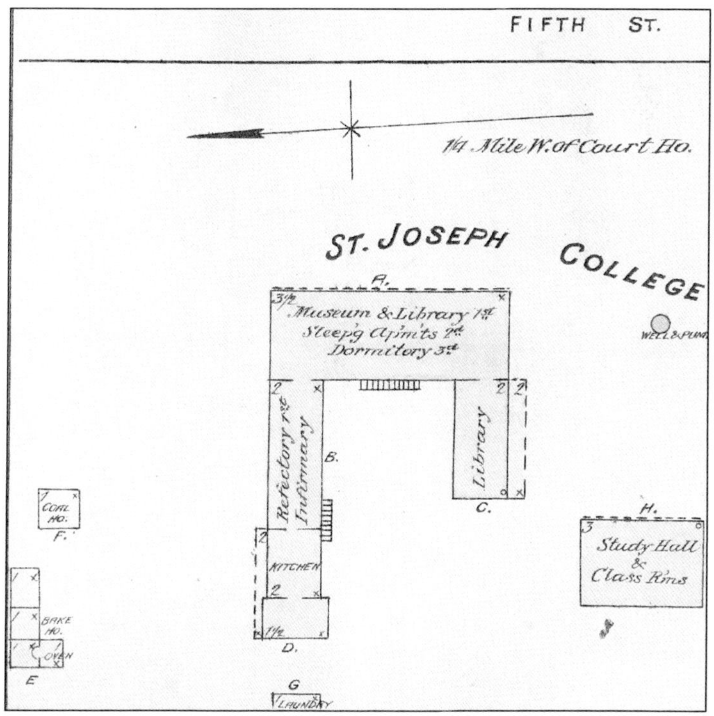

St. Joseph College was used as a seminary in the 1870s–1880s. This 1886 map shows the uses of the different buildings: (first floor) Spalding Hall and Refectory; (second floor) museum, library, and infirmary; (third floor) sleeping apartments and dormitory. Flaget Hall had a study hall and classrooms. Note the outside bake house and laundry. The Sisters of Charity and Sisters of Loretto assisted the college from 1821 to 1860 as housekeepers, nurses, and seamstresses.

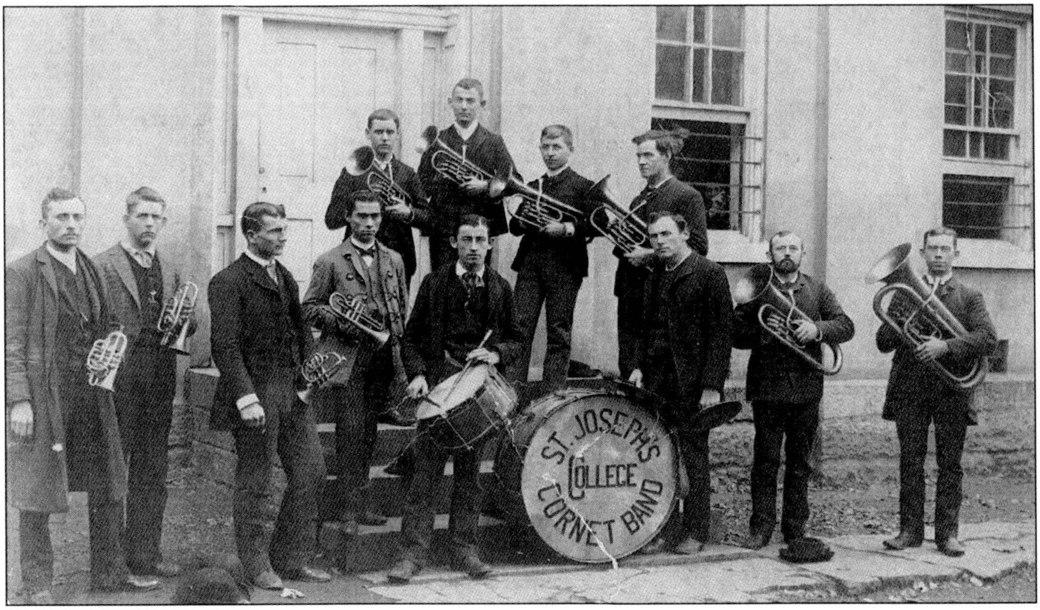

The St. Joseph College Cornet Band poses in front of Flaget Hall *c.* 1885. The Jesuits left the college in 1868. From that time to 1888, it was used as a diocesan seminary and college.

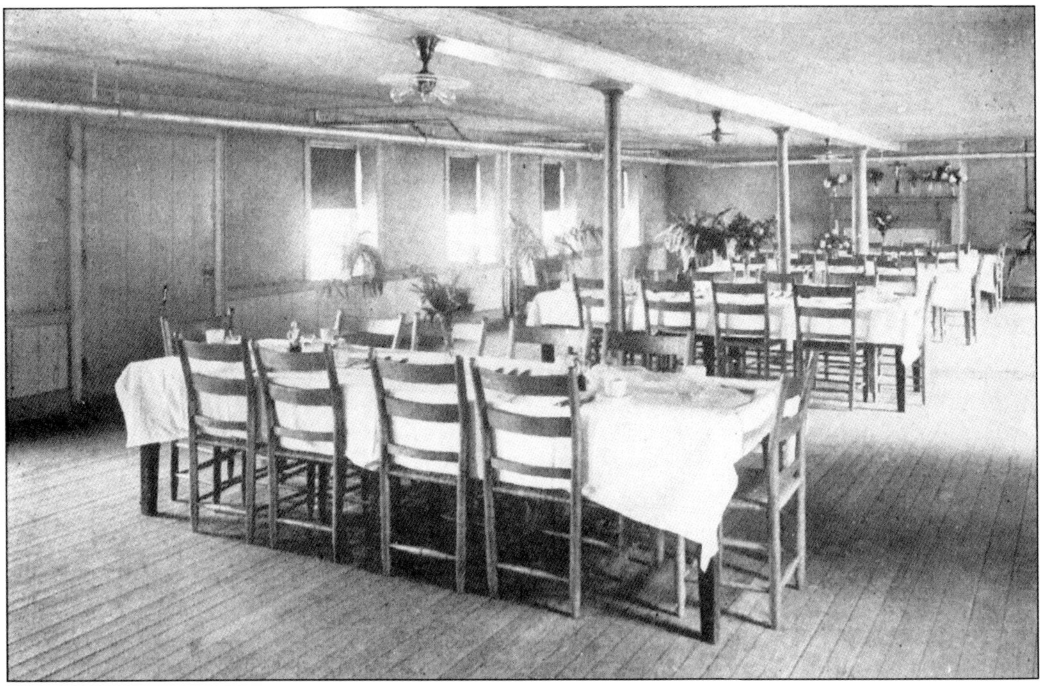
This 1926 photo of the refectory on the first floor of the "Chapel Wing" provided a dining and meeting space. The slat-back chairs were probably made locally. Do the tablecloths mean this was a special occasion?

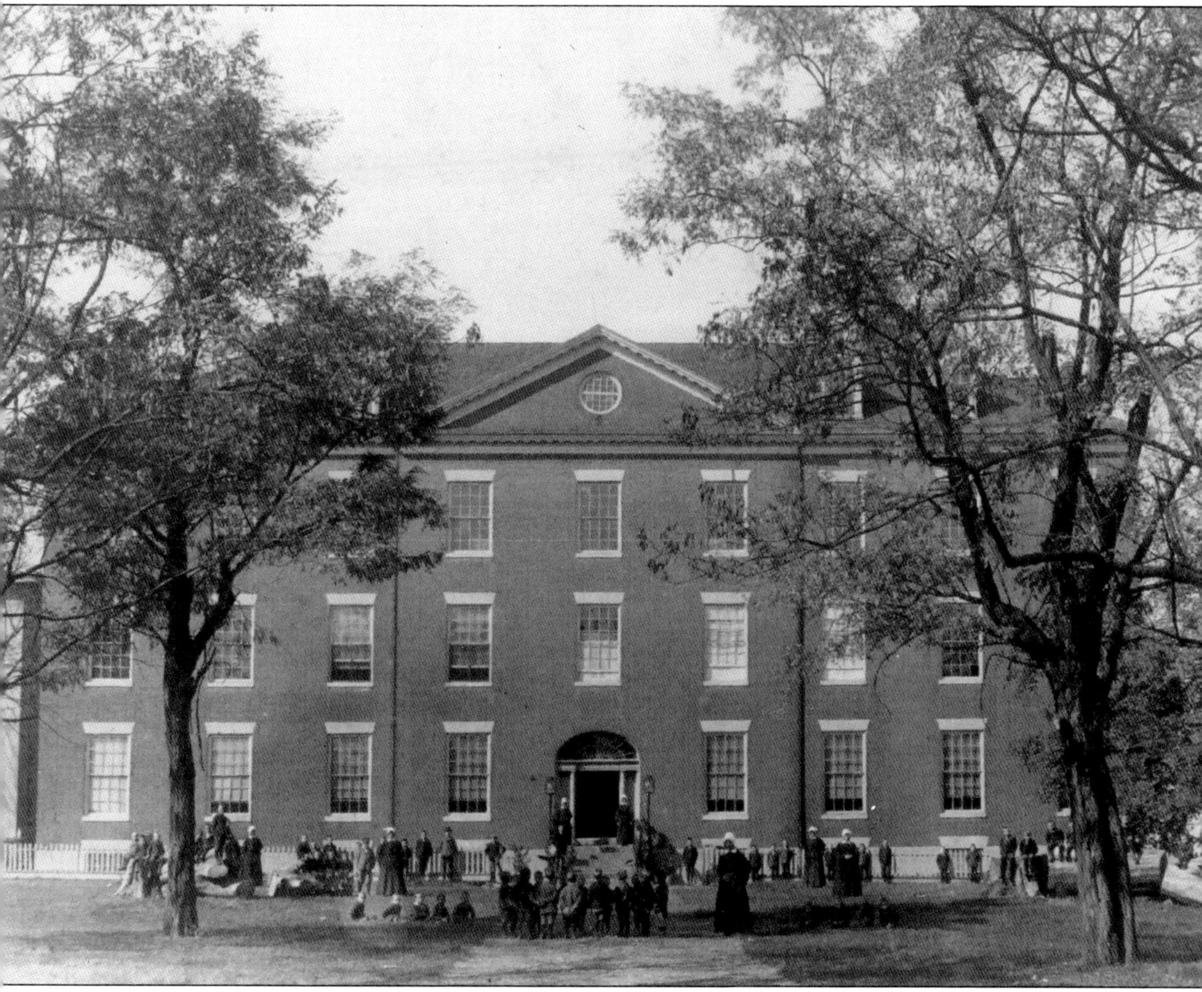

In 1889, the Sisters of Charity moved St. Thomas Orphanage to the college buildings. A fire destroyed their buildings, and since the school was closed, it was ideal for their needs. They did not occupy Flaget Hall, so the building was left unheated and sometimes open to the weather. The Sisters occupied all of Spalding Hall. This *c.* 1900 photo shows their charges playing on the large logs from trees that have been cut down. The orphanage moved to Louisville in 1910.

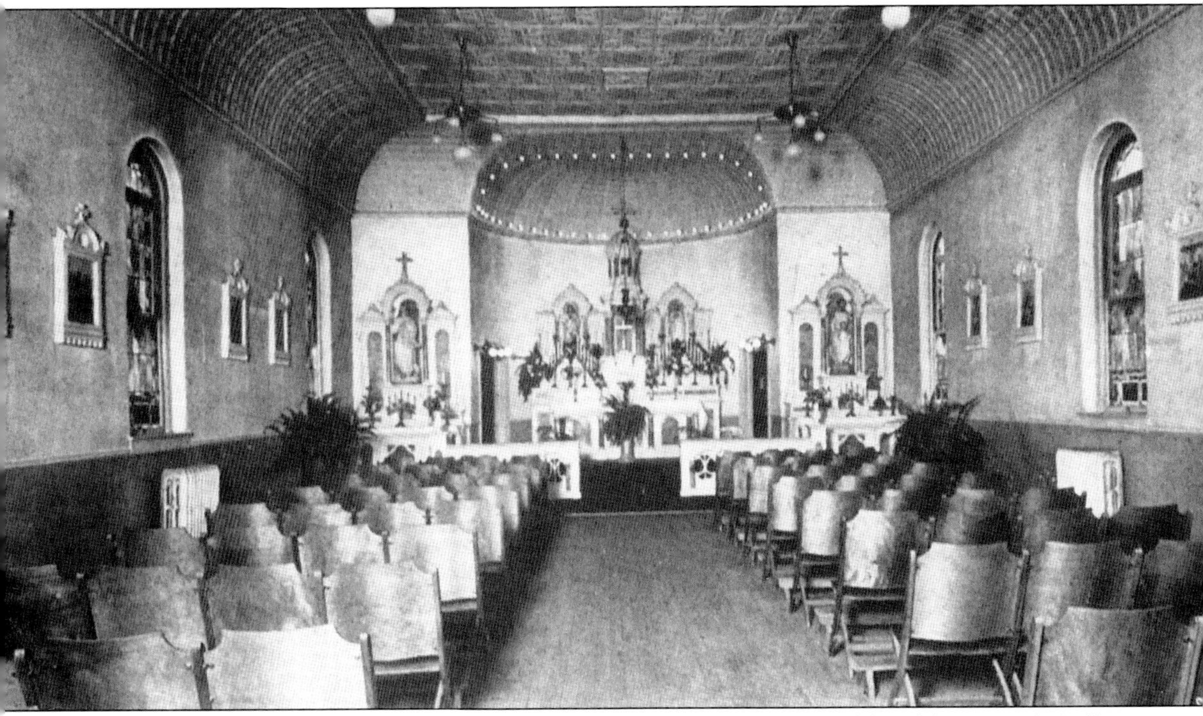

In 1911, the Xaverian Brothers purchased the buildings and grounds of the old St. Joseph College property from the diocese of Louisville in order to operate St. Joseph Preparatory School, a boarding and day school. They renovated the two main buildings and blessed a new chapel. They also began construction of a 40-by-90-foot, two-story building which, when completed, allowed indoor sports. It was destroyed by a fire in January 1932 but was later rebuilt. This is a 1926 view of the chapel, which was used until the school closed in 1968. It is presently in use as a museum.

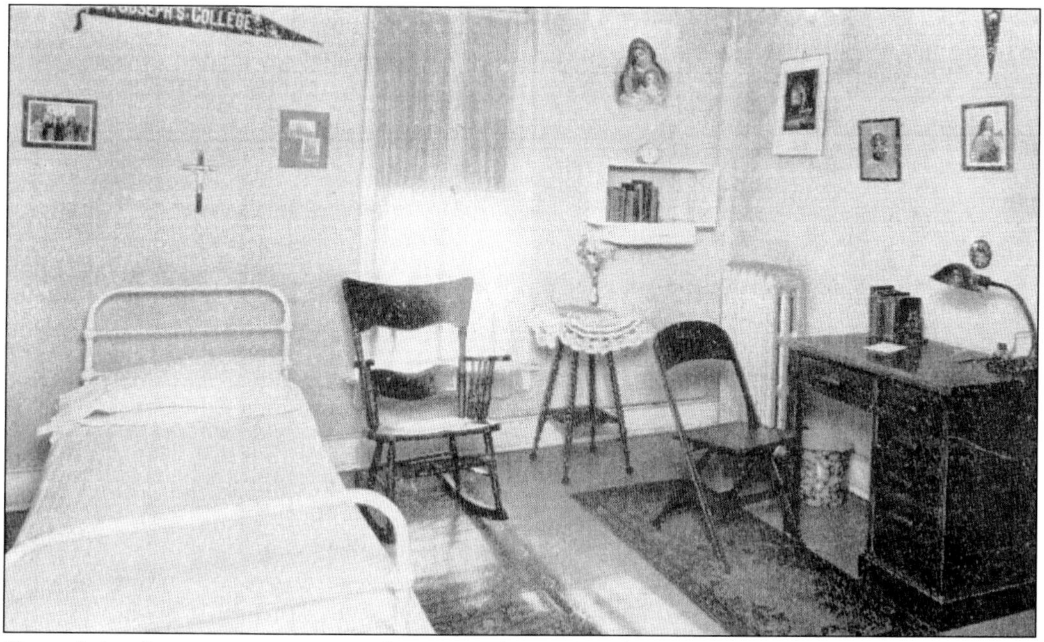

One of the few private rooms is shown in this 1932 photo. Expenses for board and tuition were $300 per year, with a private room costing an extra $60. Day students' tuition was $50 per year.

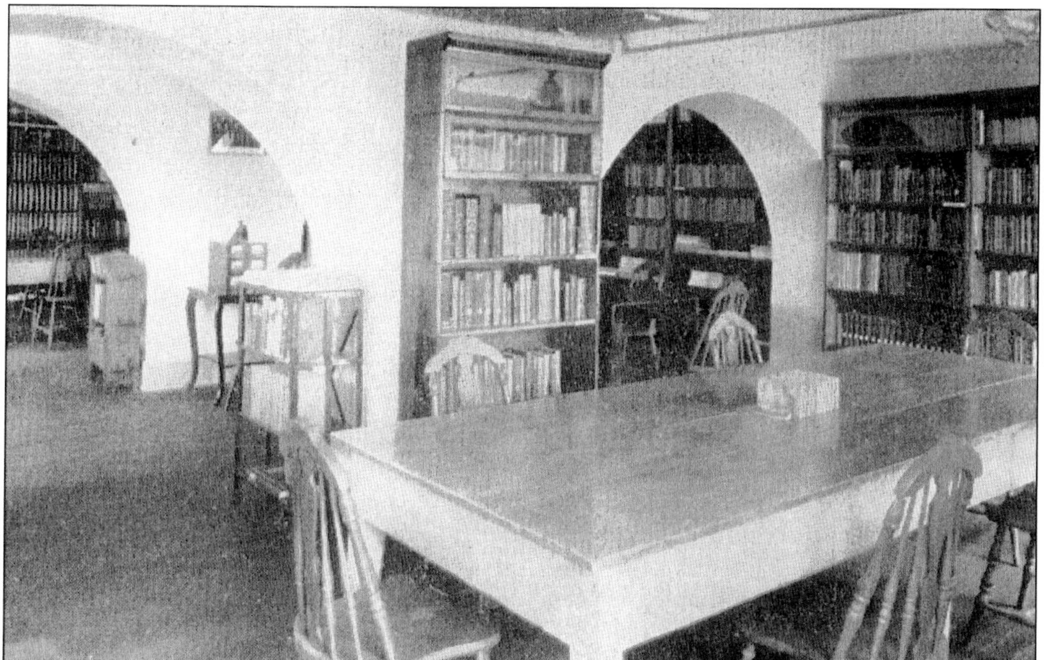

This 1932 photo is a view of the library, located on the ground floor of the central part of Spalding Hall. The brick arches are supporting three floors of solid brick walls. The area shown here is now part of a restaurant.

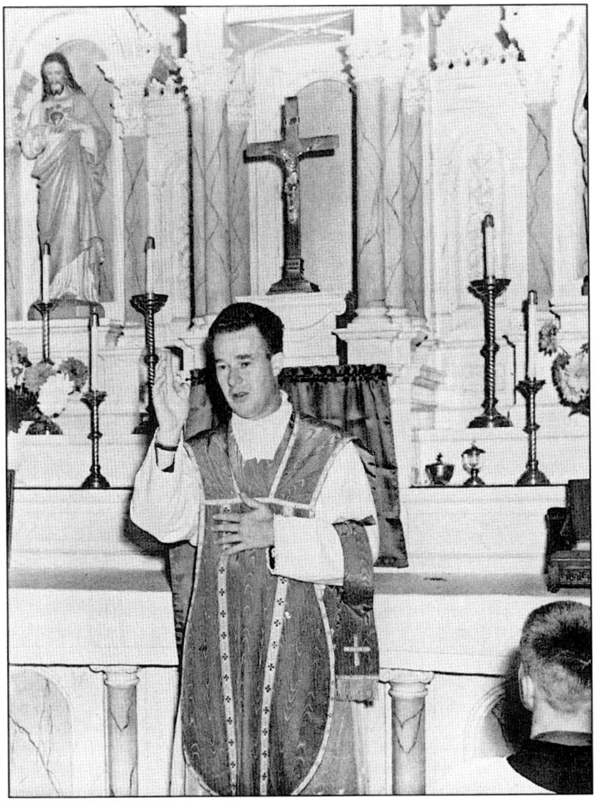

Father Michael Lally, chaplain of the preparatory school, gives the blessing at the end of the Mass of the Holy Ghost. His blessing officially opened the 1948–49 school year. This photo showing the chapel altar is from the school yearbook. The Xaverians dedicated the chapel when they renovated the college buildings in 1911.

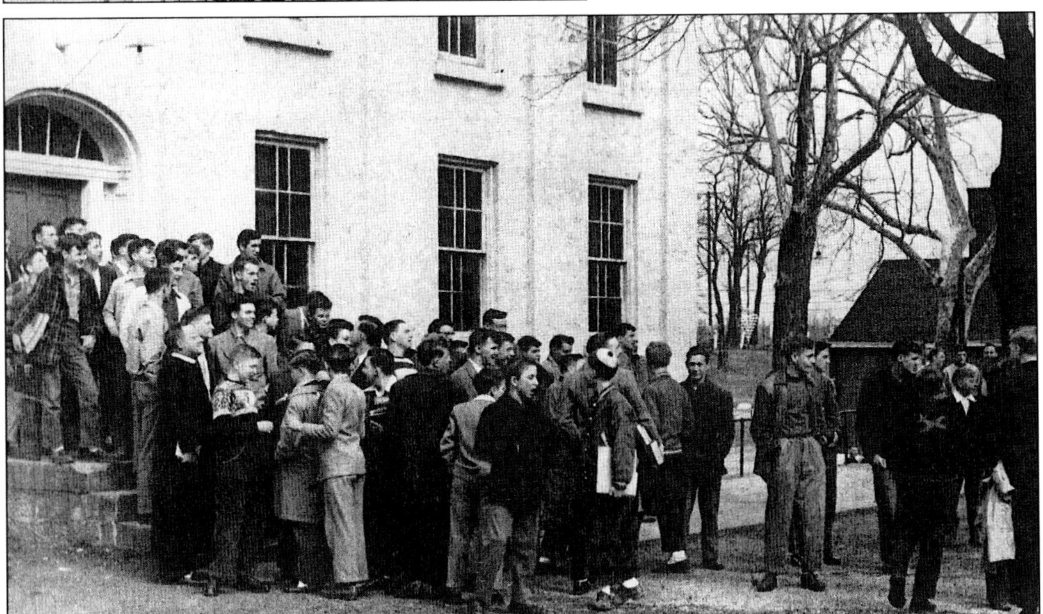

From the doorstep of Flaget Hall, Brother Walstan and 58 students turn their eyes toward the main building to nab someone within arms reach of the bell rope to signal the other 134 scholars that another school day is about to begin. At the foot of the ante-bellum steps, Brother Gerald tries to help out too. This photo is from the 1950 annual *Azuwur*.

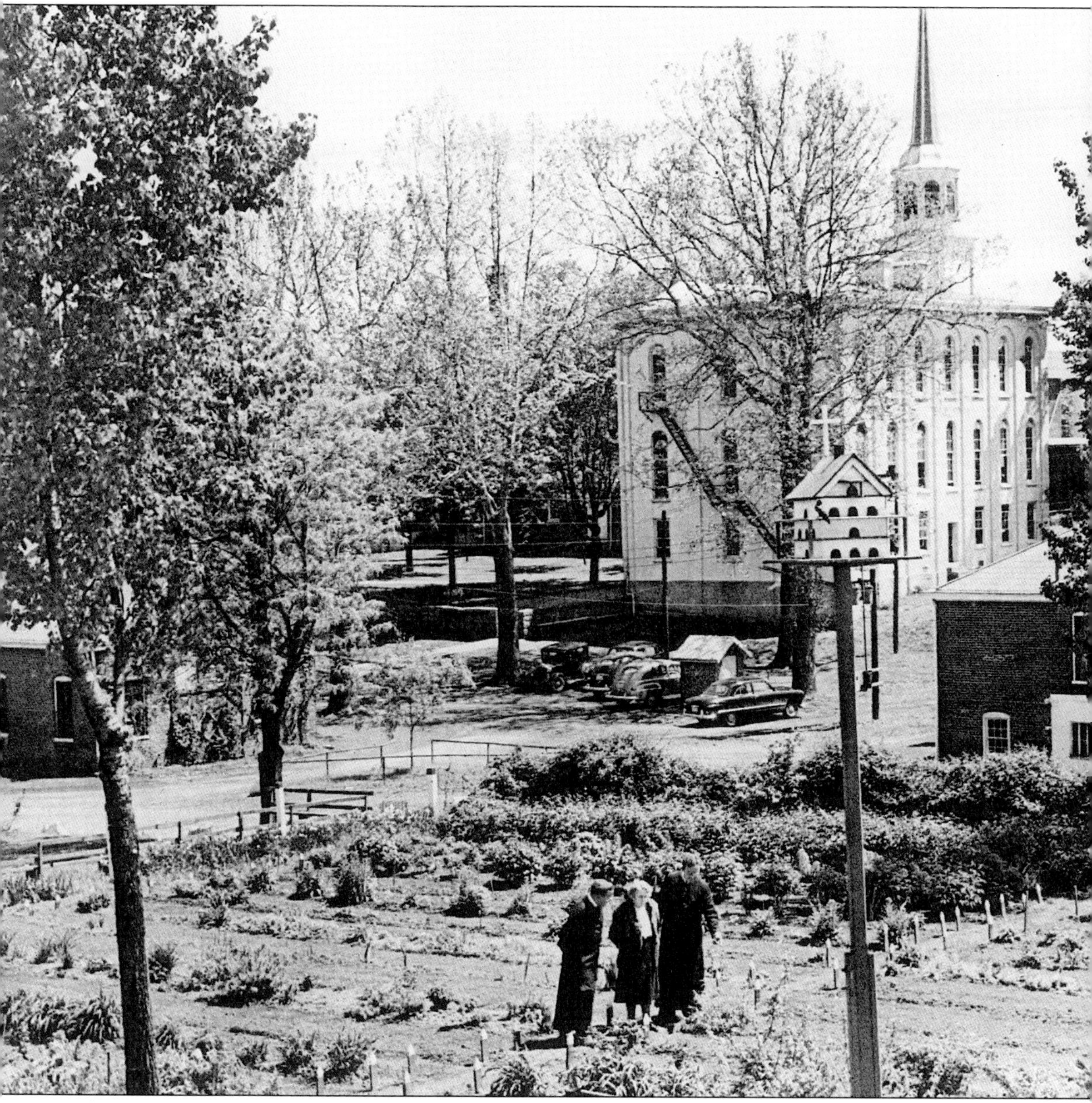

Looking south from the playing fields of St. Joe Prep in 1949, Brother Norbertus shows off his flower garden. The garden is now the site of the Bardstown Recreation Department parking lot. On the left is the chapel wing of Spalding Hall. The large white building in the background is Flaget Hall, and the St. Joseph Cathedral spire towers above it. On the right is the Infirmary building. Notice the birdhouse with its own cross.

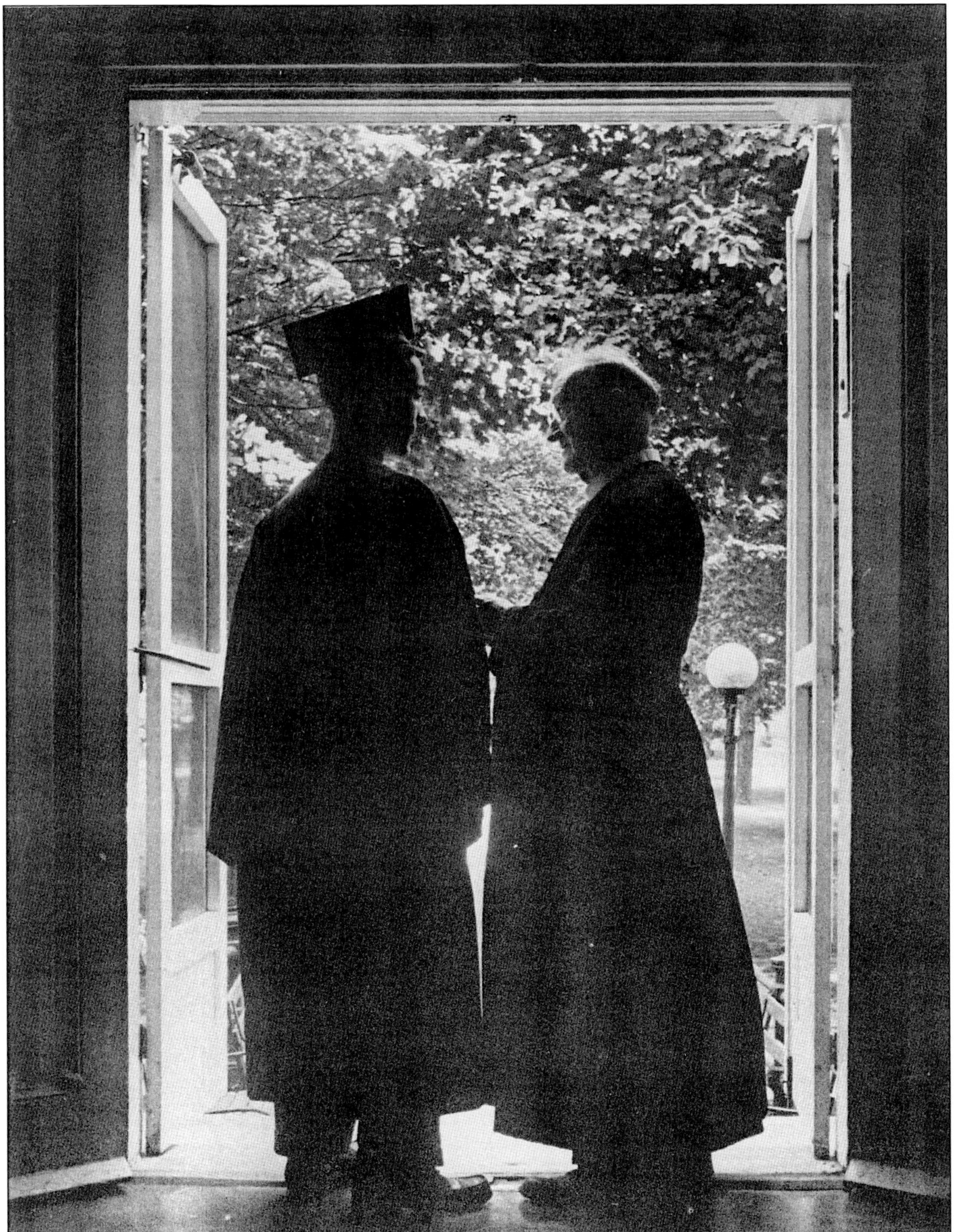

In 1968, the last students graduated from St. Joe Prep. Spalding Hall is now leased from the Archdiocese of Louisville as a non-profit community center with museums, offices, and a restaurant. The 1957 Xavier classroom building, gym, and sports fields were purchased by the City of Bardstown in 1969 for use as city government offices and municipal recreation. The Xaverian Brothers' contribution to the community continues to be used. The Prep is "gone, but not forgotten."